Evaluating the Effectiveness of Academic Development

Principles and Practice

Edited by Lorraine Stefani

Routledge
Taylor & Francis Group

NEW YORK AND LONDON

First published 2011
by Routledge
270 Madison Avenue, New York, NY 10016

Simultaneously published in the UK
by Routledge
2 Park Square, Milton Park, Abingdon, Oxon OX14 4RN

Routledge is an imprint of the Taylor & Francis Group, an informa business

Typeset in Minion and Helvetica Neue LT by Prepress Projects Ltd, Perth, UK
Printed and bound in the United States of America on acid-free paper by
Walsworth Publishing Company, Marceline, MO

Library of Congress Cataloging in Publication Data
Evaluating the effectiveness of academic development : principles and
practice / edited by Lorraine Stefani.
p. cm.
Includes bibliographical references and index.
1. Multicultural education—Case studies. 2. Educational equalization—
Case studies. 3. Comparative education—Case studies. I. Stefani, Lorraine,
1953–
LC1099.E87 2010
378.1'97—dc22
2010006075

ISBN 13: 978-0-415-87206-5 (hbk)
ISBN 13: 978-0-415-87207-2 (pbk)
ISBN 13: 978-0-203-84793-0 (ebk)

Evaluating the Effectiveness of Academic Development

How can academic developers provide evidence of the effectiveness and 'added value' of their work to the key stakeholders within their institutions?

Written for academic developers, academic administrators and others responsible for promoting organizational change, *Evaluating the Effectiveness of Academic Development* is a professional guide that shares best practice advice and provides developers with useful frameworks for effective evaluation and monitoring of their work.

Through case studies and up-to-date examples from experts in the field, this collection explores the nuances of evaluative practice and the tensions inherent in claiming a causal link between academic development and organizational transformation. As higher education institutions continue to seek effective ways to determine the impact of academic development on organizational transformation in general and student learning in particular, *Evaluating the Effectiveness of Academic Development* is sure to be an invaluable resource.

Lorraine Stefani is Director and Professor of the Centre for Academic Development (CAD) at the University of Auckland.

245 265

Contents

Tending the Secret Garden: Evaluating a Doctoral Skills
Programme   109
FRANCES KELLY, IAN BRAILSFORD AND SUSAN CARTER

Case Study 4
Evaluation as Bricolage: Cobbling Together a Strategy for Appraising
Supervision Development   117
BARBARA M. GRANT

Case Study 5
Archiving for the Future: A Longitudinal Approach to Evaluating a
Postgraduate Certificate Programme   127
HELEN SWORD

Case Study 6
Tracking the Invisible: An eLearning Group's Approach to
Evaluation   133
CATHY GUNN AND CLAIRE DONALD

Case Study 7
Continuous Improvement Projects: Whose Evaluation Matters?   143
LORRAINE STEFANI

Case Study 8
Leadership Programmes: Evaluation as a Way Forward   153
LINDA McLAIN

III Evaluation of Large-Scale Development Projects   167

  7 Accreditation, Accountability and Assessment: Addressing Multiple
     Agendas   169
     CLAUDIA J. STANNY AND JANE S. HALONEN

  8 An Institutional Programme: A National Model for Evaluation?   183
     RONI BAMBER

  9 Evaluation Matters in a National, Funded Academic Development
     Project   197
     KOGI NAIDOO AND ALISON HOLMES

 10 Impact Evaluation and its Implications   209
     KATHLEEN GRAY AND ALEX RADLOFF

 11 Evaluation of Academic Development: Looking to the Future   221
     LORRAINE STEFANI

     Contributors   227
     Index   233

Figures

Tables

Foreword

A few months ago I was at a conference on student learning where I met an academic I hadn't seen for over 15 years. He seemed especially pleased to see me. 'You know', he said, 'you changed my life!' Smiling and nodding, he told others around him: 'I wouldn't be here today if it hadn't been for her.' I'm not telling this brief tale to blow my own trumpet. This is what academic developers do. They change people's lives. Many, if not most, could probably tell a similar story. The normal business of academic developers is to bring about change. Yet this kind of transformation is not captured in institutional measures, evaluations and reports of effectiveness. Academic development is an altruistic pursuit, often going unrecognised and unrewarded. But the effects on individual academics can be profound.

In the changing and changed context of higher education, academic development has steadily developed its profile. Many, if not most, universities now boast an academic development centre. Many of these are located outside of faculties and report directly to senior personnel, but increasingly we are seeing the growth of centres located in specific faculties as well as a growth in specialist centres with a focus on, for example, assessment, research-based learning, elearning, etc.

Critical reflection on practice has made important contributions to moving forward the field of academic development. We now know much about how to engage academics, how to link with strategic priorities of institutions and about the wide variety of types of development available. There is increasing use of evidence-based practice, a substantial literature specifically on academic development and the development of professional organisations for academic developers. Through organisations such as the International Consortium of Educational Development (ICED), academic developers are now linked in international networks of like-minded people with similar commitments and focus, carrying out similar work across numerous nations. All of this attests to academic development being now a mature profession. Yet it is a curious one. Unlike many other professions, the specialist skills, values, and attributes that are required to carry out the job of an academic developer with integrity and commitment are not well recognised within the community, even and especially the academic community.

A consequence is that there is frequently a conflict between the evaluation strategies required by institutions and those that adhere to academic development values and notions of good practice. In this context, how academic development is to be evaluated has become one of the most pressing problems confronting it today. The importance of robust and compelling evidence of effectiveness has become a mantra. Evaluation in relation to academic development work is, however, multi-layered and multi-faceted. Evaluating academic development is highly problematic. This book highlights the tensions and complexities in negotiating this terrain and, as such, goes to the heart of fundamental dilemmas in academic development practice.

Academic developers are balanced on a knife-edge of what practices are in line with their academic development values on the one hand and what is in the interests of others, for example university managers, on the other. The very survival of academic development centres depends on currying favour with those in power.

To their core commitment to improving higher education, adherence to a set of altruistic values, academic integrity and an ethic of 'usefulness', academic developers have, in the last 20 years or so, had to add furtherance of the institutional mission, assistance with the institutional strategic and teaching and learning plan and responsiveness to the demands of senior managers. These managers can make or break an academic unit, and indeed the careers of developers, so they are important as stakeholders. Yet their demands can be at odds with the needs and desires of disciplinary academics with whom developers may be more in sympathy. The academic developer may be caught in the middle. Examples of this are how developers negotiate the territory between enhancement and judgement in the implementation and support of institutional evaluation strategies, or how academic developers respond to requests from heads of department to 'develop' academics identified as poor teachers. How they negotiate this space and demonstrate their own effectiveness is complex and challenging. This means that demands are placed on them which are unknown in faculties, such as the high levels of surveillance over what they do, often accompanied by continual critical questioning of their very existence. So, although developing high standards of professionalism, academic developers are often working in contexts which are just as likely to diminish, misunderstand or negate their expertise as they are to honour and reward it.

Institutional expectations and demands in relation to the evaluation of academic development practices, often expressed in the views of senior personnel, can seem to be in line with developers' best intentions, while at the same time neglecting the exigencies of the role. An example of this is in relation to changes in students' experiences and outcomes. In line with the orientation of this book, I have been talking of academic development in the sense of focusing on changing academics; not in the sense of students' academic development as it is seen in some countries. Yet a key issue is whether evaluation should focus on changes in the student experience demonstrated through student questionnaires and the like. The argument broadly goes that if many academic development practices are focused on improving teaching, surely the effects on students' learning will demonstrate effectiveness. Yet academic developers rarely work directly with students. In working with academics to achieve strategic change in teaching and learning, academic developers are always at one stage removed from the effects of their actions on students. Workshops, conversations, courses and interventions carried out by academic developers may demonstrably affect changes in academics' thinking, but the effectiveness of their actions in terms of changes in student learning is reliant on the extent to which others make changes in their practice. It is up to academics to decide to change. So academics mediate the effectiveness of academic development.

Another example, in which the values base of academic development is undermined, often with the acquiescence of developers, has been the implementation of the same strategies for evaluating courses in teaching and learning as for other courses. In this way, academics are treated as if they are students rather than professional colleagues. This, together with requirements to assess academics' work in such courses, subverts the integrity of the relationship of academic developers and their professional colleagues, changing the dynamic of the relationship and undermining the value base of academic development practice.

The value base of academic development is critical to its success. Faculty academics with whom developers work do a different kind of job from developers, so sensitivity to their needs and interests is critical if developers are to carry any authority to effect change. However, it is perhaps curious that evaluation of effectiveness in terms of improved capacity of academics to change, increased pedagogical skills and so on, is of less interest to managers than that these changes have resulted in improvements in students' learning and experiences. In contrast, commercial organisations have long recognised that the skills, well-being and opportunities for personal growth and fulfilment of their employees are vitally important to the productivity of the company; a lesson that universities appear slow to come to terms with. Student progress and well-being are dependent on the skills and well-being of university employees. A focus on student experiences and outcomes at the expense of investment in academics' training and development is not wise, and it creates a difficult terrain for academic developers to tread.

The present day effectiveness of academic development is dependent not only on what they do today, but on the history of the particular institution and centre. I was recently at an event where some senior academics were arguing that academic development workshops were useless. They were talking of the one-off workshops that they had attended some fifteen or twenty years earlier. Myths of academic development practice held by the academic community and specifically by academic managers influence the extent to which academic development practices are taken up and taken seriously, and their capacity to effect change in organisations. A recent study shows that there are some institutional differences in the extent to which people take up opportunities for development. Academic developers have limited opportunities to shift historically grounded myths and cultures, yet the effectiveness of present-day practice is affected by this.

It is pertinent to ask why evaluation has become particularly important at the present time. With the increased emphasis on performance management, centres and individuals have not just to be effective, but to be seen to be effective. What constitutes evidence of effectiveness changes over time as new senior personnel wish to make a mark. We have seen in a number of universities over recent years, the destruction of long-standing academic development centres as new managers take over and want to change institutional strategies and make their mark on teaching and learning. Restructuring an academic development centre is an easy way to demonstrate change and this can readily be effected by questioning previous evaluation strategies and data on effectiveness. A centre, which one year is held up as an exemplar of how change can happen in a department, which has programmes considered world leading, can change overnight when a new regime demands different kinds of evidence. Underlying many of the discussions in this book is the knowledge that change can happen almost in an instant. Developing a nuanced understanding of the role of evaluation in the politics of institutions is a key task facing academic developers. It is a strategy to minimize the risks of catastrophic change. This book, in providing a range of different theoretical perspectives and examples of practice, highlights the challenges, the complexity and the importance of this.

So what does the future hold? Will academic development ever be other than a troubled profession? The growth in academic development centres within faculties signals an important trend. It gives expression to the view that development of teaching and learning in a specific disciplinary context is best carried out by specialists in that discipline. Yet there will always be a need for cross-disciplinary debate that comes from bringing together academics from across the disciplinary spectrum. So academic development will continue to negotiate difficult terrain. A greater sense of the politics and practices of evaluation is an important addition to the skill set of developers. This is a much-needed and timely book which contributes a great deal to the professional debates within the field of academic development. It is my hope that it will also contribute to a greater understanding of academic managers of the complexities and multi-faceted nature of evaluating this important work.

Angela Brew
Sydney, 2010

Acknowledgments

I would like to thank all the authors who agreed to write a chapter or case study for this book and who then delivered in good time. I would also like to thank Raewyn Heays, my Research Assistant, who provided her extensive expertise in manuscript layout and who always responded promptly to each draft of the edited manuscript. Roni Bamber from Queen Margaret University in Edinburgh provided helpful and constructive comments on the first version of the completed manuscript, for which I am extremely grateful.

I would like to acknowledge the University of Auckland for its support by way of Research and Study Leave during 2009, which enabled me to take on this project.

Finally I would like to thank my partner Frances Devaney for her eternal patience with my academic career and her good-humoured support when I decide to embark on a new and generally time-consuming project.

Lorraine Stefani
Auckland, 2010

I
Evaluation of Academic Practice

1
Evaluating the Effectiveness of Academic Development
An Overview

LORRAINE STEFANI

Introduction

Academic development activities and centres are now commonplace in most universities and higher education institutions, certainly in the UK, Australasia, Canada and South Africa, whereas in the USA there is a long history of faculty development in colleges and universities. Academic development is gaining importance in higher education institutions in every country and every continent. Universities in Pakistan, Saudi Arabia and China are currently seeking advice on how best to provide academic development opportunities for their staff.

This interest at a global level gives some credence to the assertion that academic development has moved from being a highly marginal practice to a dominant discourse framing the ways university teaching is understood (Clegg and Smith, 2008; Clegg, 2009). On the other hand some would argue that, more than 40 years after its beginnings, academic development still stands uncertainly on the threshold of becoming a profession or discipline in its own right (Grant et al., 2009).

Activities encompassed within the broad field of academic development are many and varied and tend to shift in accordance with national policy developments relating to higher education; the nature and type of higher education institution; changes in institutional priorities; and changes in key personnel at senior management level.

Over the past few years there has been an interesting and not always welcome shift with national/institutional desires for strategic alignment and wider impact of academic development endeavours. Increasingly academic development initiatives are viewed as enabling activities, and developers as acceptable interpreters and framers working with both senior management and frontline academic staff.

Problematic issues for academic development and developers are a lack of coherence in the understood purpose of 'development' and uncertainty of direction within the community of developers. These issues are compounded by the lack of an agreed framework for evaluation of the impact, added value and effectiveness of academic development (Kreber and Brook, 2001; Rowland, 2002). As universities under pressure from governments and funding bodies become more concerned over measures of accountability and standardization, the field of academic development could potentially become vulnerable to imposed measures of accountability or impact.

Academic development is a highly fragmented 'project' oriented towards change and transformation (Land, 2004) thus rendering the activities encompassed under the broad umbrella term 'development' problematic to evaluate. If programmes of development activities and practices are viewed as interventions intended to effect positive change, meaningful evaluation of these practices needs to be seen in historical and contextual terms.

However, given that learning and teaching and the overall student learning experience at tertiary level are the objects of intensive scrutiny and the ultimate goal of academic development is essentially to change teaching practice to support student engagement and enhance the student learning experience, it is perhaps not surprising that the work of academic development units is also an object of scrutiny.

The academic development community is well aware of the need to develop a culture of evaluation and to develop effective evaluative tools. The genesis of this book is the ongoing dialogue at international conferences, the collaborative projects academic developers are engaged in and many recent journal articles focusing on issues of evaluation and effectiveness. The community of developers has a sense of the urgency to share best practice and out of that to seek effective models and frameworks for evaluation of the impact of the work we do within our institution(s), and for national and international collaborative development projects.

The chapters and case studies which follow will affirm the scope and influence of the academic development project; explore the relationship between academic development and the scholarship of learning and teaching; and propose new approaches and frameworks for evaluation. The book addresses the question of how we can best evaluate and evidence our contribution to strategic educational change, through an exploration of practitioners' views and understandings of the *notion* of impact or effectiveness, given the complexity of the environments within which academic development and developers operate.

The Scope of Academic Development

Despite the uncertainties that still exist over whether or not academic development meets the criteria to be defined as a profession in its own right, there can be no doubt that development in higher education is a fast-growing area. As Gordon points out in Chapter 3 of this book 'considerable proliferation has taken place in the range of roles which academics can be asked to perform'. This applies equally within the field of academic development. Clegg (2009) suggests that 'academic development is a primary site through which the "subject" of teaching and learning in higher education has come about' (p. 403). It seems timely therefore to engage in an exploration of how academic development interventions are currently evaluated and to further enhance the status of academic development through seeking tangible and transferable frameworks for evaluation of our work.

Given the broad scope of academic development and the diversity of the academic development community, this book is intended to appeal to a wide audience. Some of the ideas expressed are challenging and even controversial, which is all to the good in terms of stimulating further debate. For those interested in entering the field, this book will provide important insights into the different orientations of academic developers, the tensions inherent in academic development practice and the complexities of evaluation of that practice.

Structure and Outline of Chapters and Case Studies

There are three sections in this book. The chapters in Section I focus on defining and contextualizing academic development practice. They set the scene around the complexities of evaluation of that practice. Section II provides a range of examples of evaluation of current practice. This section comprises a series of eight case studies drawn from current practice at the University of Auckland (UoA), New Zealand. The Centre for Academic Development (CAD) at the University of Auckland is one of the largest centres of its type in Australasia. Benchmarking activities indicate that the types of programmes and academic development initiatives offered are similar to those in most higher education institutions internationally and, owing to its size, the work of CAD encompasses a very broad range of development activities and interventions. One of the case studies, focusing on leadership programmes, is written by a collaborative colleague, the Director of the Staff and Organisational Development Unit based within Human Resources at the University of Auckland. The chapters in Section III are primarily concerned with evaluation of large-scale projects at faculty, institutional and national level. The penultimate chapter in this section provides a salutary message about the language we use around evaluation. Terms such as 'impact' and 'effective', for example, are loaded terms that can be interpreted in different ways depending on context. The message is that the language of evaluation may be as important as evaluative practice itself. The final chapter summarizes the future potential for evaluation of the effectiveness of academic development.

Setting the Scene for Evaluation

In Chapter 2, Shelda Debowski maps out the context for and the scope of academic development highlighting the challenges in forming 'a comprehensive approach to evaluating the impact and outcomes of the extensive range of activities carried out by academic developers.'

Although the changing roles and responsibilities of academic development units have been the subject of extensive research (e.g. Gosling, 2007; Harland and Staniforth, 2008; Clegg, 2009), Debowski, in her chapter, discusses a subtle but important shift in the status of academic development and developers through the expansion of executive appointments in many universities to include the role of Pro Vice Chancellor Learning and Teaching. On the one hand, this reflects the elevated status of learning and teaching, now part of the international policy agenda in higher education as universities compete for students in what is now a global industry. On the other hand, the role of Pro Vice Chancellor Learning and Teaching generally includes strategy and policy formation; consequently the focus for academic developers, particularly Academic Development Directors, may have shifted to implementation of these policies rather than acting as influential agents for learning and teaching policy and change across the senior leadership community.

Debowski states that the 'focus of academic development is to influence and transform academic practice and communities and that the measurement of how these agencies encourage reformed practice needs to be carefully considered.' She presents a potential model for documenting and evaluating both inputs and outputs, taking into consideration the different levels at which academic development operates, including individual/group learning, influencing and culture setting, and institutional organization and transformation.

A further important matter highlighted in this chapter is the evaluation of the management of the academic development unit as a service agency in the university community, a subject well worthy of further research. Debowski offers a model which she believes has the potential to support a cohesive analysis of the overall functioning of academic development units.

In Chapter 3, George Gordon questions where academic development sits within the spectrum of quality assurance and quality enhancement. Gordon explores the question in relation to aligning academic development work with the bottom line of externally led quality/assurance/enhancement agendas – which is the quality of the student experience. Although Gordon acknowledges that this idea may be contested or even contentious, he outlines and then expands upon the long list of significant changes in higher education in recent times, all of which impact on the quality agenda and which in turn have the potential to influence the definition and direction of academic development.

Like Debowski in Chapter 2, George Gordon sets out the scope of academic development. There are similarities, differences and overlaps between the meanings and definitions of academic development work, highlighting again the complexities of the project and the difficulties in setting out a framework for evaluation of effectiveness.

In common with other contributors to this book, Gordon points to the many agencies, professional bodies and individuals involved in promoting the enhancement of academic practice. He suggests that with the sheer scale of activities taking place at any given time, the academic development activities being reported on may be only the tip of the iceberg. He calls for the development of visual tools or models to promote a shared understanding of interconnections, structures and relationships to guide reflection on and evaluation of the academic development enterprise.

Gordon also points to the important work of Land (2004) in outlining the range of different orientations to academic development and suggests that 'where academic development sits in relation to quality agendas will be coloured by the orientations of the various players and their experiences, preferences, aspirations and values.' This comes close to suggesting that Land's work (2004) on discourse, identity and practice as related to academic developers and development could provide a useful tool for aligning academic developers with particular aspects and facets of the development project.

In his concluding remarks Gordon suggests that academic developers and development perhaps need to change with the times. Our agenda needs to be transformative as opposed to compliant. This necessitates more risk taking and of course recognizing that transformation is not easily amenable to simple evaluation.

In a thought-provoking, conceptual chapter, Carolin Kreber poses the question 'how might we demonstrate the "fitness for purpose" of our academic development work?' (Chapter 4). Her backdrop for this questioning is, in common with other chapter authors, the often conflicting agendas and expectations of the development project. Drawing on the extensive literature on the philosophy of learning and teaching, Kreber takes on the challenge of exploring what kind of a practice academic work essentially is, and from this exploration attempts to define academic development itself.

Kreber puts enhancement of the student learning experience to the forefront in her treatise on the meaning and purpose of learning and teaching at university level. Whereas Debowski and Gordon essentially map out the scope of academic development in the previous two chapters, Kreber picks up on the idea of the bottom line of accountability being the quality of the student learning experience. She interrogates what it means to teach such that students will have a quality learning experience and what that then implies for the practice of academic development.

Kreber deplores the often simplistic responses to the UK-wide National Student Survey outcomes. She takes issue with knee-jerk reactions to low survey scores – one response being that academic developers need to provide academics with hints and tips to improve some aspects of teaching; the idea behind such a response being that this will improve the scores next time around! Such responses add weight to Kerri-Lee Krause's view, expressed in Chapter 5, that institutions do not interrogate survey outcomes in a scholarly manner with the intention of enhancing the student experience.

Kreber's in-depth exploration of the purpose or goals of teaching and teaching practice at higher education levels takes us to the heart of what academic practice and development should be about. We are taken on a journey that reaches the conclusion that 'if universities are to achieve the goal of emancipating learners, setting them free through their learning so that they can use their critical capacities, apply and invest themselves and thereby begin to address the problems confronting humanity' – then evaluation of academic development should focus on the 'processes' by which we enable, support and inspire academics to take a courageous and authentic approach to teaching.

Whereas Carolin Kreber suggests evaluation of academic development should focus on the processes by which we support academic staff in their role as facilitators of student learning, in Chapter 5 Kerri-Lee Krause advocates an evidence-based approach to evaluation. In a view not dissimilar to that expressed by Gordon in Chapter 3, Krause advises academic developers to make their mark by developing an evidence-based agenda. In her chapter Krause discusses the benefits of using student survey data to shape academic development priorities and approaches.

Although academic development units are constructed in different ways in different universities and have varying remits, in essence there is a shared understanding amongst developers that we are engaged in a project to improve the quality and status of university teaching and to improve the student learning experience (Stefani and Elton, 2002; Prebble et al., 2004; Buckridge, 2008).

Krause emphasizes the importance of addressing the questions of relevance, purpose and effectiveness of academic development in a climate of reduced government funding and increased scrutiny of all aspects of academic practice. She believes that one purposeful means of showing relevance is to engage with and respond to student survey data, using it to 'inform academic development strategic and operational plans, policy development, targeted workshop programs and discipline-based professional development.'

Krause provides extensive information on types and purposes of student learning experience data that are now available to us, from the suite of surveys encompassed within the Cooperative Institutional Research Program in the United States; through the National Survey of Student Engagement (NSSE) used in the United States and Canada; the Course Experience Questionnaire and the First Year Experience Questionnaire both developed and administered in Australian higher education institutions; the National Student Survey in the UK; and a recent instrument, the Australian Survey of Student Engagement (AUSSE). The point Krause is making is that the rapid emergence of a number of influential survey tools aligns clearly with the increased focus on institutional accountability, quality assurance and performance-based funding arrangements.

But Krause sees this intensive survey activity as an opportunity for academic developers to bridge the data gap by using the information collected by means of student surveys to work in partnership with stakeholders across the institution, interpreting and using the data to effect culture change and enhance practice. She provides a model that places an emphasis on 'academic development activities that are sensitive and responsive to institutional structures, processes and cultures', and argues that academic development approaches that are underpinned by strategic use of student data could enable better alignment between the experience of staff and students, the institutional values and culture, policies, practice and resourcing.

Such an approach would undoubtedly be helpful in aligning evaluation of academic development work with strategic endeavours to enhance the student experience. In the latter part of Chapter 5, Krause conveys the importance of academic developers and other key stakeholders having the skills to interpret student data. She suggests this is often a barrier to effective use of the rich data being gathered.

In the final chapter in this section (Chapter 6) Cathy Gunn provides an insightful analysis of the 'challenges facing academic developers in the influential but unpredictable area of digital technologies in tertiary education', and a conceptual overview of the changing terrain of learning and teaching as a result of technological advances. With clear links to the earlier case study on elearning (Case Study 6), Gunn questions and provides a response to the question 'what is it that is being evaluated?'

In common with Kerri-Lee Krause in the previous chapter, Gunn is clear that evaluation at any stage of implementing innovative strategies must be first and foremost evidence-based. She eschews the notion that we should evaluate the impact of specific activities either by isolating them from other activities or by comparing them with others. She argues that such techniques may work well in some areas of study but do not fit the different paradigm of development. Instead she argues for the ongoing development of 'qualitative, interpretive and critical methods of evaluation fine tuned to the study of learning in naturalistic settings.'

There are also interesting parallels between Gunn's viewpoint on evaluating the processes by which we build elearning capacity within an institution and Kreber's view (Chapter 4) that we should evaluate the processes by which we as developers support teachers to achieve the goals of higher education teaching.

Although the focus of Gunn's chapter is on academic development relating to elearning and effective embedding of technology in learning and teaching, the design-based research approach that she suggests is the best approach to evaluating the impact of such work could well be applied to many more aspects of academic development.

Case Studies of Evaluative Practice

Section II showcases academic development practice and approaches to evaluation of the effectiveness of that work, in a large, top one-hundred, research-intensive institution with eight faculties, a diverse population of students and one of the largest academic development centres in Australasia.

The purpose of the case studies is primarily to show approaches taken to evaluating the effectiveness of a range of academic development inputs with different facilitative strategies and different goals. There are two strands to the overarching objectives of the inputs, one being to enhance learning and teaching and the student experience and the other to effect organizational change and development. These two strands resonate well with the purpose of academic development as articulated by the authors of the chapters in Section I. Overall the case studies give a sense of the range of activities that fall within the remit of academic development. There will be similarities and differences between different institutions depending on the nature of any particular higher education institution, the socio-political environment, the size of the institution and the mission. What becomes apparent from this series of case studies is the absence of an overarching evaluative framework for the academic development enterprise.

However, many of the key themes that can be drawn from the chapters in the previous section can be glimpsed through the case studies, for example taking a longer (historical) perspective on evaluation, examining the processes by which we endeavour to enhance learning and teaching and the student experience, the multi-agency nature of academic development and providing the evidence base for our activities. Taking these together with the themes from Section III, it becomes possible to see ways forward to develop more robust and compelling ways of providing evidence of the effectiveness of academic development.

Overall the case studies highlight a number of important points. In the institution showcased here, three of the case studies focus specifically on different aspects of building research capacity and capability. This is not too surprising given the nature of the institution. Different types of institution will encourage different sorts of academic development input, hence making it difficult to suggest common frameworks for evaluation. Other issues explored include the unpredictability of academics' immediate responses to academic development inputs. A prime example here relates to academics' views on the institutional Postgraduate Certificate in Academic Practice programme described by Helen Sword (Case Study 5). Evaluations carried out during or immediately after engagement with such programmes may differ markedly from views expressed at a different point in time – which resonates well with the notion that meaningful evaluation of interventions intended to effect positive change needs to be seen in both historical and contextual terms (Land, 2004).

The case studies show little in the way of generic workshops. In common with many similar academic development units or centres, the staff within the CAD at the University of Auckland recognize the limitations of generic workshops. Anecdotal evidence from faculty indicates a preference for contextualized development opportunities or defined development programmes. The cases here tend to relate to institutional strategic priorities actioned through specific interventions such as the institution-wide Doctoral Skills Programme described by Kelly et al. (Case Study 3), mandatory supervision training as discussed by Barbara Grant (Case Study 4) or high-level activities such as facilitation of departmental strategic development events (Stefani; Case Study 7). The outcomes of such interventions or activities are not amenable to immediate simplistic evaluations, nor is it easy to predetermine the tangible outcomes of such work.

Most institutions have an interest in building elearning capacity and the University of Auckland is no exception. As Gunn and Donald show in Case Study 6, the evaluation of academic development relating to elearning capacity building poses a number of challenges. Once again the question can be asked, 'what is it that is being evaluated?' Is it enhanced student learning outcomes? Is it the expertise of those enabling capacity building or is it the iterative processes involved in developing online resources intended to engage the learners?

The first case study of the series (Case Study 1), written by Matiu Ratima, gives an indication of one institution's response to the importance of culturally relevant academic development, whereas the last case study, by Linda McLain (Case Study 8), focuses on leadership development within the institution. These two cases in particular show the need for multi-agency input to organizational change and development, which adds further layers of complexity to the 'who, what, why, where and when?' issues associated with evaluation of effectiveness. They also link well with the ideas expressed in George Gordon's chapter in which he suggests we need some form of visualization of the connections and relationships between different academic development inputs to support shared understandings of the development project and to provide a tool or a model to inform reflections and guide evaluations (Chapter 3).

In Matiu Ratima's case, it is clear that the institution has some way to go to fully live up to the principles outlined in the Treaty of Waitangi (Case Study 1) but the Centre for Academic Development is making strenuous attempts to promote and support excellence in teaching and learning for Māori staff and students.

Barbara Kensington-Miller describes well the strategies she uses to set up peer mentoring pairs with early-career academics. She also presents the ways in which she is currently attempting to evaluate this work. However, as with many interventions of this nature, it will be immensely difficult to determine or even suggest a causal link between the developmental inputs and the future attainment of the peer mentoring participants. Providing peer mentoring is an institutional strategic priority, to support staff in all aspects of their academic career, but it may well require longitudinal studies to determine the impact.

Barbara Grant, in her case study on academic development activities intended to improve or enhance supervision skills, describes her evaluation practice as 'bricolage' (Case Study 4), a term often used to refer to the construction or creation of a work from a diverse range of things which happen to be available.

The term describes well the measures she uses to evaluate her practice; but her case also shows the problematic issue of assuming a causal link between academic development work and improved practice.

The case study on facilitating a departmental strategic planning retreat for the purpose of 'continuous improvement' poses the question 'whose evaluation matters?' (Case Study 7). On the one hand the role of facilitator requires the academic developer to be a substantively neutral third party, but on the other hand there is an involvement in the group's discussions and decision making as an 'expert consultant'. The facilitative role has to be seen by the group as appropriate to its needs in order for the group to be legitimately influenced in their future direction. However, what matters most is whether the group achieves its goals within a reasonable time frame (as decided by the group itself). McLain, in detailing the sorts of evaluative measures that may be used to determine the effectiveness of leadership programmes, concludes that 'we do what we can to evaluate as best we can' (Case Study 8).

Large-Scale Evaluative Endeavours

In the first chapter of Section III (Chapter 7) Claudia Stanny and Jane Halonen, from the University of West Florida, provide a useful set of strategies for evaluating the impact of a teaching centre on institutional culture. The authors here examine the evaluation of their academic development unit as a whole, taking assessment/evaluation of student learning outcomes as a primary focus of the work being carried out by the centre.

The backdrop of their chapter is the pressure on universities in the United States to enhance their accountability practices with respect to providing valid and reliable information about the quality of student learning. Institutions are expected to satisfy the complex demands of Federal government, State government, regional accreditation bodies and discipline-specific accreditation bodies. The major external drivers of quality assurance in this heady mix are the accreditation bodies. The accountability agenda with respect to assessment of student learning involves evidencing high quality learning and academic performance, accommodating teaching practices to a changing academic environment, making expectations of student performance explicit and measuring the impact of the learning experiences designed/delivered.

There are two paradigms in operation regarding assessment; one being focused on continuous improvement of student learning outcomes and the student experience and the second focusing on the accountability 'regime'. Faculty development within this context poses some serious challenges.

Stanny and Halonen describe different orientations to the accreditation, accountability and assessment agendas and, importantly, describe the sorts of indicators, both direct and indirect, that determine the success of development strategies. The important message the authors convey that perhaps should be heeded by all academic developers is that 'we must be fearless in the measurement of our own evolution' (Chapter 7). Although the authors fully recognize that the 'journey for faculty developers can be a hazard-filled one', they believe that the growth of a culture of development makes the journey worthwhile. What needs to be understood within this chapter is that, in the United States, the terms 'assessment' and 'evaluation' are used differently from in other parts of the world. In this chapter, the 'assessment agenda' has similar connotations to a quality assurance agenda.

In Chapter 8, Roni Bamber questions whether an institutionally derived model of evaluation of Lecturer Development Programmes (LDPs) could be applied nationally. Bamber takes the position that LDPs are underpinned by a 'theory of change' but, wisely, she advises that different theories of change will be in operation in different types of institution. The evaluation strategies in use will also have a particular philosophical and theoretical basis and these factors tend to mitigate against a national framework for evaluation of LDPs. Despite her argument for caution Bamber believes that a national framework or large-scale evaluations could provide a useful backdrop for local evaluations and could also provide benchmark data. In Chapter 8 she provides a thorough review of small-scale local evaluations and describes in detail the evaluation strategy for the LDP within her own institution.

The overall position Bamber is taking is that the links between learning and teaching could be strengthened and enriched 'if educational developers took a research-informed approach to evaluating their programmes and published their findings.' She suggests that 'if this were to happen systematically educational development may move into a more positive space than is currently ascribed to it'. This premise sits comfortably with the views expressed by chapter authors in Section I.

Following on from this, Naidoo and Holmes (Chapter 9) provide an account of a nationally funded project aimed at demonstrating the impact of academic development on teachers' and students' success. The project described was undertaken partly in response to the report of a study commissioned by the New Zealand Ministry of Education which signalled that there was little evidence of a causal link between the work of academic developers and student learning outcomes (Prebble et al., 2004).

The overall premise of the research project described by Naidoo and Holmes was to have academic developers in all eight New Zealand universities implement a Teaching and Learning Enhancement Initiative (TLEI) in a large first year class where there were perceived to be completion and retention issues. The academic development input, lecturers' responses and student learning outcomes would be monitored through three iterations of the academic course within which the TLEI was being implemented.

What is clear from Holmes's and Naidoo's account of this project is the multi-layered, multi-faceted nature of the evaluation strategies put in place for the duration of the funded project. In fact it could be concluded that the regular monitoring and updating of the project outcomes to satisfy the funders was more complex than the academic development work itself, to the point that the positive outcomes of the work were almost buried under the evaluations.

Like Bamber in the previous chapter, the authors argue strongly for a research informed approach to evaluation, but developers need to exercise some caution regarding making evaluation overburdensome, such that the key outcomes and messages deriving from action-research academic development projects are not undermined by the evaluation.

Kathleen Gray and Alex Radloff in Chapter 10 present a note of caution on the language of evaluation. They make a plea for caution in using the term 'impact' in relation to academic development work, either to describe its aims or as a criterion for its evaluation. Their review of the academic development literature indicates the high value that the academic community places on the concept of 'impact'.

Gray and Radloff interrogate the interpretations/meanings of the term 'impact' and how they may skew the expectations of what academic developers can achieve towards reporting only 'the high point attained in a piece of AD work' or 'constantly demonstrating the usefulness, effectiveness and value of academic development units.' They argue that this negates the big-picture issues that can influence the advancement of learning and teaching.

Through an interrogation of annual reports presented over a period of years by an academic development unit in a large multi-campus university, the authors describe not only the changes in reporting style and content according to what template is being used in any one year, but also that each year's report was crafted to convey the impact of their work in such a way as to make a good impression. Annual reports are in essence a form of reflection and evaluation, but by focusing overwhelmingly on the positive impression, what are not documented are the factors that impede our work such as intractable staff, disengaged managers, administrative inertia and the sheer person hours taken to achieve the outcomes that are reported on positively.

Although in no way negating the importance of critically examining and presenting evidence to stakeholders about the effects of what we do, Gray and Radloff suggest that to use impact assessment to evaluate academic development work requires rigorous evidence drawn from multiple sources and that to improve impact requires being open about the barriers to effecting positive change – the unforeseen and unwanted effects – as well as the good news!

The final chapter of Section III (Chapter 11) explores the potential of the high-level patterns and evaluative strategies that the contributors to this book have put forward and the implications for the further development of the field of academic development.

References

Buckridge, M. (2008) Teaching portfolios and their role in teaching and learning policy. *International Journal for Academic Development* 13 (2), 117–127.

Clegg, S. (2009) Forms of knowing and academic development practice. *Studies in Higher Education* 34 (4), 403–416.

Clegg, S. and Smith, K. (2008) Learning and teaching and assessment strategies in higher education: contradictions of genre and desiring. *Research Papers in Education* 25 (1), 115–132.

Gosling, D. (2007) Context and organization of educational development. In Tompkinson, B. (ed.) *Leading educational change* (SEDA special, 20). London: Staff and Educational Development Association.

Grant, B.M., Lee, A., Clegg, S., Manathunga, C., Barrow, M., Kandlbinder, P., Brailsford, I., Gosling, D. and Hicks, M. (2009) Why history? Why now? Multiple accounts of the emergence of academic development. *International Journal for Academic Development* 14 (1), 83–86.

Harland, T. and Staniforth, D. (2008) A family of strangers: the fragmented nature of academic development. *Teaching in Higher Education* 13 (6), 669–678.

Kreber, C. and Brook, P. (2001) Impact evaluation of educational development programs. *International Journal for Academic Development* 6 (2), 96–108.

Land, R. (2004) *Educational development: discourse, identity and practice.* Buckingham: SRHE and Open University Press.

Prebble, T., Hargraves, H., Leach, L., Naidoo, K., Suddaby, G. and Zepke, N. (2004) *Impact of student support services and academic development programs on student outcomes in undergraduate tertiary study: a synthesis of the research.* Report to the Ministry of Education, New Zealand.

Rowland, S. (2002) Overcoming fragmentation in professional life: the challenge for academic development. *Higher Education Quarterly* 56 (1), 52–64.

Stefani, L. and Elton, L. (2002) Continuing professional development of academic teachers through self-initiated learning. *Assessment and Evaluation in Higher Education* 27 (2), 117–129.

2

Locating Academic Development
The First Step in Evaluation

SHELDA DEBOWSKI

Introduction

Academic development centres emerged in the 1970s to encourage better academic practice and improved student outcomes (Sorcinelli et al., 2006). They commenced in Australia, for example, as various individuals gained executive sponsorship to establish centralised academic units that could promote better understanding of academic work (Lee et al., 2008). Subsequently these units became common practice in most western nations, although their structure, nature and focus vary considerably. This movement has continued throughout the intervening years across many different countries, with China now commencing the process of establishing its centres for teaching and learning enhancement.

The central precept of academic development units relates to improving the effectiveness of academic outcomes. However, as this chapter will show, the foundational concepts for academic work remain loosely defined, with many implicit rather than explicit assumptions. Three main issues will be explored: first, the nature of academic development work and its positioning in university settings; second, how academic development work operates; and third, the consequent challenges of evaluating impact and effectiveness of academic development outcomes.

The Context for Academic Development

Academic development units have been somewhat unusual in their university placement. In most cases, the staff appointed to these units hold academic positions. They are generally located in central administrative units (or sometimes within faculties), and have responsibility for guiding the academic community toward better practice – most commonly, with respect to learning and teaching applications. There are few avenues for gaining professional qualifications in academic development. For the most part, the majority of staff have moved from other disciplines into their new field of work. Academic developers may therefore come from many different backgrounds, including a long teaching track, organisational development, educational disciplines, doctoral study focusing on higher education development or any number of other paths. Although this diversity of background has many benefits, it also offers many challenges in building a professional base and accepted practices that can be broadly accepted and adopted across the sector.

The concept of academic development has been variously scoped to mean many things. It can, for example, encompass services and support relating to:

- academic skills and capability enhancement in the areas of teaching and learning and, in some cases, research and leadership
- curriculum reform and development
- student support services
- student management
- learning technologies
- educational evaluation and measurement
- educational research and scholarship
- policy and organisational practice
- university change and system enhancement.

Although the selection of a particular service mix may have been partly determined by the capabilities of the available academic developers, it also relates to the particular choices that university leaders make in scoping, staffing and funding these units. The absence of a long-established theoretical and professional base has encouraged variable interpretation of the academic development concept, with institutions constructing their services in many different configurations. Certainly, we see a long history of redesign of academic development centres as new imperatives emerge within an institution. The location of academic development units may shift across broader administrative structures as new executive portfolios are scoped. They can also be reconstructed to better match the prevailing ideology or political context of the institution. In recent years in Australia and the United States we have seen a tougher line being taken with academic developers who have not demonstrated sufficient agility to adapt to changing institutional expectations.

Over this new century the status and functions of academic development units have also shifted markedly. Initially, they were established as highly influential change agencies with high-level sponsorship; the directors reported to a very senior executive member and actively contributed to many strategic committees and working groups. In recent years universities have expanded their range of executive appointments to include additional senior leadership roles that oversee broad portfolios. It is not uncommon now, for example, to have a Deputy Vice Chancellor (Education) and a Pro Vice Chancellor (Learning and Teaching) sitting on the Executive. The Academic Development Director, once an influential agent for learning and teaching policy and change across the senior leadership community, now reports to these senior appointments, receives advice on the priorities that should be addressed and guides policy into practice across the university community. For some, this has meant a stronger focus on implementation rather than strategy and policy formulation. The increased range of executive appointments has also led to increased fracturing of academic development work. It is possible, for example, to see various agencies tasked with elements of academic development work. Teaching and learning, evaluation, student support, research development and leadership development might be located in a range of different service areas, supporting different executive member portfolios, with each envisioning the role of the academic developer in very different ways. Academic developers may also be located in different communities, with some operating as central appointments in the main administrative hub of the university, whereas others are placed in faculty locales. This can also affect their orientation, alignment and engagement with university priorities and directions. Few disciplines have experienced the same degree of fractured identity as academic development.

In some professions external organisations have taken a leadership role in scoping and defining the standards, principles and expectations that should underpin the professionalisation of a discipline. Academic development has been slow to develop focused support of this nature. On the whole, academic developers work from a notion of community, encouraging the sharing of good practice and a gradual accretion of knowledge that can be shared and adapted to meet the institutional needs. A good example is the strengthening focus on foundational skill programmes for new teachers in Australia and New Zealand. Starting as an initial forum for exchange and learning, the Foundations Colloquium has evolved into an ongoing collaborative initiative that seeks to formalise the programmes and recognition for new teachers (see http://www.tedi.uq.edu.au/evaluations/index.html). Similarly, the Future Research Leaders Program aimed to provide a body of learning that would enhance researchers' professional capabilities (see http://frlp.edu.au/public.html). However, each of these initiatives stemmed from committed individuals identifying a need to collaborate, rather than a cohesive mapping of the work that is undertaken by academic developers. The nature of academic development work has therefore coalesced around the areas of interest or need that have emerged in different communities, rather than through a focused attempt to clarify where it should best be oriented. This has resulted in a somewhat piecemeal approach to depicting academic development work.

The discipline is made more challenging as the necessary competencies for academic developers also remain ill-defined. People generally learn their profession on the job, drawing on their own background knowledge and the modelling of those around them. There is no established syllabus for preparing academic developers and few formal professional recognition channels for those wishing to develop their skills. It can be argued that three different professional knowledges are required. First, the developer requires an understanding of the academic activities that are being supported (which may be teaching and learning or a wider suite of support). The research base around these areas is still developing, and so the academic developer often operates as the interpreter of past research and an action researcher investigating their own context and community to build common meaning. Second, a knowledge of organisational development principles and strategies enables effective facilitation, leadership and organisational development support, although the lens of working with academics continues to challenge some of these concepts. Third, knowledge of adult learning principles informs the design and implementation of effective programmes and assistance. At its annual meetings the International Consortium for Educational Development (http://www.osds.uwa.edu.au/iced), which comprises the major international network for academic development, notes the challenges of building a common language, theory base and principles that will readily translate across national boundaries and communities. However, it also notes the importance of developing a framework that will better articulate the basic concepts that guide this important work. In the coming years it will be important to develop a professional academic development knowledge and capabilities framework to better assist those moving into the field.

Despite these contextual complexities, it would be fair to suggest that the following statements are true of most academic development communities.

1. The primary role of academic developers is to educate, influence and enhance academic practice.
2. Academic developers will normally work closely with faculty members and faculty leaders to encourage improved knowledge and skills in their designated portfolio areas.
3. Their professional practice is informed by research, promotes ongoing scholarship and research, and prompts further exploration of the discipline.
4. They interact with a diverse range of stakeholders, including executive members, academic leaders, and experienced and new academics.
5. Their scope of responsibilities, performance expectations and required outcomes can shift as institutional priorities evolve.

Given this contextual framework, it is easy to see why academic development has found it difficult to form a comprehensive approach to evaluating its impact and outcomes. With each developer coming from a different disciplinary paradigm, professional associations operating as agencies for communication, rather than accrediting bodies, and each institution interpreting its service mix to suit its own perceived needs, the challenges are many.

Despite this complex setting, it is clearly time to start the process of building some stronger frameworks and principles to better evaluate the impact and effectiveness of the discipline.

The Nature of Academic Development Work

To evaluate academic development outcomes, it is first important to understand the way in which this role operates. In general, the aim is to educate, influence and enable change across the community.

Developers *educate* the community by providing a range of programmes, workshops and customised support to individuals and groups. Although their primary focus has been at the new entry level for academics, there is increasing concern for providing more effective guidance for academic heads and coordinators in their work (Scott et al., 2008). This formal educative role focuses on areas such as building capacity for effective academic practice across the community, promoting communities of practice, encouraging higher-order thinking and reflection about academic work and, in some cases, certifying staff as being sufficiently educated to undertake their core academic roles. Although the general model is to provide these services through a centralised agency, there is considerable value in locating this work in a faculty where the barriers to learning transfer are diminished and the building of a supportive community is increased. The academic developer might also act as a broker to enable groups to meet and explore common issues. This can be a very powerful educative process operating through peer learning partnerships, with the developer taking more of a facilitative role than a direct educational role.

Influencing work operates from an advocacy and partnership model in which the developer works closely with stakeholders to guide their ongoing learning and increase their understanding of their roles, responsibilities and capacity to improve the work context. Many of these activities take place in the local community, where a cohort of engaged colleagues may be brought together to address a common issue or challenge. This responsive approach has the potential to be most influential in shifting cultures, community practice and leadership capabilities. However, it is intensive work and requires high-level relationship, facilitation and consultative skills. Stakeholders choose to work with the developer based on their assessment of that individual's competence, reputation and credibility. It is therefore important for the developer to have a good profile, a credible body of work and a reputation for effective outcomes. A further complication is that critical stakeholders with whom the developer will work change regularly. Heads of school, for example, fill their role for only a set period of time before resuming their academic position. Associate deans and other coordinators similarly fill roles for a period of time and then head to other roles. This means that the developer is on a constant cycle of meeting, establishing trust, building credibility, initiating partnerships, educating the new incumbent and then transitioning to an ongoing supportive relationship with the new incumbent.

The third level of academic development work is often hidden to the wider community. Academic agencies *enable institutional change* through their ongoing development and refinement of policies, technology, systems and processes that support the academic enterprise. This work can be time consuming and may require considerable consultation. The development of policies on academic integrity, for example, requires considerable research, discussion, mapping of existing practice and translation into student record systems, academic staff education and design of student information packages. Work of this nature is largely unsung, but of critical importance in building a more effective outcome for the institution. The academic development unit may also play a large role in capacity building across the broad university community – particularly if it has responsibility for leadership enhancement and large-scale reform initiatives. This transformational focus encourages a wider outreach role and increased interaction with diverse leaders and university groups, as well as a stronger emphasis on consultation and marketing of new initiatives to the entire university community.

From this brief overview, it can be seen that academic development operates across a continuum of professional support. Developers are educators, change agents, brokers, consultants, facilitators, system and policy experts, and relationship managers. They need not only to build a body of professional practice that is pertinent to their institution, but also to market their services to the wider community. They operate from both a push and a pull paradigm: pushing services, policies and systems out into the community and pulling stakeholders into a stronger focus on enhancing academic practice. The ultimate goal of these dual foci is to transform academic practice across the community so that the university prospers and flourishes.

Currently the main focus of academic development work emphasises providing academics with the capabilities they require to successfully execute their complex roles. In most universities, participants in academic development programmes attend centrally conducted programmes and workshops attended by a diverse mix of staff from many different university areas. Every individual is exposed to new techniques and practices and then moves back into their individual work context where support and encouragement is unpredictable. The influence of the local culture, leadership and the individual academic's own work role and capabilities all influence the overall transfer of the new knowledge and skills. Academic developers' impact on capability enhancement is thus hard to demonstrate, given the many other variables that also contribute to the final outcome. Although we measure the initial inputs with alacrity, the ultimate impact of educational programmes and workshops on academic practice is much harder to affirm or test. These challenges are also evident when we consider the academic developer's contribution to institutional transformation.

Academic Development as a Transformative Agency

Recently Australian higher education was extensively reviewed in the Bradley Review – a wide ranging and in-depth evaluation of the effectiveness and impact of higher education policy and practice on student learning and outcomes. The review revealed an alarming decrease in student satisfaction across a number of areas, including student and staff interactions, enriching student experiences and feedback provision (Bradley et al., 2008). Many factors have contributed to this slippage, including the decreasing funding base that operates in Australian higher education. However, it also challenges claims that academic development units positively impact on their wider communities. Do they really make a difference to educational quality and outcomes? On the face of it, the degradation of the student experience could be argued to be a broad indicator that academic development agencies have not markedly shifted community attitudes and values. Are they a good investment for universities? How do we know? Are our methodologies and strategies the best approaches to encouraging ongoing higher education transformation? Could we do better by focusing our work in different ways? Or possibly, some might argue, are these outcomes for which academic developers should not take responsibility?

If the focus of academic development is to influence and transform academic practice and communities, the measurement of how these agencies encourage reformed practice needs to be carefully considered. The cultivation of a strong relationship with academic leaders and the move toward a stronger partnership model with those leaders opens new avenues for creating a stronger impact within specific communities. However, this approach generates considerable resource implications, since it requires an intensive and continuous focus on one group. At the University of Western Australia, for example, faculty-based early-career academic development programmes generally encourage a range of strategies that will benefit the local area, including mentorship support, better induction processes, increased academic awareness of organisational data and metrics, wider engagement of the community in academic matters and increased interaction across different levels of the community. These interventions generate significantly enhanced outcomes in academic practice, but they do not happen by simply suggesting ideas to the relevant leaders. Instead, a partnership between the academic developer, other specialists, the academic leader and relevant members of the community needs to be formed and cultivated. Although the subsequent shifts in cultural outcomes and practice are extremely important, the resource implications for the academic consultant are high. This work has the capacity to transform a local community, but the results of that work also need to be more widely promulgated. The academic developer needs to be able to show the impact of this approach and to demonstrate how they have contributed to the outcomes.

Role-based development programmes also have the potential to be highly influential in shifting organisational practice. Scott et al. (2008) undertook a comprehensive review of the need for improved leadership development of academic leaders. Their work highlights the importance of focusing more intensively on the groups that have the most impact on the academic community: heads of school, course coordinators and others with major functional responsibilities. Some of the work that might be undertaken in this context includes the development of peer learning and problem-based approaches to emergent issues (see, for example, Blake et al., 2009, who illustrate the use of institutional case studies to promote better academic practice across the wider community).

Academic development units have the potential to enhance competitive advantage, improve staff engagement with academic outcomes, lower duplication, increase knowledge exchange and promote innovation. Developers work across boundaries and gain an intensive knowledge of the broader context. They see the work being done by various communities and operate as conduits for sharing and exchanging that knowledge and experience. Innovation can be cultivated in a number of ways, including the contribution of stakeholders to the development of innovative practice; the reuse of existing knowledge and strategies; the invention of new approaches; and the ongoing melding of practices from different communities (Dvir et al., 2002). By operating as an agent of change, the developer encourages more rapid shifts in organisational practice and increased efficiency in building viable solutions. The development of an institutional focus on innovation and interactive exchange of knowledge takes considerable time to cultivate. It requires careful development of a range of initiatives that encourage stronger staff engagement. In facilitating institution-wide transformational processes, the developer needs to employ a wider repertoire of strategies, including practices such as Open Space Technology (Owen, 1997). The overall impact of these strategies is likely to be significant as deeper engagement and exchange are achieved across the community (Debowski and Blake, 2007).

The progressive enrichment of academic development strategies to support institutional, community and individual outcomes requires careful management of resources and ongoing consideration of how best to support the institution's priorities. In reviewing the overall impact of the academic development agency, the goal is to establish a robust link between the agency's activities and the subsequent improvement of organisational practice. However, the causal relationship can be hard to demonstrate as it operates through the activities and demonstrable change achieved across the organisation by local academic communities and through individual academics. The ultimate proof of impact relies on others taking up the concepts and ideas that have been shared or stimulated. It could be argued that the best work is done when others have taken up the message and acted on the principles. In the process, however, they become the visible agents of improvement, not the academic developer. The challenge of articulating and demonstrating the relationship between the academic developer's work and changes to organisational outcomes therefore requires careful consideration. How can we show that academic developers make a difference?

Evaluating the Impact of Academic Development

Evaluation of outcomes and impact provides evidence of the degree to which investments in academic development (money, time and effort) are justified. It offers guidance on whether existing strategies should be continued or amended to better match the university's goals. Evaluation should address two questions:

1. How are we progressing in improving our impact and effectiveness?
2. How does academic development make a difference to this organisation?

The first question anticipates a progressive enhancement of institutional support as educative techniques, interventions and services are regularly refined to better match the institutional needs. The second question explores the broader context in which academic development operates, focusing on the transformational role that a well developed service can achieve.

There are many ways in which evaluation might be enacted. Table 2.1 depicts some of the approaches that might be employed in an academic development context across the various forms of support that might be in operation.

Evaluative processes directed toward assessing the impact of academic development interventions commonly explore *input* measures of effectiveness, particularly the cost of activities, participant responses to the learning experience and the numbers of people who engage with the programmes and workshops on offer. *Output* measures focus more intensively on how much difference the academic development strategy has made to the individual, the community and the institution as a whole. As Table 2.1 illustrates, there is considerable potential to better measure the impacts or outputs of academic development interventions if a more rigorous evaluative process is implemented. Although some measures, such as evaluations of the student experience, can be attributed to the work of many individuals across the community, they might also provide a proxy measure of particular change strategies that have been part of the academic development strategy. With a broader range of evaluative measures, academic developers are better able to review the degree to which their work makes a difference. They can triangulate data sources to clarify consistent trends, look for cultural shifts, identify communities at risk and build a longitudinal picture of how the institution is evolving in terms of the desired practices. They can also better identify issues or areas of concern that may require more concerted focus in the coming year(s). The granularity of the evaluation can be adapted to reflect the purpose and audience which will be privy to the outcomes. The impact of workshops and programmes on individuals, for example, might be explored by the developer, or by their sponsor, or as part of a more detailed programme review that will guide further programme development.

The measurement and reporting of impact is an important element of academic work. The reporting of academic development centre outputs encourages ongoing institutional resourcing of the agency and also affirms the strategic

Table 2.1 Evaluating Academic Development Educational, Community and Institutional Impacts

Focus	Examples of activities	Evaluative methods / indicators
Educational role (individual/group learning)		
Entry-level capabilities, e.g. teaching, research, management skills, elearning	Educational programmes Graduate certificate qualifications Self-selected workshops Mentorship schemes Website support Online learning Teaching excellence submissions support Grant-seeking assistance	*Inputs* Hours of development offered Participant feedback/satisfaction Participation in programmes and activities Expenditure on academic development activities *Outputs* Increased quality of participant work/ submissions Submission success rate Supervisor feedback on changes in practice/ outcomes Increases in student ratings/feedback on individual's work activities Pre-test/post-test of participant knowledge, skills, attitudes and work patterns
Community engagement (influencing and culture setting)		
Cohort (role-based) networks and learning Local community support	Leadership/role-based programmes Customised support/bespoke programmes Case studies Peer exchange and learning Communities of practice support and brokering Cross-disciplinary peer learning projects Role-based forums Website guidance Online forums	*Inputs* Hours of support provided Participation of target audience in programmes, communities of practice Activity costs and expenditure *Outputs* Changes to leadership/community practice Shared strategies and resources Completed projects Changes to systems/practices Pre-test/post-test measures Measures of staff engagement Student experience feedback Focus groups/interviews Self-report surveys Attitudinal surveys Experiential stories Number of areas that have adopted new practices
Institutional influence (organisational transformation)		
Organisational development Organisational change Cultural change	University forums Staff retreats Policy development System enhancement Website development Guidelines Project management/delivery Peer-learning projects	*Inputs* Hours of development Staff participation/engagement *Outputs* Project outcomes Policy implementation/adoption Cultural analyses/surveys Action research Student engagement metrics Staff engagement metrics Institutional performance

impact of the work that is done. Richer evaluative approaches also encourage closer evaluation of impact and may assist in making decisions as to where future resources are best deployed. Research and scholarship activities are also better supported by more thorough analysis of the data. In addition, as Table 2.1 demonstrates, whereas much of this material is readily captured, there is a need to think more carefully about the indicators to be measured, the timing, the messages they convey and the intended audience for those outputs.

Evaluating the Management of the Academic Development Unit

So far, this chapter has focused on the broad service roles that the academic development unit fulfils in the university community. It has emphasised the need to think about the ways in which services are perceived and deployed in the various communities and how the individual developers are received by their 'clients'.

A largely underdiscussed element in the academic literature relates to the overall evaluation of the unit's management as a service agency in the university community. Many of the measures outlined in Table 2.1 explore the causal effect of a particular intervention on the relevant community. The measurement of the overall management and positioning of the academic development unit generates some additional evaluative processes. There are three evaluative elements that contribute to this assessment: the efficiency, effectiveness and strategic relevance of the agency.

Efficiency relates to how much throughput and activity is achieved by the unit. Increased efficiency can be generated through careful management of workflows, system management and streamlining of processes. An increased emphasis on group as opposed to individual consultancies, for example, has been driven by the need to provide more support with fewer additional resources. A key consideration in determining efficiency relates to where resources can be put to make the most difference. This encourages regular review of how academic work is undertaken and related cost–benefit analyses.

Effectiveness concerns the quality of the outcomes, services or processes that are generated by the academic development agency. The demand for the services provided is one measure of effectiveness, demonstrating ongoing user satisfaction with the offerings and standard of assistance provided. User satisfaction measures might also be employed, ranging from a wide ranging survey to a more targeted interview of key stakeholders. More formal measures of user satisfaction with the service quality could also be undertaken, possibly adapted from the well regarded SERVQUAL used by many service sectors (http://www.businessadvantageuk.biz/SERVQUAL.htm). This survey explores five perspectives: reliability, responsiveness, quality assurance, empathy and tangible outcomes, and has been adapted for use in a variety of contexts, including higher education (Tan and Kek, 2004; Fitzsimmons and Fitzsimmons, 2006). The use of a standard instrument could also facilitate benchmarking with other, similar agencies in different universities.

Strategic relevance relates to how the unit parallels the university's ongoing priorities and foci. Academic development units are increasingly required to respond to the shifts in organisational priorities to ensure their communities are equipped to meet the new challenges that are emerging. At the same time, they need to maintain existing core services. It is most important to manage the balance between these two spheres of activity to ensure they can support the university's goals. However, the determination of relevance is a value laden word: the academic developer is somewhat challenged by working among a number of different stakeholders – all of whom may have a different view as to what is strategically relevant. One of the relationship management roles then is to guide stakeholders toward an increased understanding of academic development and its possibilities.

A risk in evaluating the management of the academic development strategy is that a piecemeal approach might be employed, thereby failing to recognise the high level of inter-relationship which exists. To build a more cohesive examination of the entire functioning of the academic development unit, a balanced scorecard approach (BSC) could be beneficial (Kaplan and Norton, 1996). The BSC recognises that a focus on dollars expended is less critical than the overall consideration of how the service impacts on users and their ongoing practice; in other words: how has the service contributed to the transformation of the university? This evaluative process draws on stakeholder feedback and encourages stronger consideration of the cultural and social dimensions that are inherent in academic development work. Table 2.2 illustrates the focus an adapted BSC for academic development might explore. Five core aspects are reflected: financial management; customers/stakeholders; internal management; research and scholarship; and learning, growth and innovation. The adoption of a BSC framework helps to balance the long- and short-term imperatives that operate in an academic development context.

Table 2.2 Balanced Score Card Approach to Academic Development Evaluation

Financial investment	Customers/ stakeholders	Internal management	Research and scholarship	Learning, growth and innovation
Are funds appropriately expended and exploited?	Does the service achieve what customers/ stakeholders need/expect?	Is the service operating effectively, efficiently and in a strategically relevant way?	Does the service operate from a scholarly focus that applies and builds good theory and measurement?	Does the service encourage the ongoing learning, growth, change and improvement of individuals, teams and the organisation?

Conclusion

The evolving nature of academic development work and its positioning in university settings parallels the changing nature of higher education institutions themselves. There is a need to be flexible and adaptive, responding to the different forces that are operating, while also ensuring that the service is as strategic and effective as possible. The variability of concept and service design creates some challenges for academic development units in developing effective evaluation strategies. However, it is important that academic development agencies monitor their performance, relevance and effectiveness in responding to institutional and stakeholder needs. The process of evaluation encourages reflection, innovation and careful consideration of the changing context in which the discipline works, thus ensuring it remains a vital component of higher education's development.

References

Blake, V., Debowski, S. and Sharma, R. (2009) Internal and external quality assurance: tensions and synergies. *Internal and external synergies: tensions and synergies.* Alice Springs: Australian Universities Quality Forum, 1–3 July. Available at: http://www.auqa.edu.au/files/auqf/paper/paper_9_paper.pdf (accessed 15 September 2009).

Bradley, D., Noonan, P., Nugent, H. and Scales, B. (2008) *Review of Australian higher education: final report.* Canberra: Commonwealth Government. Available at: http://www.deewr.gov.au/HigherEducation/Review/Documents/PDF/Higher%20Education%20Review_one%20document_02.pdf (accessed 15 September 2009).

Debowski S. and Blake, V. (2007) Collective capacity building of academic leaders: a university model of leadership and learning in context. *International Journal of Learning and Change* 2 (3), 307–324.

Dvir, R., Pasher, E. and Roth, N. (eds) (2002) *From knowledge to value: unfolding the knowledge cube – a balanced approach to new product development.* Herzliya: Edna Pasher.

Fitzsimmons, J.A. and Fitzsimmons, M.J. (2006) *Service management: operations, strategy and information technology.* 3rd edn. Singapore: McGraw-Hill.

Kaplan, R. and Norton, D. (1996) *The balanced scorecard.* Boston: Harvard University Publications.

Lee, A., Manathunga, C. and Kandlbinder, P. (2008) *Making a place: an oral history of academic development in Australia.* Milperra, NSW: HERDSA.

Owen, H. (1997) *Open space technology: a user's guide.* San Francisco: Berrett-Hoehler Publishers.

Scott, G., Coates, H. and Anderson, M. (2008) *Learning leaders in times of change: academic leadership capabilities for Australian higher education.* Sydney: University of Western Sydney and Australian Council for Educational Research.

Sorcinelli, M.D., Austin, A.E., Eddy, P.L. and Beach, A.L. (2006) *Creating the future for faculty development: learning from the past, understanding the present.* Bolton, MA: Anker Publishing.

Tan, K.C. and Kek, S.W. (2004) Service quality in higher education using an enhanced SERVQUAL approach. *Quality in Higher Education* 10 (1), 17–24.

3
The Quality Agenda
Where Does Academic Development Sit?

GEORGE GORDON

Introduction

For many outside the academy the question of where academic development sits within the quality agenda can appear to be an important one that should be comparatively simple to answer. Yet for many within the academy the question is complex, nuanced, situated, conditional and even contested or contentious.

This chapter seeks to explore key dimensions of such perspectives and how these affect attitudes to attempts to align academic development with the now commonplace bottom line of externally led quality assurance/quality enhancement agendas, namely the quality of the student experience.

Quality assurance and quality enhancement may present different challenges and opportunities for academic development and developers. Assurance expects systems, policies, procedures and practices to be in place and operating effectively for each and every student whatever their stage or programme of study. The assurance measures that are in place should be appropriate and equitable. Such strictures do not preclude localised flexibility but, arguably, they do constrain and shape it. It is hard to escape the conclusion that having in place an array of threshold standards and/or standardised approaches is a rational institutional strategy for much of the mainstream functioning of a robust set of quality assurance policies and procedures. By contrast, quality enhancement may offer greater scope for localised initiatives and ownership. It also has the natural advantage, in terms of alignment with academic development, of encouraging attention to improvement of the quality of the student experience rather than the compliance focus, which is often perceived within the academy as the main thrust of assurance.

In reality the distinction is often subtle. In Scotland, for example, the external process, entitled enhancement-led institutional review (ELIR), places primary responsibility for assurance with institutions but tests the institutional evidence for effective assurance during the process of ELIR. Moreover, institutions are expected to carefully assess any risk to students which might occur during an enhancement initiative, for example a new curriculum for a course or class, a new form of assessment or a new approach to placements, and have in place processes for quickly identifying and addressing any issues or problems. Thus enhancement is expected to occur within a strong assurance framework and culture.

The focus of the quality agenda is highly appropriate, salutary and challenging. Enhancing the quality of the student experience provides an agenda so vast, it is difficult not to conclude that there is ample scope for academic developers to align their agenda to this overarching goal.

The potentially overlapping challenges between the quality agenda and the academic development project include the scoping of the student experience, measurement of that experience and identification of causal links between developmental policies, initiatives and actions, and improvement to the student experience. The following sections of this chapter will explore the complex range of issues that impact or potentially impact on the learning experiences of our students.

Defining the 'Student Experience'

Baird and Gordon (2009a) argue that the literature suggests at least six possible definitions of the student experience, namely:

- all life experiences of all students
- all experiences of a student while a student
- all experiences whilst in the identity of a 'student'
- all experiences of facets of the institution such as a sense of belonging
- consumer experiences of the institution as a student
- the student learning experience, that is, personal development as a learner (p. 194).

Harvey (2004–8) favours reference to all aspects of the engagement of students with higher education. Others, including Krause et al. (2005), emphasise all student experiences, during and as part of studies. A subtle distinction could be introduced if one substituted 'across' for 'during'. The latter highlights a time envelope whereas the former might surface issues of connectivity, intentionality, coherence and alignment. Baird and Gordon (2009a) deduced that, for example, an institutional response to interpreting the student experience as being constituted 'during all or part of their studies' might be to highlight layered strategies, namely induction, the first year experience, transition to majors/honours, pre-graduation, transition to postgraduate studies, etc., rather than. for example, prioritising the relationship of formal to informal learning, the role of peer communities, or reflecting upon definitions of the curriculum and the potential consequences for quality assurance, quality enhancement and academic development.

Of course it is possible to operate multiple definitions in parallel, and indeed any sampling of institutional documents would suggest that is sought in policy and practice.

Indeed, given the powerful roles of academic tribes (Becher and Trowler, 2001) and the traditions and cultures of disciplines, it can be argued that a degree of breadth and measure of flexibility for detailed interpretation and prioritisation is both desirable and realistic.

The Changing Landscape of Higher Education

Many changes are affecting higher education worldwide, albeit there are local and national differences in scale, balance and detail. Each of the following factors has the potential to impact on student perceptions and attitudes, influence operational definitions of academic development and guide institutional strategies and policies: globalisation; internationalisation; widened access; the knowledge explosion; the implications of generational shifts in the student body (and indeed in faculty); shifts in curriculum delivery (e.g. blended learning); the diversification and multiplication of roles within the academy and of funding streams for higher education; legislative changes relating to equality, employment and health and safety; shifts in governmental and employer expectations of graduates and of the primary roles of higher education institutions; developments in the organisation of academic research and scholarship, commonly subsumed under the Mode 1/Mode 2 thesis (Gibbons et al., 1994); emerging communities of practice and their relationships to more established disciplines and thematic groups; the continuing debates about the relative importance of Boyer's four forms of scholarship (Boyer, 1990) and about the impact of the various pressures for change upon academic and professional identities (Gordon and Whitchurch, 2009; Henkel 2009); and the influences of the trend towards inter-institutional rankings (league tables).

Looking briefly at these different factors, globalisation, for example, is eroding the capacity of nation states, especially those which espouse free markets, to single-handedly steer or determine the nature, structure, framework and key objectives of publicly funded provision of higher education within their territories. Increasingly, the potentialities for borderless education (CVCP 2000) are materialising, although to date national states have succeeded in continuing to exercise considerable influence over what might be described as the big picture, the macro features of academic development.

The Bologna process (see http://www.ond.vlaanderen.be/hogeronderwijs/bologna/about/) can be viewed, at least in part, as a strategy by participating European nations to seize an opportunity presented by globalisation and gain an advantage in an increasingly competitive international market for student recruitment, as well as addressing distinctively European political ideals and aspirations.

Over a period of two decades, internationalisation may have had a massive impact upon academic development, transforming the nature and structure of the curriculum and facets of the student experience. To date, the reality is that the impact has been much more modest and specific. Certain programmes have been developed for international markets, many provided at offshore locations. These present developmental opportunities and challenges. Where provision is offshore the quality assurance expectations are comparability of standards, appropriately prepared staff, suitably supported students with access to high-quality facilities and security of arrangements for assessment. It could be argued that such arrangements should be seen as offering opportunities for experimentation, something which may not be easily reconciled with the demands of quality assurance. Yet some adjustment is almost inevitable and, arguably, desirable so that the provision pays due attention to the experiences and expectations of the students.

Part of the huge increase in participation rates in higher education has followed from the widespread migration towards higher education provision of a range of professions such as nursing, radiography, physiotherapy and social work. That shift has presented particular developmental challenges to practitioners in those disciplines, to staff such as educational/academic developers charged with providing support and to relevant professional bodies and communities of practice. Many of these programmes are governed by professional body accreditation. Such scrutiny often considers the appropriateness of staffing in terms of criteria such as qualifications, developmental experiences and opportunities, range of expertise and quality of leadership and evaluation.

More generally, higher participation rates are commonly perceived as entailing a more diverse student body, with a wide range of entry qualifications and prior educational experiences. They have also been associated with a shift in the balance of provision with greater scope for part-time study and for study using a wide range of modes of learning provision. This has impacted upon academic development and quality assurance/enhancement, particularly in relation to specific cohorts, such as students with disabilities. Nowadays legislation often requires developmental actions, including anticipatory policies and practices, clear and systematic procedures, coherent policies and integrated approaches to learning provision, student support, and academic and related staff development. However, the connection between systemic institutional approaches to quality assurance and the enhancement of the learning experiences of a diverse student body is less clear.

Exploring systemic quality assurance for diverse student experiences, Baird and Gordon (2009b) suggested that an institution-centred perspective might recognise:

- the distinction between academic activities and the other services
- the role of the institution in maintaining the credibility of awards
- the importance of student engagement and transformation
- how the diversity of students might affect academic processes and outcomes.

The knowledge explosion has impacted upon all disciplines and academic activities including academic development. The increase in the volume of output and the expansion of channels of dissemination, in combination, present daunting challenges in terms of keeping abreast with the literature of even a comparatively specialised subfield of study. The task escalates as the domain expands, especially when the field of interest spans disciplinary boundaries, as would characteristically be the case for the community of practice of academic developers and in large measure for the growing communities of developmentally oriented academics within disciplines, especially those in centres or units dedicated to supporting academic development within the discipline. Notable examples of the latter include the subject centres of the Higher Education Academy in the UK and the Centres for Excellence in Learning and Teaching (CETLS) in England. Equally, it embraces national support centres established by specific disciplines as well as units which over time acquire a national, even international, reputation such as the National Resource Centre for the Student Experience in the USA.

Gibbons et al. (1994) believed that an important shift had occurred in the production of scientific knowledge with a heightened role for interdisciplinary and multi-disciplinary, often fluid, teams of researchers. Some 15 years later, traditional discipline-based (Mode 1) research remains strong, and a major source of the generation of new knowledge and the testing of potential of existing knowledge. Nonetheless a substantial volume of findings stem from Mode 2 research. Where academic programmes, perhaps initially at postgraduate level, emerge from Mode 2 work, the connection between research and teaching, the closing of the circle of academic development, is readily enabled.

Considerable proliferation has taken place in the range of roles that academics can be asked to perform (Gordon, 2004). Additional, new professional roles have emerged in what Whitchurch (2009) describes as third space, territory between more traditional academic and administrative domains. Indeed, academic developers often occupy such third space even when they hold academic positions.

Notwithstanding the numerous forces for change impacting upon higher education institutions and academic life and practice, Henkel (2000) found that the identities were primarily founded upon the twin pillars of research and teaching, although the degree of interconnectedness did differ between disciplines. Nonetheless many new communities of practice have emerged. Academic developers would be an example, as would specialists in learning technologies or student support. One thing which these various emerging communities of practice have in common is that each in its own distinctive manner contributes to the quality of the student experience.

The key point that emerges from this brief overview of the changing landscape of higher education is that obvious synergies are emerging between the quality enhancement agenda (within the overarching framework of quality assurance), the role of academic development and the changing nature of the student experience. The next section explores the positioning of academic development within this complex picture.

Where Does Academic Development Sit?

Academic development can have several meanings. These include the development of:

- academics (initially and continuing) for their various roles
- curricula, facilities, support for learning and services which contribute to the quality and improvement of the learning experiences of students
- knowledge creation through research and scholarship and the furtherance of knowledge transmission/exchange
- the skills, competencies, qualities and attributes of students
- communities of practice and networks of learning
- the whole academic endeavour, that is, all aspects of the work of a higher education unit.

Each of these is considered in the following discussion. Moreover various meanings can, and do, coexist and interact with each other.

Whilst typically externally led approaches to quality assurance and enhancement primarily concentrate upon the learning and teaching domains, some specifically include research, most embrace postgraduate education, and all expect that provision is up-to-date and appropriate, and that staff members are suitably qualified and knowledgeable.

Moreover quality assurance and enhancement can, and arguably should, be viewed as scoping much more widely than simply the requirements of national quality assurance agencies. Reference has been made earlier to the roles of professional bodies in relation to both accreditation (quality assurance) and development (quality enhancement).

The professional standards framework of the Higher Education Academy in the UK and broadly similar schemes for recognising the professional development of individuals within academia such as those operated by the Staff and Educational Development Association (SEDA) and the Higher Education Research and Development Association (HERDSA), although primarily enhancement and capacity-development oriented, embody elements of quality assurance. They also promote enhancement of academic practice.

In a similar vein many research councils have put in place schemes to support and promote various dimensions of the development of newer researchers (e.g. doctoral students, research assistants and postdoctoral fellows). In the UK these endeavours have been lubricated by money from government (frequently described as 'Roberts funding' after the late Sir Gareth Roberts). Additionally a raft of independent organisations and learned societies which fund research have also widened and deepened their range of developmental awards. All such initiatives are intended to encourage and enable enhancement of specific sets of academic skills and/or forms of academic practice. Often the symbolic dimension is crucial, making visible the commitment of prestigious bodies that are held in high esteem by the relevant peer communities. When such bodies combine, for example to produce a concordat on the development of newer researchers, that symbolism is greatly magnified. In some senses, that may be further advanced through multi-national pronouncements such as the European Union stance on the development of newer researchers. However, such intergovernmental initiatives can encounter a variety of responses from academics, since, for some, they can be perceived as representing political interference in the donnish dominion, the province of peer communities, in this case, of researchers.

Undergirding all of these important and laudable initiatives is the vast panoply of development support and activities operating within institutions and through disciplines and related professional bodies. Finally, and most significantly, are the countless enhancement actions of members of staff and students, individually or in groups such as teaching teams, departments and peer communities.

One of the challenges both for academic development and for quality assurance/enhancement is the sheer scale of activities that are taking place at any moment in time. Much reported academic development may represent only the visible part of the iceberg, with numerous actions being undocumented.

As McInnis (2009) has argued, such realities demonstrate the exceptionalist professional claims made for academics, notably in terms of personal academic freedom. They also reflect both the autonomy which higher education institutions typically assert and the special relationship between academic tribes and their members.

In combinations, these sets of relationships can be visualised in various ways. For example, the foregoing points might suggest a pyramidal formation with a broad base of localised actions and a small central steering core. Another depiction is that of a hub and spokes model, with the supporting functions at the hub having clear connections via the spokes (faculties/schools or disciplines/other groupings). Both visualisations provide useful insights into intra-institutional structures and relationships but are less suited to situations, which are increasingly commonplace, where numerous interactions transgress institutional boundaries. Here Venn or systems diagrams may have more to offer.

One might wonder why it is necessary to seek some form of visualisation of relationships. The principal reasons are to facilitate communication, promote the emergence of shared understandings and provide a tool (model) that can be used to inform reflections and guide evaluation.

Opportunities and Challenges for Academic Development

On balance the viewpoint of the author is that quality assurance and enhancement agendas offer significant opportunities for academic development and developers. For example, each of the several interpretations of academic development outlined earlier features in quality assurance/enhancement agendas. Often there is an expectation that provision is in place for both the initial and continuing development of all staff concerned with and contributing to the learning experience of students. In some countries, such as the UK and Sweden, such provision is widely available and schemes for inter-institutional endorsement of standards are in place. In other domains localised provision is in place, sometimes institutionally accredited. Generally participation is voluntary, although it may be a contractual requirement for certain groups of individuals. The balance of focus is upon teaching, learning and assessment, although a proportion of programmes adopt a more comprehensive definition of academic development to include, for example, research supervision, pastoral duties and academic leadership.

Another area of substantial growth has been the nurturing of the scholarship of teaching and learning (SOTL). Since this incorporates reflection and evaluation as well as development it sits comfortably with quality assurance/enhancement agendas even when not specifically identified in assurance/enhancement guidance documents.

Over the past 10–15 years personal development planning (PDP) for students has attracted developmental attention. The approach offers the opportunity to engage students in active reflection and decision making about developmental options and choices. Electronic portfolios provide a neat means of recording information and, if necessary, sharing it with others. In the UK the Royal Society of Chemistry has developed sets of trigger questions that can be used by undergraduate and postgraduate students respectively, thereby contextualising the process for the students. This resonates with experiences which suggest that students are most likely to recognise and value the benefits of PDP when it is contextualised and relates to expectations they need to meet such as the recording of experiences which registration requirements place upon trainee nurses.

All of these initiatives and projects outlined offer opportunities for academic developers to influence institutional strategies and policies and to provide the necessary expertise and support across the institution to achieve the goal of enhancing the student learning experience.

More generally work has taken place, such as an initiative in Scotland to develop simple framing for PDP, the Effective Learning Framework (QAAHE, 2007), which is intended to allow students to interrogate the relationships between three domains (personal, academic and career). What is notable in this context is that the PDP framework is promoted by the Quality Assurance Agency for Higher Education (QAAHE) and the implementation and contextualisation of the process to the needs of different institutions and student cohorts is carried out and promoted by academic developers.

One recurrent development theme from quality audit or review reports has been the identification of examples of good practice, attempts to make these more visible to others and encouragement to institutions to promote wide-ranging and diverse ways of fostering sharing of good practice and reflection upon practice. Responses have been varied and include awards and developmental projects, showcasing events and the formation and support of learning enhancement networks and communities of practice.

The following cameo indicates just how closely linked are the quality enhancement agenda and aspects of academic development.

A component of the Quality Enhancement Framework in Scotland has been a programme of nation-wide Quality Enhancement Themes (see http//:www. enhancementthemes.ac.uk). There have now been several themes, with the current one focusing on Graduates for the 21st Century. The two preceding themes were Research-Teaching Linkages and The First Year Experience.

This work is overseen by the Scottish Higher Education Enhancement Committee (SHEEC), whose members are drawn from Scottish higher education institutions, typically the relevant senior academic officer from each institution. Each theme has a dedicated Steering Committee chaired by a senior academic officer from a Scottish higher education institution and with members drawn from a range of relevant interests including student representation. Indeed, student involvement is a distinctive feature of the enhancement-led process in Scotland, with ELIR review teams always including one student member as a fully fledged reviewer.

The Enhancement Theme programme is sponsored by the Scottish Funding Council, which in turn commissions the QAA Scottish Office to manage the programme. It is recognised that most of the work associated with a theme should take place within each institution. Modest funding is given to each higher education institution to assist with that work. Additionally, the Steering Committee for a theme determines what broader project support should be provided, selects the successful tenders, and steers and oversees the progress of each project. The reports from the projects are published on the Enhancement Themes website.

There are organised conferences and seminars around the themes such as an annual two-day Enhancement Themes national conference, and generally international experts are recruited to support each theme. These experts also make visits to Scottish higher education institutions and give presentations at national events. Many academic developers are involved in these projects.

Scotland also provides an illustration of the coincidence of whole institutional endeavours with quality assurance/quality enhancement agendas. Drawing upon European work (Bollaert et al., 2007), the Scottish Funding Council expects institutions to promote the development of a culture of quality, which is interpreted widely to incorporate all facets of enhancing the student experience.

In 2008 the SHEEC commissioned work on the dual and related topics of developing a culture of quality and developing effective quality systems. The projects, undertaken by Gordon and Owen (2008), duly reported to SHEEC. Subsequent actions primarily rest with institutions, although the SHEEC has commissioned some additional desk research on international examples of good practice. Once again, this work shows a close relationship between academic development and the quality agenda.

Even this selective illustrative sample provides ample evidence that interesting opportunities for academic development are associated with quality assurance/ quality enhancement agendas. Those engaged in academia, especially those closely involved in academic development, know that there are also some significant challenges, many of which pertain to issues of ownership of the development enterprise, engaging staff in development initiatives, appropriateness of the inputs or interventions, timeliness and the language of development. As alluded to earlier, activities such as those encompassed within the Scottish Quality Enhancement Framework can be viewed, at best, as coming from the narrow end of the developmental pyramid and, at worst, as an unwelcome external intrusion into the territories of the academic tribes and institutional gatekeepers.

Furthermore, there is an unavoidable element of administrative documentation associated with quality assurance/quality enhancement. Indeed, whilst efforts have been made to reduce or to restrain some of that burden, at least in part, it has merely involved a shift to heightened internal monitoring and evaluation to address the devolved responsibilities that are coming to characterise many review/audit frameworks.

Such stresses and strains are exacerbated by the perceived growth of workload demands upon staff in higher education and, often, by competing calls upon their time (for research, for teaching and learning, for third stream activities, etc.). Yet, this author would argue, there is an innate well of personal support within the academy for enhancement. For example, academic staff members pursuing the Postgraduate Certificate Programme in Advanced Academic Studies at Strathclyde University recurrently highlight the satisfaction they get when students show greater levels of engagement in their learning. This observation is replicated across many institutions.

Orientations to Academic Development

Academic developers are known to have different orientations to the work they do and this will almost inevitably have a bearing on how they respond to institutional agendas. From his research into the views of educational developers Land (2004) outlined a range of orientations, namely:

- managerial
- political–strategic
- entrepreneurial
- romantic (growth of individual practitioners)
- opportunist
- researcher
- professional competence
- reflective practitioners
- modeller-broker
- interpretative–hermeneutic
- provocateur (discipline-specific).

Although it is beyond the scope of this chapter to give extensive detail on the nature and characteristics of these orientations, suffice it to say that individuals with a leaning towards some of the orientations listed would not necessarily agree with the notion that there are clear linkages between the quality agenda and academic development.

One might expect shifts in the profile of orientations of the academic development community depending on location and scoping of the role, that is, whether the academic development unit is a central service, faculty-based, department-based or sitting within the umbrella of human resources. As was apparent from Land's study, features such as institutional mission, traditions, experiences and personal values would also shape orientation profiles. Senior managers might be expected to incline more towards some orientations than others, again allowing for effects of personal and institutional factors.

Individual practitioners might favour particular mixes of orientations. For example, experience suggests that, at any point in time, only a proportion might seek to act as modeller-broker or provocateur. Moreover, their effectiveness in impacting upon their colleagues varies, in large measure depending upon factors such as history (track record), role, esteem and powers of persuasion. It may be the case in the future that Land's typology becomes a useful tool for building academic development teams for particular institutional development initiatives.

Conclusion

The University of Dundee in Scotland used enhancement funding to send a group of participants on the Postgraduate Certificate in Teaching in Higher Education to the 2009 Quality Enhancement Themes Conference. Discussing their experience, Walsh et al. (2009) reported that one participant felt reassured from finding that it was not unusual to encounter problems with progressing initiatives aimed at enhancement (p. 24).

Taking the lead from Barrie et al. (2009), Walsh et al. (2009) suggested a need to support and foster engagement with curriculum renewal and new learning experiences which address the diverse needs of mass higher education, capitalise upon staff motivations, take a long-term view and address 'all aspects of the puzzle'.

Academic development subsumes educational development but it is more than that, not only spanning all dimensions of academic practice (including research, management and leadership, and third stream activities), but also encompassing more comprehensive views of the entire academic endeavour.

The nature of such scoping is pertinent to a key question of this chapter, the degree of beneficial overlap between academic development and quality assurance/quality enhancement agendas. Narrow interpretations of the student experience could mean a corresponding reduction in the degree of overlap. More comprehensive definitions increase the potential range of overlap but also raise questions about the nature and strength of some connections between academic development and the student experience.

Walsh et al. (2009) ponder the extent to which, and the ways whereby, the work of Quality Enhancement Themes 'trickles down' to the student experience (p. 26). In a similar vein, although connections exist between research and teaching as the various reports of the Research–Teaching Links Quality Enhancement Theme and other writing demonstrate, these connections are complex, multifarious and may not necessarily be transparent to students (Land and Gordon, 2008). Activities relating to the academic development of researchers sit in an even more distant location from the student experience unless there are opportunities through internships or equivalent means for students to gain greater insights into the processes of research and of the skills needed.

The issue of language was neatly captured by Webb (1996), who viewed 'development' as a cursed word (p. 65). It is to be hoped that it now sits a little more comfortably in the lexicon of higher education and is less readily reduced to any sense either of a deficit model (you need development) or of an inevitable focus upon individuals, rather than embracing activities, processes, policies, objectives, methodologies, techniques, knowledge, roles, practices, etc., in the spirit of continuing reflection and lifelong learning.

Where academic development actually sits in relation to quality assurance/enhancement agendas will be coloured by the orientations of the various players and their experiences, preferences, aspirations and values. These are not fixed and unchangeable, but if there is any analogy to identities there may be comparatively high levels of short- to medium-term stability characterised by gradualist evolution. Could arguments about the nature of shifts in the scientific paradigm (Kuhn, 1970) apply to academic development? If so, what circumstances might foster a shift? How would discontentment with the prevailing paradigm surface, given the multiplicity of players and perspectives? A managerial impetus might favour strategic dimensions, something which could resonate with external stakeholders. Perhaps many of those with formal developmental roles are shifting to a strategic–professional–reflective practitioner hybrid. Could generational shifts that are taking place in the profile of practitioners affect views of academic development?

If transformative learning is one of the key purposes of higher education should that not apply with equal force to academic development? If so, a level of discomfort may be an inevitable correlation as the provisionality of knowledge of academic development is explored, unpacked and interrogated. Perhaps the last thing we should seek is a stance that could be characterised as representing comfortable accommodation.

References

Baird, J. and Gordon, G. (2009a) Beyond the rhetoric: a framework for evaluating improvements to the student experience. *Tertiary Education and Management* 15 (3), 193–207.

Baird, J. and Gordon, G. (2009b) Systematic quality assurance for diverse student experiences. Paper presented at 32nd HERDSA International Conference: The Student Experience. Charles Darwin University, 6–9 July 2009.

Barrie, S., Hughes, C. and Smith, C. (2009) *The national graduate attributes project: integration and assessment of graduate attributes in curriculum.* Sydney: Australian Learning and Teaching Council.

Becher, T. and Trowler P. (2001) *Academic tribes and territories:* Buckingham: SRHE/Open University Press.

Bollaert, L., Brus, S., Curvale, B., Harvey, L., Helle, E., Jensen, H.T., Komljenovic, J., Orhanides, A. and Sursock, A. (eds) (2007) *Embedding quality culture in higher education.* Brussels: European University Association. Available at: http://www.eua.be/quality-assurance/past-qa-forums/qa-forum-2006/ (accessed 19 August 2008).

Boyer, E.L. (1990) *Scholarship reconsidered: priorities for the professoriate.* Princeton, New Jersey: The Carnegie Foundation for the Advancement of Teaching.

Committee of Vice-Chancellors and Principals (2000) *The business of borderless education: UK perspectives.* London: CVCP (now Universities UK).

Gibbons, M., Limoges, C., Nowotny, H., Schwartzman, S., Scott, P., and Trow, M. (1994) *The new production of knowledge: the dynamics of science and research in contemporary societies.* London: Sage.

Gordon, G. (2004) University roles and career paths: trends, scenarios and motivational challenges. *Higher Education Management and Policy* 18 (2), 135–155.

Gordon, G. and Owen, C. (2008) *Cultures of enhancement and quality management: structures and processes in a reflective institution.* Available at http://www.enhancementthemes.ac.uk/themes/QualityCultures/default.asp (accessed 15 June 2010).

Gordon, G. and Whitchurch, C. (eds) (2009) *Academic and professional identities in higher education: the challenges of a diversifying workplace.* New York: Routledge.

Harvey, L. (2004–8) Analytic quality glossary. Quality Research International. Available at: http://www.qualityresearchinternational.com/glossary/ (accessed 20 August 2009).

Henkel, M. (2000) *Academic identities and policy change in higher education.* London: Jessica Kingsley.

Henkel, M. (2009) Change and continuity in academic and professional identities. In Gordon, G. and Whitchurch, C. (eds) *Academic and professional identities in higher education: the challenges of a diversifying workforce.* New York: Routledge.

Krause, K.-L., Hartley, R., James, R., and McInnis, C. (2005) *The first year experience in Australian universities: findings from a decade of national studies.* Canberra: DEST (Department of Education, Science and Technology).

Kuhn, T.S. (1970) *The structure of scientific revolution.* 2nd edn. Chicago: University of Chicago Press.

Land, R. (2004) *Educational development.* Maidenhead: SRHE/Open University Press, McGraw Hill.

Land, R. and Gordon, G. (2008) *Research–teaching linkages: enhancing graduate attributes. Sector-wide discussions: executive report.* Glasgow: QAA.

McInnis, C. (2009) Traditions of academic professionalism and shifting academic identities. In Gordon, G. and Whitchurch, C. (eds) *Academic and professional identities in higher education: the challenges of a diversifying workforce*. New York: Routledge.

QAAHE (2007) *Effective learning framework*. QAA Scotland/Universities Scotland: QAA 183, 02/07.

Walsh, L., Comber, D. and Oberski, I. (2009) Dreams and aspirations of what might be achieved: the Quality Enhancement Themes Conference 2009. *Educational Developments* 10 (2), 24–27.

Webb, G. (1996) Theories of staff development: development and understanding. *International Journal for Academic Development* 1 (1), 63–69.

Whitchurch, C. (2009) The rise of the blended professional in higher education: a comparison between the UK, Australia and the United States. *Higher Education* 58 (3), 407–418.

4

Demonstrating Fitness for Purpose
Phronesis and Authenticity as Overarching Purposes

CAROLIN KREBER

Introduction

The question that intrigues me, and which I would like to explore in this chapter, is how, in the context of various, often conflicting, agendas and expectations, we might conceive of the overarching purposes of academic development and what we might look for in order to satisfy ourselves and others that our work is worthwhile, or 'fit for purpose'. Drawing on the ancient Greek concept of 'praxis', and the two virtues of 'phronesis' and 'authenticity', I explore what kind of a practice academic work essentially is and what this essence might imply for the kinds of knowledge academic developers could sensibly be expected to support academic colleagues in attaining.

Although I argue largely from an Aristotelian virtues framework I do not stay entirely faithful to it. I integrate into this discussion also more recent communitarian perspectives on authenticity (e.g. Taylor, 1991), as well as the modern notion of empowerment or emancipation articulated in critical social theory (Habermas, 1971). The latter I think usefully enriches the idea of practical knowledge, particularly in the context of academic work, a practice rife with traditions, shared understandings and values, which, one might contend, ought to serve not only as a context for socialization and future action but also, from time to time at least, as a candidate for critical interrogation by its members (Barnett, 1992).

Based on the view that the purpose of academic development is to provide learning environments that support academics in moving towards phronesis and authenticity in relation to academic practice, I conclude the chapter by proposing that critically inspired phronetic studies (Flyvbjerg, 2001) would offer most useful insights into whether the programme's purposes and processes are suitably aligned.

The Purposes of Academic Development in Light of the Nature of Academic Practice

Conflicting Agendas and Expectations

Despite their distinctiveness and embeddedness in local cultures, one observes, across academic development programmes, a considerable degree of commonality. Some consistency may not be surprising given that most academic development professionals share the experience of having to respond to a series of fairly predictable expectations. However, these expectations, some voiced from within the academy itself and others by external bodies, are at times in tension, requiring the academic developer to continuously negotiate these. Common expectations include that academic development should:

- acknowledge the disciplinarity characterizing higher education yet also deal with issues that are common to all subject areas;
- be situated within departmental cultures and structures yet also encourage exchanges across the institution;
- be sensitive to local needs yet also adhere to national standard frameworks (where these exist);
- promote 'reflective practitioners' and yet also encourage so-called 'evidence-based practice';
- offer opportunities to learn about various performative aspects of teaching yet also promote a richer understanding of student learning;
- problematize the first year experience and yet also pay due attention to the challenges of working with postgraduate students;
- consider the challenges posed by increased numbers of non-traditional local students and yet encourage sensibilities for the rather different needs of international students;
- focus on academics' teaching function yet also consider how it is firmly integrated within the whole of academic practice (including also research and scholarship, and collegiality; Nixon, 2008).

Other, perhaps more significant, claims found in the higher education literature include that academic development programmes should encourage academic workers to:

- strengthen teaching and research synergies in their practice;
- reflect on the local norms, values and traditions within which present practices are nested and on the extent to which these structures are provisional and offer opportunity for agency;
- reflect on their responsibilities as 'scholars' in the broader context of society;
- reflect on how students could be supported in becoming participants in the academics' particular disciplinary communities;
- reflect on the barriers different students might experience not only in

becoming participants of specialized disciplinary discourse communities but in developing a basic sense of belonging to the academy;

- reflect not only on how students could be supported in their academic learning in the discipline but also on developing so-called 'graduate attributes' relevant for the world of work where transdisciplinary knowledge and skills are increasingly expected;
- reflect on how students may develop graduate attributes relevant not so much for work but for active and critical engagement in the public sphere as citizens of the world.

Given these wide-ranging expectations, the prospect of identifying an overarching purpose of academic development may seem idealistic, particularly if we add to the above list yet another frequently emphasized maxim, namely that in order to be effective academic development should fit the institution's own strategic goals. I would like to take this last point as an example to illustrate how very different orientations can be identified in how certain expectations might be met. This will lead me into a discussion of the kind of practice teaching is and which orientations to academic development seem most suitable for supporting it.

At my own institution, concern has been expressed over low scores, for some schools, on the feedback scale of the annual UK-wide National Student Survey (NSS). In order to meet the institution's strategic goals of achieving higher scores next year, an immediate response has been to offer academics some concrete advice, 'techniques', on how to improve their feedback practices with the goal of attaining higher scores in the NSS next year. An alternative way of responding to the goal of enhancing feedback might be to invite academics to reflect on what such a score might suggest in light of the realities, challenges and tensions inherent in academic work. Reflection could be encouraged on the virtues we consider as characterizing professionalism in academic practice, and on what a high or low score on feedback might suggest in relation to the extent to which these virtues are actually enacted (for a virtues approach to academic practice see also Nixon, 2008 and Macfarlane, 2004).

Although the first response is consistent with an orientation that considers the purpose of academic development essentially as offering a means to a predetermined end, the second response is perhaps more consistent with an orientation that considers the purpose of academic development as encouraging participants to move towards greater authenticity, and where teaching is considered essentially as a moral (rather than technical) practice (Carr, 2000). Although there seems to be value in both responses described, the distinction identified here invites a more careful analysis of the kind of practice that teaching embodies.

What Kind of a Practice is Teaching?

In the realm of teacher education, Aristotle's classic distinction between two different forms of practical activities ('poiesis' and 'praxis', as articulated in Book

VI of the *Nicomachean Ethics*; Thomson, 1976) has long been recognized as essential for identifying the forms of knowledge deemed necessary for teachers to attain (Dunne, 1993; Carr, 2000; Korthagen et al., 2001).

Aristotle used the term 'poiesis' to refer to an activity aimed at production or making where the ends and means are separate; the term 'praxis' (also referred to as 'action') he used to refer to an activity of conducting oneself within a web of social relations. The end of action or praxis is to act *well*; that is, the ultimate end is 'to lead a good and worthwhile life, an activity that inevitably involves relationships with other people and the intertwining of ends and means' (Coulter et al., as cited in Hansen, 2007). The notion of praxis emphasizes our social interdependency as human beings and our embeddedness in social relations. Praxis demands of the actors not so much a command of skills and techniques (as is the case with poiesis or production) but a disposition to find their unique way of responding to the constant flow of concrete and varying situations they encounter in their relations with others.

These two basic practical activities (poiesis and praxis) correspond to two distinct rational powers: 'techne' (i.e., the knowledge of the expert) and phronesis (i.e., practical wisdom). A person who has acquired techne 'understands the principles underlying the production of an object or state of affairs' (Dunne, 1993). Techne involves much of what we have come to consider theoretical scientific knowledge: it is explanatory, generalizable, systematic and, for this reason, relatively easily teachable. Models of how to promote self-regulated learning derived from empirical studies or so-called evidence-based strategies for enhancing student motivation would fall in the realm of techne. This form of knowledge is pervasive in our culture and hence well understood. For this reason, I will now focus my discussion on the special nature of phronesis.

The Nature of Phronesis (Practical Wisdom)

Aristotle's key insight was that the knowledge needed in the realm of praxis or human affairs is of an entirely different nature from that required for production. The significant aspect of phronesis (the knowledge needed for praxis) is not just that it is a form of practical knowledge but that it is intrinsic to character. It is also essentially of an experiential nature. In defining phronesis, Dunne (1993) highlights next to its experiential grounding the

> immediacy of its involvement in concrete situations, and the responsiveness and resourcefulness in these situations that come to it only from the character and dispositions of the person, formed in the course of his life-history, and not from any knowledge that can be made available in treatises or manuals.
>
> (p. 228)

The person who acts phronetically (and thereby ethically) is someone who, as a result of experience, is particularly able to perceive, within a concrete situation, an indeterminate number of potentially relevant factors; who is able to recognize among these those that are particularly important; and who is able to select, from among all the possible ways in which he or she could act, the one that is most appropriate for the situation at hand (Bowman, 2002). To act phronetically means to abandon the security offered by rules and regulations for the sake of meeting 'the other' in his or her concrete uniqueness. In short, phronesis refers essentially to the capacity to make good judgements in concrete social situations.

However, it would be false to conclude that good judgement would be possible without any universal and systemized knowledge. Importantly then, universal (also theoretical) knowledge is not denied by, or in conflict with, phronesis. Rather, as Dunne and Pendlebury (2003) make clear, one of the crucial functions of phronesis is to facilitate exactly the mediation between the universal and the particular. It is:

> an ability to recognize cases, or problems of this kind (which are precisely of *no* clearly specified kind) and to deal adequately with them. A person of judgement respects the particularity of the case – and thus does not impose on it a procrustean application of the general rule.
>
> (p. 198)

This latter point is important with respect to the relationship between theory and practice in academic development, as I will discuss below.

By drawing attention in this chapter to the significance of phronesis I certainly do not wish to argue against the inclusion of theory in postgraduate programmes in academic practice, for example. On the contrary, I think that an analysis of phronesis offers us a plausible argument against frequently voiced claims that theory is irrelevant for practice. Although it makes intuitive sense that the 'wise thing to do in a teaching-student-relation can seldom – if ever – be deduced from general rules and prescriptions or methods but has to be sensed in the situation in a more experienced and intuitive way' (Hansen, 2007), one of the key roles of phronesis is to mediate between theory and the particulars of the situation. As Norris (2001) argued, this is the only way that theory can be expected to enrich practice, namely not as situational or context-specific problem-solving strategies but precisely as general models which teachers need to adapt to their specific context. Whether a certain theory applies to a teacher's given situation is a question that only those who know the particulars of the situation can answer.

Moreover, by privileging phronesis I am not against participants in academic development initiatives having the opportunity to acquire basic teaching skills (how to pace and organize one's lecture, make good use of visual aids, design tests). Acquiring these basic skills is important. However, the key is not to follow a checklist but to know how to vary one's approach according to the particulars of the situation. So again, what is needed is good judgement or phronesis. What we certainly want to resist is a view of academic development as 'technology', that is a matter of handing down certain means (rules, techniques, algorithms, tricks and hints, etc.) to be employed to attain certain ends. Fortunately, the academic development community is much more enlightened and will recognize this latter perspective as merely a caricature of what would generally be considered poor practice.

Authenticity and Links to Phronesis

Dunne (1993) comments that a person involved in praxis 'becomes and discovers "who" he is through his actions' (p. 263). He goes on to explain that according to Aristotle 'The self is revealed only within a network of relationships and communal responsibilities, and the function of "phronesis" is not to maximize a "good" that one already knows and can come to *have*, but rather – a much more difficult task – to discover a good that one must *become*' (p. 270). Similarly, Arendt (1958), in her classic text *The Human Condition*, reminds readers that 'In acting and speaking, men show who they are, reveal actively their unique personal identities and thus make their appearance in the human world' (p. 179).

To be authentic then inevitably involves investing one's *self* in one's actions. There is no one who makes the decision for me: I have to decide and take responsibility for my actions in the light of uncertainty and contingency; I cannot hide behind any evidence-based rules or algorithms. I would like to explore this notion of authenticity a bit further.

Focusing on Authenticity: Why is it Important in Human Relations?

Authenticity is typically associated with a certain sense of personal commitment, ownership and responsibility for one's decisions. Bonnett and Cuypers (2003) argue that:

> Significant interpersonal relationships require a developed sense of ownership and responsibility for one's own life and its consequences upon others, as a prerequisite both for showing consideration to others and for *understanding* them – knowing from the inside what it is to be responsible and thus to participate in the human condition.
>
> (p. 337)

Taylor (1991) reminds us that authenticity has two dimensions that are in tension with one another, thereby demanding continuous negotiation by the actor. On the one hand, authenticity is linked to creativity, originality and at times even opposition to existing rules; on the other hand, to be really authentic demands recognition of the fact that we are part of a community by whose socially constructed and historically shaped norms, traditions, and values (which he also refers to as 'horizons of significance') we are already bound and shaped (see also Mead, 1967). In other words we are always already actors in a praxis, together with other actors with whom we aim to negotiate and agree the norms that bind us. Authenticity is not just a matter of 'being true to oneself' in the narrow sense of being guided only by one's own deepest wishes, desires or callings; real authenticity is given when I strive to assert my uniqueness within this framework of existing social norms and relations.

Grimmet and Neufeld (1994) interpreted Taylor's communitarian perspective on authenticity within the context of teacher development, suggesting that authentic teachers are bound by a moral obligation to do what is in the important interest of students. The latter, one might say, is the horizon of significance to which the teaching profession, as a community, is committed. However, given multiple pressures (e.g. from within oneself, the institution, government agencies, research councils), doing what is in the best interest of students is not always easy; but through acting in the world, Arendt (1958) argues, I reveal the 'who' that I am. This disclosing and exposing one's self by leaving one's private hiding place requires courage.

Nixon (2008) views a person's disposition towards authenticity as being underpinned by the virtues of courage and compassion. He argues that 'through courage I assert my own claims, or those of my clan, to recognition; through compassion I assert the rights of others to recognition' (p. 89). Showing compassion I allow for the authentic engagement of others who without my compassion would remain unrecognized. In explaining the compassion we feel when we encounter suffering in others (for example the student who struggles with organizing the term paper or never speaks in seminars), Nussbaum (2004) emphasizes the importance of recognizing our related vulnerability, which implies that we see others as important to our own flourishing. Encouraging authenticity in others is linked to my own authenticity.

It should be obvious that there are no rules or guidelines to be followed in the striving for authenticity in academic practice. I move towards greater authenticity through experience of the unique situations I encounter in my daily work in which I have the choice to act courageously or compassionately (or not) and the opportunity to learn and grow through this experience of acting. I therefore become 'virtuously disposed through my developing relationship with myself and others' (Nixon, 2008). This applies to the virtue of phronesis as well as to the virtue of authenticity.

How might a disposition towards authenticity assert its influence in academic practice? In relation to teaching, Nixon (2008) suggests that authenticity is underpinning practice when teachers show the willingness and capacity to share, or 'profess' (p. 90), their own unique perspective on the ideas or facts that make up the content of the courses they are teaching; when they invite students into *their* authenticity to achieve authority as learners; when they develop their own pedagogical style. In each of the above three examples 'the courage of the teacher is put at the disposal of the student, with a view to encouraging learning' (Nixon, 2008). In terms of the virtuous disposition of compassion, Nixon proposes that it allows us to be perceptive of the actual and unique needs of varying groups of learners and resist instrumentalist approaches to teaching that claim that the needs of our students can be met by following a certain set of means, thereby ignoring the contingency, particularity and variability of teaching and learning.

Phronesis, then, can also be understood as that virtue which guides academic workers in deciding to what degree it is called for, in a given situation, to act courageously and/or compassionately, and thereby authentically.

Empowering Phronesis

We have seen that phronesis is the personal knowledge needed for making good judgements in particular social situations, and develops through extended experience of relations within a community. This community itself is bound by 'horizons of significance' (Taylor, 1991). Applied to teaching in higher education, one might say that the horizons of significance are given, for example, by how the academic community understands itself, national standards frameworks agreed upon by the sector, and the teaching and learning traditions that have developed in institutional and departmental cultures.

Now, one might suggest that these traditions, norms and values, and the purposes and means that spring from them, also need to be kept under review from within the community itself. Authenticity in teaching, for example, is described by Cranton and Carusetta (2004) as a process of 'being conscious of self, other, relationships, and context through *critical reflection*' [emphasis added] (p. 288). It is this idea of critical reflection to which I now wish to turn.

In his early work, Habermas (1971) expanded Aristotle's framework of poiesis and praxis by distinguishing not two but three knowledge-constitutive interests which could be summarized as the technical (an interest in controlling and predicting the environment), the practical (an interest in arriving at shared understandings and getting along with one another), and the critical (an interest in developing or becoming empowered). The critical interest brings about critical reflection which by 'grasping the genesis of the tradition from which it proceeds and on which it turns back, ... shakes the dogmatism of life-practices' (Habermas, cited in Dunne, 1993). It involves tracing the origins of certain norms and values that have evolved within a community and exploring alternatives. The critical interest leads to 'emancipatory knowledge', a concept which usefully extends how we might understand phronesis.

The criticality implied in autonomy or emancipation is, of course, not foreign to institutions of higher education. To set students free through their learning, to invite them to find their own voice amidst established ones and become authors of their learning, and hence their lives, through critical dialogue with others, is a widely shared goal of higher education (Barnett, 1992). Such notions are linked to the understanding that students shall not be bound by the courses or topics they are studying but shall develop a capacity to do something with their learning. Through their higher education experience, so it is hoped, students will develop and then use their critical thinking capacities, will come to apply and invest themselves, and thereby will address the problems confronting our humanity.

One purpose of academic development then is to support academics in developing the ability to promote these learning and developmental processes in students. However, it will be clear from the previous discussion that this is not principally a matter of academics attaining more and more techne. First of all, there is the uniqueness of each individual student with his or her particular needs that must be acknowledged no matter how daunting this might seem (particularly when classes continue to grow larger and student diversity richer as a result of widening participation and internationalization), which involves making judgements about what is the 'wise' thing to do, meaning what to do with whom, when and to what degree. Importantly, a focus on the development of techne alone would not involve reflection among academics on what the goals of higher education teaching should be, let alone on what the role of the scholar (academic worker/teacher) should be in contemporary society. These questions, however, seem fundamental for any meaningful understanding of student learning and how to encourage it. Apart from these issues there are also the varying contexts, and particular local cultures, in which academics do their work to be considered. Techne does little by way of helping academics develop a disposition towards acting in courageous and compassionate ways towards students so as to support their learning.

I suggest, therefore, that the purpose of academic development might be conceived as supporting academics not so much in attaining techne but rather phronesis (in a classical sense), and principally a *critically inspired* phronesis. When academics come together to engage in critical dialogue about what it means to teach and learn in the context of our times – or perhaps 'let learn' [to borrow a term from Martin Heidegger (1968)] – there is opportunity for a critically inspired phronesis to develop. When such dialogue occurs not only among members of the same departmental/disciplinary culture but across different cultures, the likelihood for a critically inspired phronesis to thrive is greater because taken-for-granted assumptions and values are more easily surfaced.

We have seen earlier that phronesis crucially depends on experience. It develops through 'reflection on action' and largely through 'reflection in action'. It would seem particularly relevant, therefore, to encourage academics to reflect on their experiences, and specifically on why they made certain decisions in particular situations.

So what does all this mean for evaluating academic development programmes? How do we know – and how can we demonstrate – that we are 'fit for purpose'?

Evaluating Academic Development Practice: Towards Critically Inspired Phronetic Studies

What I have been trying to do up to this point is to explore whether in the context of various, often conflicting, agendas and expectations, there can be an overarching purpose of academic development, one that academic developers as a group could subscribe to, despite the necessary distinctiveness of their local programmes. Based on a view of teaching as praxis, I have suggested that the purpose of academic development could be conceived of as encouraging critical reflection on how to *act* or make good decisions. The concepts (or virtues) of 'authenticity' and 'phronesis' are dominant in this discussion.

In relation to phronesis, I have explored its role in the mediation of theory and practice and also its linkages to authenticity. Implied in the discussion is the argument that teachers whose work is guided by authenticity invite students into their own authenticity and to gain authority over their learning. I have emphasized that teaching understood as praxis demands of us considerable investment of *self*. We can't hide behind any proven rules – we need to find our own solutions and take responsibility for these. This takes courage. Taking this particular view of the overarching purpose of academic development as my premise, I now want to comment on how we might demonstrate that our programmes are 'fit for purpose'.

I propose that evaluation studies addressing questions of 'what works, how and why' make sense in the context of clearly defined outcomes [for example, participants will enjoy the course, will include assessment guidelines in the syllabus, will pace their lectures appropriately, or perhaps even adopt student-focused conceptions of teaching (the latter, of course, becomes much more problematic if one moved away from using established questionnaires to find out whether this happened)]. The moment the expected outcomes are less tangible, however, or invite greater investment, engagement and interpretation of those who are expected to achieve them, these questions become problematic. How would we know that it worked if the purpose of our work was to encourage phronesis and authenticity in academic teachers? How would we measure these outcomes? How would participants themselves know that they have developed these virtues [are they a matter of being (an endpoint) or a matter of becoming]?

In response to this problem I suggest that evaluations focus not on outcomes but instead on *processes*. What we would want to know then is whether the processes that characterize the programme are aligned with its purpose; or put differently, whether the processes can be assumed to support the expected outcomes. We might look, for example, for evidence of processes through which participants are encouraged to engage in the kinds of reflection discussed earlier. We would like to know whether, and to what extent, participants are encouraged to engage in reflection leading to instrumental learning (that is the development of techne) and, more importantly, whether they are encouraged to engage in reflection leading to communicative and emancipatory learning about teaching (see also Kreber and Cranton, 2000; Kreber and Castleden, 2009), assuming that the latter would be particularly important for moving towards phronesis and authenticity.

Several years ago, Bent Flyvbjerg (2001) argued for a critically inspired 'phronetic social science', as it would offer greater insight into matters of real social relevance than efforts geared towards generating predictive theories. The latter he recognized as appropriate for the hard sciences but entirely inappropriate for the social sciences, which deal with human phenomena that are, by their very nature, characterized by contingency, particularity and variability. In line with his general argument, which resonates throughout this chapter, I propose that what we need in academic development are critically inspired phronetic evaluation studies that take account of the numerous factors that affect our practice in the particular contexts in which we work (here I have in mind, for example, the specific policy context, institution, group or individual we work with), and help us to make appropriate judgements about how to enhance our practice. Such studies would seem to be most appropriate for evaluating a practice whose principal purpose it is to support the development of critically inspired phronesis among its participants.

Comprehensive case studies, given their reliance on thick descriptions of context and careful attention to the particulars of the situation, would seem especially suitable. Importantly, such studies would address four questions that Flyvbjerg proposed as general guidelines for critically inspired phronetic studies. These are: '(1) Where are we going? (2) Who gains, and who loses, by which mechanisms of power? (3) Is this desirable? (4) What should be done?' (p. 162). Certainly, programmes whose purpose it is to promote among academic workers greater authenticity and (critically inspired) phronesis would encourage participants to pose these same questions about their own practice. The question 'Who gains, and who loses, by which mechanisms of power?', in particular, seems pivotal to developing a meaningful understanding of how to support the learning of *all* students (meaning not just the privileged).

What then might be some of the questions we would ask as part of a critically inspired phronetic evaluation? Under 'Where are we going?' we might want to look for evidence of processes [for example, course activities (discussions, small group work, individual work, debates, role play, case studies, demonstrations, peer observation, etc.), assignments (inquiry work, portfolios, journals, etc.), resource materials (readings, films, websites, etc.)] that are likely to encourage participants to engage in reflection and dialogue, within and across disciplines, on issues such as:

- their own specific teaching experiences (particular instances with students that felt challenging, rewarding, disturbing, disappointing, and why);
- the various and at times conflicting views on the purposes and goals of higher education;
- different instructional approaches (also techniques and methods) and why, in particular situations, they seemed to have worked (or not) for whom (who got served well and who got ignored?);
- whether the approaches they have taken were compatible with what they

hoped to achieve (and whether, given the particulars of the situations, what was deemed a desirable goal changed, and why);

- the consequences of their decisions/actions for themselves and others;
- different theories of student learning and the extent to which these seemed to explain their own experiences of helping different students to succeed;
- how different approaches and conceptions of teaching relate to the values they hold as persons (are participants invited to develop their own pedagogical style?);
- the meaning of professionalism in academic practice, on what it means to be a good teacher, and how teaching relates to their other academic roles;
- diversity and uniqueness in relation to the students they work with and how to respond to this;
- departmental teaching and learning regimes, how they have come about, and their own opportunities for agency;
- the values that govern their work, and the extent to which these are their own values;
- the relationship between their work and wider society.

Of course other foci for reflection are possible. The idea is to look for evidence that the programme is characterized by processes that can be assumed to encourage phronesis and authenticity. However, the other questions, 'Who gains, and who loses, by which mechanisms of power?', 'Is this desirable?' and 'What should be done?', are no less significant. The evaluation study, therefore, would want to explore to what extent programme participants engage in these activities, why some engage more fully than others, and why some withdraw entirely. It would explore whether the programme's own particular teaching and learning regime makes engagement easier for some participants and harder for others. It would look for the discourses that are dominant in the programme, and for those which are marginal or missing entirely. Participants' own views would be particularly valuable on these latter questions. If some individuals or groups were systematically marginalized by certain mechanisms of power this would clearly not be desirable, and more inclusive ways of engaging colleagues would need to be identified and implemented.

Conclusion

What I have been able to do here is offer no more than a sketch, and I confess that I have not yet fully worked out in my own mind what a critically inspired phronetic evaluation study would look like in detail. However, it strikes me that if academics moving towards phronesis and authenticity in relation to their practice were indeed the desired ends of our academic development work, and if we wanted to know and demonstrate to others that our programmes were fit for *this* purpose, studies that yield the most meaningful and useful insights would need to be of this kind.

References

Arendt, H. (1958) *The human condition*. Chicago: University of Chicago Press.

Barnett, R. (1992) *Improving higher education*. Buckingham: Society for Research into Higher Education and Open University Press.

Bonnett, M., and Cuypers, S. (2003) Autonomy and authenticity in education. In Blake, N., Smeyers, P., Smith, R. and Standish, P. (eds) *The Blackwell guide to the philosophy of education*. Blackwell Philosophy Guides. Oxford: Blackwell Publishing. pp. 326–340.

Bowman, W. (2002) Theorie als Praxis. Urteilskraft, Ver-Antwortlichkeit und der Wert philosophischer Praxis. *Zeitschrift für Kritische Musikpädagogik*. Available at: http://home.arcor.de/zf/zfkm/bowman1.pdf (accessed 12 September 2009).

Carr, D. (2000) *Professionalism and ethics in teaching*. London: Routledge.

Cranton, P.A., and Carusetta, E. (2004) Developing authenticity as a transformative process. *Journal of Transformative Education* 2 (4), 276–293.

Dunne, J. (1993). *Back to the rough ground: 'phronesis' and 'techne' in modern philosophy and in Aristotle*. Notre Dame: University of Notre Dame Press.

Dunne, J., and Pendlebury, S. (2003) Practical reason. In Blake, N., Smeyers, P., Smith, R. and Standish, P. (eds) *The Blackwell guide to the philosophy of education*. Blackwell Philosophy Guides. Oxford: Blackwell Publishing. pp. 194–211.

Flyvbjerg, B. (2001) *Making social science matter: why social inquiry fails and how it can succeed again*. Cambridge: Cambridge University Press.

Grimmet, P., and Neufeld, J. (1994) *Teacher development and the struggle for authenticity. Professional growth and restructuring in the context of change*. Columbia University, NY: Teachers College Press.

Habermas, J. (1971) *Knowledge and human interests*. Boston: Beacon Press.

Hansen, F.T. (2007) Phronesis and authenticity as knowledge for philosophical praxis in teacher training. *Paideusis: Journal of Canadian Philosophy of Education* 16 (3), 15–32.

Heidegger, M. (1968) *What is called thinking?* New York: Harper and Row.

Korthagen, F.A., Kessels, J., Koster, B., Lagerwerf, B., and Wubbels, T. (2001) *Linking practice and theory: the pedagogy of realistic teacher education*. Mahwah, New Jersey: Lawrence Erlbaum Associates.

Kreber, C., and Castleden, H. (2009) Reflection on teaching and epistemological structure: reflective and critically reflective processes in pure/soft and pure/hard fields. *Higher Education* 57 (4), 509–531.

Kreber, C., and Cranton, P.A. (2000) Exploring the scholarship of teaching. *Journal of Higher Education* 71 (4), 476–495.

Macfarlane, B. (2004) *Teaching with integrity: the ethics of higher education practice*. London: RoutledgeFalmer/Taylor and Francis Group.

Mead, G.H. (1967) *Mind, self and society (from the standpoint of a social behaviourist)*. Chicago: University of Chicago Press.

Nixon, J. (2008) *Towards the virtuous university: the moral bases of academic practice*. New York: Routledge.

Norris, S.P. (2001) The pale of consideration when seeking sources of teaching expertise. *American Journal of Education* 108 (3), 167–196.

Nussbaum, M. (2004) *Upheavals of thought*. Cambridge: Cambridge University Press.

Taylor, C. (1991) *The ethics of authenticity*. Cambridge, MA: Harvard University Press.

Thomson, J.A.K. (1976) *The ethics of Aristotle: the Nicomachean ethics*. Harmondsworth, Middlesex: Penguin Books.

5
Using Student Survey Data to Shape Priorities and Approaches

KERRI-LEE KRAUSE

Introduction

This chapter examines ways in which student survey data may be used to shape the priorities and approaches of academic development units and their work. In particular, the chapter focuses on survey data relating to students' evaluative feedback on their learning experiences, rather than on broader student satisfaction surveys, though it is acknowledged that such a distinction is not always feasible given the strong connections between all elements of students' experiences both within and beyond the formal curriculum (Krause, 2007; Krause and Coates, 2008). Examples are drawn from student experience surveys currently in use, particularly in the UK and Australia, and the possibilities they offer for enhancing the work of academic development in a rapidly changing higher education context.

Collection of valid and reliable data on the student experience has become a high priority for universities. National benchmarking instruments such as the National Student Survey (UK), the Course Experience Questionnaire (Australia) and the National Survey of Student Engagement (US) represent a few of the more widely used student surveys. Institution level policy makers tend to occupy themselves with the role that such student data play in performance-based funding, institutional benchmarking and quality assurance exercises. However, these institutional datasets also represent a rich source of information for academic developers charged with the responsibility of working with colleagues to enhance the quality of learning, teaching, assessment and curriculum design.

Evaluative data in the form of the student voice offer a rich vein of information to guide strategic approaches to academic development. This voice may be heard in a range of ways, including through student involvement in university committees and governance, through focus groups, and through student feedback on surveys. The last of these is the focus of this chapter. Survey data may comprise reflections on the quality of students' experiences in academic programmes and courses, and their overall engagement with university life. Academic developers have a key role to play in bridging the gap between centrally held student experience data and the day-to-day practices of academics in disciplinary contexts. These data also have an important role to play in shaping the strategic planning and policy advice that academic development units arguably should be providing to institutional leaders and managers.

Academic Development Practice in Context

Academic development units and the institutions within which they operate are posing important questions about the relevance, purpose and impact of academic professional development in higher education. Although these questions are not new, the imperative to address them critically and in an evidence-based manner has assumed new significance in a climate of reduced government resourcing for higher education and a greater emphasis on accountability and performance-based funding. In such a policy environment, every function of the university is scrutinised for the value it adds and the function it performs. Academic development is no exception.

The issue of the function, positioning and reporting lines of academic development units within institutional structures is a perennial source of debate. In a study of academic development in the Australian context, Ling (2009) found that the majority of academic development units were stand-alone centralised units (p. 35). A notable proportion were also located in human resources departments, education faculties, or information technology and library services. The study notes that no uniform organisational model of academic development exists. Rather, academic development units tend to be differentiated according to such variables as institutional type, unit size, whether or not the unit is responsible for learning technology or managing the institution's student evaluation function, and whether the unit comprises academic staff with a scholarly research brief or professional staff with no mandate to conduct research.

Discussion of the merits, or demerits, of these various structures lies beyond the scope of this chapter. Nevertheless, the strategic positioning of an academic development unit plays a key role in such areas as capacity of the unit to harness resources; involvement in institutional governance and committee structures; strategic influence on policy; relationships with other elements of the university such as institutional research offices, student support services and the like; and perceptions of the purpose, relevance and value of academic development across the institution (see Bath and Smith, 2004).

The institutionally mandated mission and structural positioning of an academic development unit also shape its engagement with student survey data in various ways. For instance, if an academic development unit includes in its core business responsibility for managing student surveys, such as student evaluations of teaching or internally managed student experience surveys, this will influence its engagement with survey data and, in turn, will shape university colleagues' expectations of how the data might be incorporated into academic development practice (Dearn et al., 2002; Sorcinelli et al., 2006). On the other hand, if an academic development unit is structurally separate from the university's institutional data collection and analysis functions, there may be very limited connection between the work of academic developers and the student learning experience data available. Regardless of structural positioning it is vital for academic development units to engage with the rich vein of student datasets that are increasingly available in universities. Judicious use of these data should inform academic development strategic and operational plans, policy development, targeted workshop programmes and discipline-based professional development with course developers and teaching teams.

This chapter argues for a systems approach to interpreting how student survey data can and should be used to build synergies between and among elements of the university in order to bring about sustainable change (Ackoff, 1999) and improvement in learning, teaching and student outcomes. Strategically designed, collegial and collaborative academic development activities have the potential to play a key role in building these synergies and relationships across the institution, underpinned by high-quality student data (Figure 5.1). Given the range of

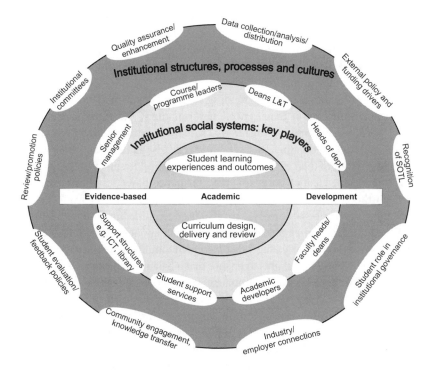

Figure 5.1 A Systems Approach for Interpreting Evidence-Based Academic Development.

ways in which academic development units and their roles are configured, the chapter explores various approaches for using student data strategically, rather than advocating a single approach. A brief overview of a selection of student experience surveys is followed by discussion of a systems model for interpreting how data from such surveys might contribute to a joined-up, data-driven approach that connects academic development activities with student feedback on learning experiences, with curriculum design, review and reform, and with institutional social systems, structures and processes.

Types and Purposes of Student Learning Experience Data

Student experience data, in the broadest sense, take various forms within institutions and across the higher education sector nationally and internationally. The United States has a long and distinguished history of longitudinal analyses of the student experience. One of the most widely known initiatives is the Cooperative Institutional Research Program (CIRP) which was initiated in 1966 with a focus on the impact of higher education on students' cognitive and affective outcomes (Astin, 1993; see also Pascarella and Terenzini, 2005). The suite of surveys included in the CIRP include the Freshman Survey for incoming first year students, the Your First College Year Survey (YFCY) and the College Senior Survey (CSS).

Since 1999, the National Survey of Student Engagement (NSSE) College Student Report has been prominent in the United States and Canadian higher education systems with its focus on gathering data on how undergraduate students spend their time and what they gain from attending university (see http://nsse.iub.edu/html/about.cfm).

In Australia, the most long-standing instrument on the student learning experience is the Course Experience Questionnaire (CEQ). Originating in the early 1980s, it has been administered across the Australian higher education sector since 1993 and in the UK since 2005. The CEQ gathers data about graduates' perceptions of their higher education experience. Results from this survey have underpinned federal government performance-based funding in Australia through the Learning and Teaching Performance Fund since 2003.[1] In many Australian universities, these data are also used to guide institutional planning and resourcing. However, one needs to be cautious about interpreting CEQ data in isolation as this is clearly a lag indicator which should always be supplemented with a range of other measures to ensure that a balanced approach is adopted.

One of the more targeted national surveys of the student experience both within and beyond the classroom is the First Year Experience Questionnaire (FYEQ) which has been in operation across the Australian higher education sector since 1994 (see Krause et al., 2005). This instrument has been successful in documenting trends in the first year experience for the purposes of guiding institutional planning and for benchmarking purposes for 15 years.

Other national surveys of the student experience have gained particular prominence in Australia, New Zealand and the United Kingdom (UK) since 2005. In the UK the National Student Survey was first conducted in 2005 and is now widely used as part of the UK quality assurance framework for higher education. In Australia and New Zealand, the Australian Survey of Student Engagement (AUSSE) – specifically the Student Engagement Questionnaire (SEQ) – was administered for the first time in 2007 in selected universities across Australasia. The survey, based on the US-developed NSSE College Student Report, comprises six scales covering various elements of the learning experience including academic challenge, active learning, work-integrated learning and the nature of the learning environment (ACER, 2008).

The International Student Barometer (ISB) (see http://www.i-graduate. org/services/student_insight--student_barometer.html) is an internationally administered survey that has been in operation since 2005. It provides an example of an independently operated benchmarking instrument focused on the international student experience in a range of areas, one of which includes the learning experience.

In addition to nationally and internationally administered instruments, universities typically operate locally developed student evaluations of teaching and courses/units as well as various other forms of formative and summative data collection processes designed to gather information about different dimensions of the student experience (Table 5.1). The instruments listed here are representative of the rapid emergence of a number of influential student survey tools developed since 2005. This is no coincidence. It has occurred during a period of intense sector-wide activity in relation to performance-based funding and the associated emphasis on institutional benchmarking (see Bradley et al., 2008), along with a range of other accountability mechanisms in the university sector internationally. In this climate, there has been amplified interest in understanding how to capitalise on student data for a range of purposes including benchmarking, quality assurance and enhancement of learning and teaching practices. Several comprehensive analyses of student feedback instruments have been published since 2005, in particular. Richardson (2005) provides a comprehensive review of the research evidence concerning the use of formal instruments to measure students' evaluations of their teachers, satisfaction with their programmes and perceptions of the quality of their programmes. Abrami et al. (2007) conducted a major review of the research literature on the dimensionality of student feedback on teaching. Barrie and colleagues (2008) conducted a sector-wide analysis of student evaluation of teaching surveys and practices in Australian universities.

Table 5.1 presents a summary of instruments designed to gather data on students' learning experiences in different contexts and for a range of purposes. It is recognised that a single survey may perform several functions. Moreover, there is merit in considering a suite of approaches to gathering both qualitative and quantitative data on students' experiences (Stake and Cisneros-Cohernour,

Table 5.1 Student Survey Types, Purposes and Typical Levels of Application

Survey type	Purpose	Typical levels of application
Student evaluation of teaching/subject	Summative student evaluation of a subject/ unit, focusing on day-to-day experiences of a particular teacher or teaching team, typically conducted at the end of a teaching session. Locally developed formative instruments are also used to supplement summative data	Individual and/ or teaching team, subject/unit
Student evaluation of degree programme (e.g. Course Experience Questionnaire)	Students' retrospective evaluation of whole-of-programme experiences (e.g. CEQ: conducted post graduation)	Degree programme within or across departments or faculties
Student satisfaction surveys (e.g. National Student Survey, UK)	Students' evaluation of the overall experience of higher education, including extra-curricular dimensions (e.g. NSS: distributed to final year students). Institutionally developed satisfaction surveys are also used to target specific issues (e.g. satisfaction with information technology provision of student services)	Institution level, national
Targeted student experience and engagement surveys (e.g. AUSSE, First Year Experience Questionnaire)	Students document behaviours, experiences within and beyond the formal curriculum, and amount of time spent on study-related and other (e.g. paid work) activities (e.g. AUSSE: distributed to first and third year students; FYEQ: distributed to first year students)	Institution level, national, international

2000). Table 5.1 is, therefore, intended simply as a guide for considering the broader implications for academic development approaches in the section to follow.

Having identified several types and examples of surveys designed to gather data of various kinds in relation to the student learning experience, attention now turns to consideration of ways in which academic developers might use student data to shape their work across the institution.

Academic Developers Bridging the Data Gap: a Whole-of-Institution Strategy

Although there has been considerable interest in analysing the range and extent of student learning experience surveys in recent years, simply collecting such feedback is unlikely to contribute to improvements in the quality of learning and teaching (Brennan et al., 2003). The key lies in how the data are interpreted, communicated and integrated into the day-to-day operations of the university, including department-level discussions about learning and teaching quality; curriculum review and reform; assessment practices; the connectivity between student support services and academic departments; and institutional planning, policy making and resourcing.

An analysis of the ways in which 29 Australian universities used student evaluation data (Barrie et al., 2008) revealed that these data were used for such purposes as internal course and programme reviews, to inform strategic planning processes and to inform curriculum design and review processes. Notably, the report makes no mention of institutional responses that refer to the role of student evaluation data in academic development activities, although it is acknowledged that academic developers may well be involved in using data to provide advice on curriculum design or on course and programme reviews.

Richardson (2005) proposes four reasons for the apparent lack of attention to information gleaned from student learning experience surveys:

1. lack of guidance available for academics, managers and administrators on how to interpret the data
2. lack of external incentives to make use of such information
3. lack of feedback to students regarding the results of their feedback and how it is being used, that is, closing the feedback loop
4. lack of clarity about ownership of student data – academics are more likely to be sceptical if it appears that student evaluative data are divorced from the immediate context of learning and teaching, particularly when data are collected, analysed and published by their institution's central administration.

Academic developers play a key role in addressing these missed opportunities. Figure 5.1 highlights the pivotal role of data-driven academic development activities in institutional operations. In order to facilitate high-quality organisational learning and cultural change (Senge, 1990, 1999), characterised by trust and collaboration, academic developers may use a range of approaches and access myriad connections as part of an evidence-based approach to staff development. The model reflects the fact that academic development activities in universities tend to be characterised by a hub and spoke model (Ling, 2009), typically comprising an academic development unit which connects with individuals, groups and institutional elements with a remit for supporting the development of academics as teachers, as well as informing strategic policy making in relation to the quality of learning and teaching. Ling (2009) notes that academic development responsibilities may be variously assumed by, for example, deans/associate deans (learning and teaching), faculty learning and teaching coordinators, programme convenors. Thus academic development is presented as a shared responsibility and a partnership between academic developers and colleagues across the institution.

In all aspects of this partnership, student survey data have a key role to play. Smith (2008) proposes an instructive model for linking student evaluation data with staff development among these academic staff groups, drawing attention to the importance of building faculty learning communities who engage with and support one another in interpreting and using these data to enhance practice. Informed by data about the student learning experience and outcomes, from a range of sources, academic development priorities should focus in the first instance on tailoring data to the needs of different groups, such as deans, heads of department, programme or course leaders and senior management. Strong partnerships should also be forged with colleagues from student support services and representatives from various service elements of the university to ensure strategic collaboration and a holistic approach to supporting academics as they support students in their learning. The central focus should be on using a range of evidence-based strategies, including student data, to enhance the student learning experience and outcomes by means of concentration on scholarly curriculum design, delivery and review.

This model also places emphasis on academic development activities that are sensitive and responsive to institutional structures, processes and cultures (Smart et al., 1997). It recognises the power of academic development partnerships that are enriched by targeted student survey data, analysed and communicated in a fit-for-purpose manner to a variety of staff groups – particularly academic staff and leaders – across the university as part of a coordinated approach to enhancing the quality of learning, teaching and the student experience.

Kuh and colleagues (2005) argue for the value of two meta-principles underpinning successful institutional implementation of strategies for student success. These principles are alignment and sustainability. Figure 5.1 highlights the way in which academic development approaches underpinned by strategic use of student data might serve as a focal point for achieving greater alignment between the experience of staff and students of the university, the institutional mission, values and culture, and institutional policies, practices and resourcing. In order for these alignments and the associated learning and teaching initiatives to be sustainable, the evidence base underpinning academic development needs to be rigorous, effectively embedded into the core business of the academic development unit and various satellite activities, and responsively targeted to the wide-ranging needs of different stakeholder groups across the institution. Strategies for sustaining and embedding data-driven and evidence-based academic development are explored in the following section.

Principles and Strategies to Guide Evidence-Based Academic Development Priorities and Approaches

Five principles and associated strategies are proposed to guide academic developers and units in designing and implementing priorities and approaches to staff development that are informed by strategic use of student learning data.

Principle 1: Pursue a Joined-Up, Holistic Approach

Strategic partnerships, cross-functional collaborations and responsive units are fundamental to high-performing organizations (Kuh et al., 2005). As part of this joined-up approach, a 'loose–tight' organisational property (p. 311) is one characterised by a delicate balance of carefully managed and prescribed processes (such as student data collection) on the one hand, and autonomy, entrepreneurship and innovation, on the other. Although data collection, analysis and reporting need to be rigorous and characterised by the highest standards, academic development activities that incorporate these data to support staff equally need to be characterised by innovation and creativity. Individual departments and disciplines may have particular needs to address; deans (learning and teaching) may wish to design targeted workshops in innovative ways to encourage staff engagement with the datasets. This fine balance is not always easy to achieve, but is fundamental to successful academic development approaches that seek to bridge the gap between centrally held student datasets and academic staff in departments and faculties (Yorke et al., 2005).

Principle 2: Delve into the Datasets and Interpret them Strategically

The following warning is timely in relation to student data: 'Never make the mistake of judging teaching or overall performance on the basis of ratings alone' (Theall and Franklin, 2001). This is a salutary caution about the importance of interpreting data within a broader context when determining academic development priorities and approaches. It is critical to recognise the range of data sources available, including peer- and self-feedback. When making decisions about strategies for integrating student data into academic development activities, it is important to pose questions such as:

- What is the purpose of the instrument?
- What are the theoretical underpinnings?
- What are the psychometric properties?
- What methodology and sampling approaches were used?
- What was the timing of the survey?
- What was the response rate and how representative are the data?
- How were the data analysed and interpreted?
- What triangulation has taken place to ensure a balanced interpretation of data?
- What other data sources are available and how might these be useful?
- Is there an appropriate balance of qualitative and quantitative data?

Delving into the data is important for a range of reasons. For instance, frequency data should focus on distribution of responses across scales and items, rather than mean scores alone. The role of institutional factors, such as student demographics, campus, discipline and programme, needs to be taken into account and more detailed analysis may be required to provide depth of information for staff at the local level. Longitudinal presentation of data may be important for depicting trends. Correlational data might be considered as a means of identifying connections between various scales and items, whereas multiple regression analysis assists in determining the unique and shared influence of a selection of survey scales on a particular outcome measure. This may assist in identifying which scale or scales would be the most effective target for academic development support and intervention (Hanbury, 2007). These are just some of the ways in which academic developers may wish to interrogate student datasets in order to be able to advise and support academic colleagues as they work towards targeted strategies for enhancing student learning.

Principle 3: Adopt a Variety of Approaches for Reporting Student Data

Kuh and colleagues (2005) astutely observe that it is not uncommon to encounter opposition when trying to bring about change, particularly in relation to enhancing educational practice. Their advice is to 'move forward with eyes wide open and alternative strategies in mind to deal with possible multiple scenarios' (p. 297). Gardner (2004) also talks about the importance of using a range of strategies to present data in order to optimise one's chance of bringing about change. These principles are usefully applied to the work of academic developers who seek to use data in a range of ways to reach a variety of audiences. Some strategies might include:

1. Target specific staff groups and provide datasets relevant to their roles and needs. For example, first year coordinators/advisors will be most interested in data on students' early perceptions of their university learning experience, and programme-level reporting of data will probably be of most immediate relevance to program leaders, whereas heads of school and deans (learning and teaching) are most likely to be interested in school- and faculty-level data respectively. Consider the needs of each group in developing professional development activities and approaches. Focusing on how the data might support their particular needs in relation to programme planning, assessment or student engagement will ensure greater buy-in from different staff groups.
2. Integrate a module on strategic use of student data into your university's Graduate Certificate in Learning and Teaching (or equivalent).
3. In multi-campus universities, host campus-based forums to discuss student learning experience data from a campus perspective. This will help staff to understand more about the student cohorts on their campus and will add value to the information-sharing process.
4. Showcase examples of good practice in use of student learning experience

data. These examples may be presented at institution-wide events to celebrate teaching, or may be targeted at disciplinary contexts.

5. Include regular reporting on available datasets and strategic uses of student learning experience data to learning and teaching committees at institution and local department/faculty levels.

6. When presenting workshops based on the student data, consider ways to integrate students as part of the presentation. This will add authenticity to the presentation and will help to bring the data alive.

7. Challenge academic staff to consider the explanations behind student responses, rather than focusing on mean scores only. This requires that they engage with informed analyses of the qualitative as well as the quantitative data. They may be encouraged to conduct follow-up investigations by means of student focus groups and the like.

8. Ensure that due consideration is given to gathering and reporting data on the learning experiences of postgraduate coursework and research students to ensure that the experiences of all student groups are represented.

Principle 4: Support Academic Developers to Ensure Informed Use of Data

If student data are to be used effectively to enhance the quality of curriculum design, assessment and the student learning experience, academic developers themselves require professional development. They need to understand the purposes of the various student survey instruments, they need to engage with both quantitative and qualitative data, and they need resources and support to be able to analyse data in a range of ways. Prebble and colleagues (2005) observed that building staff capacity in understanding how to accurately interpret and use student data was a critical first step in using the data to contribute to teaching effectiveness (p. 40). This principle applies as much to academic developers as it does to their academic staff colleagues and to university managers (Brennan et al., 2003). There may be a lack of understanding on how to analyse and interpret data in meaningful, fit-for-purpose ways. Although some academic developers may have the necessary skills, it is most likely that they would need support in terms of skills, time and resources to enable more sophisticated analysis and reporting of the data to address specific needs in different contexts across the university.

Principle 5: Look for Opportunities to Build Capacity and Trust in a Collegial Environment

Feedback on ways to interpret and use student learning experience data to improve teaching and to inform improvements in curriculum design and delivery has an important role to play in the professional development of academic staff, particularly when presented in a supportive and consultative way (Roche and Marsh, 2002). However, it is only when staff learn how to make best use of the data themselves that they will truly engage with it and the benefits it might bring. In turn, they may also make helpful suggestions to improve the collection, analysis and reporting of data and should be encouraged to do so.

A key to success is building capacity by encouraging colleagues such as course and programme leaders, heads of school and deans with responsibility for learning and teaching to initiate local discussions around use and application of data to optimise the quality of learning and teaching (Guerra, 2008). This may extend to research in a range of areas including investigation of the most effective ways to use evaluative data to inform curriculum design and reform (Menges and Austin, 2001). The key message is that academic colleagues need to be empowered and supported to take ownership of institutional datasets and the processes for learning from them and using them strategically.

Conclusion

Student survey data represent a powerful addition to the suite of professional development activities that characterise successful academic development units. Although the interest in survey data has intensified in recent years, and the number of student surveys has increased significantly, it is important for academic developers to maintain their perspective in this context. Student learning experience data should be integrated into an evidence-based approach to academic development that helps to align the social and structural elements of the university in order to bring about sustainable and continuous improvement in relation to the student experience and the curriculum that supports it. This chapter argues for the importance of a whole-of-institution strategy for building capacity and leadership among academic staff so that they will engage with student data in an informed and strategic manner, with a view to continuously improving practice. The challenge for academic developers in this regard is not to be underestimated. Engaging with student data in meaningful ways requires an investment of time and resources which, arguably, is no longer an option but a necessity.

Endnote

1. At the time of writing, this scheme has been discontinued and is under review. See http:// www.i-graduate.org/services/student_barometer.html (accessed 3 June 2010).

References

Abrami, P.C., Rosenfield, S., and Dedic, H. (2007) The dimensionality of student ratings of instruction: an update on what we know, do not know, and need to do. In Perry, R.P. and Smart, J.C. (eds) *The scholarship of teaching and learning in higher education: an evidence-based perspective*. Dordrecht: Springer. pp. 385–445.

ACER (2008) *AUSSE 2008 Australasian Student Engagement Report*. Available at: http://www.acer.edu.au/ausse/reports.html (accessed 12 July 2009).

Ackoff, R. (1999) *Ackoff's best: his classic writings on management*. Hoboken, NJ: Wiley.

Astin, A. (1993) *What matters in college*. San Francisco: Jossey-Bass.

Barrie, S., Ginns, P., and Symons, R. (2008) *Student surveys on teaching and learning: final report*. Sydney: Australian Learning and Teaching Council. Available at: http://www.itl.usyd.edu.au/projects/studentsurveys.htm (accessed 12 July 2009).

Bath, D., and Smith, C. (2004) Academic developers: an academic tribe claiming their territory in higher education. *International Journal for Academic Development* 9 (1), 9–27.

Bradley, D., Noonan, P., Nugent, H., and Scales, B. (2008) *Review of Australian higher education: final report*. Canberra: Department of Education, Employment and Workplace Relations. Available at: http://www.deewr.gov.au/highereducation/review/pages/reviewofaustralian-highereducationreport.aspx (accessed 24 July 2009).

Brennan, J., Brighton, R., Moon, N., Richardson, J., Rindl, J., and Williams, R. (2003) *Collecting and using student feedback on quality and standards of learning and teaching in HE*. A report to HEFCE by the Centre for Higher Education Research and Information, NOP Research Group and SQW Ltd. Available at: http://www.hefce.ac.uk/Pubs/RDreports/2003/rd08_03/ (accessed 22 July 2009).

Dearn, J., Fraser, K., and Ryan, Y. (2002) *Investigation into the provision of professional development for university teaching in Australia: a discussion paper*. Canberra: Department of Education, Science and Training. Available at: http://www.dest.gov.au/sectors/higher_education/publications_resources/other_publications/professional_development_for_university_teaching.htm (accessed 12 July 2009).

Gardner, H. (2004) *Changing minds*. Boston, MA: Harvard Business School Publishing.

Guerra, D. (2008) Superperformance: a new theory for optimization. *Performance Improvement* 47 (8), 8–14.

Hanbury, A. (2007) *Comparative review of British, American and Australian national surveys of undergraduate students*. York: The Higher Education Academy. Available at: http://www.heacademy.ac.uk/resources/detail/ourwork/research/NSS_comparative_review_resource (accessed 13 July 2009).

Krause, K. (2007). Social involvement and commuter students: the first-year student voice. *Journal of the First-Year Experience and Students in Transition* 19 (1), 27–45.

Krause, K., and Coates, H. (2008) Students' engagement in first-year university. *Assessment and Evaluation in Higher Education* 33 (5), 493–505.

Krause, K., Hartley, R., James, R., and McInnis, C. (2005) *The first year experience in Australian universities: findings from a decade of national studies*. Canberra: Australian Department of Education, Science and Training.

Kuh, G., Kinzie, J., Schuh, J., Whitt, E. and Associates (2005) *Student success in college: creating conditions that matter*. San Francisco: Jossey-Bass.

Ling, P. (2009) *Development of academics and higher education futures: Vol. 1*. Sydney: Australian Learning and Teaching Council. Available at: http://www.altc.edu.au/resource-development-academics-higher-swinburne-2009 (accessed 24 August 2009).

Menges, R.J., and Austin, A.E. (2001) Teaching in higher education. In Richardson, V. (ed.) *Handbook of research on teaching*. 4th edn. Washington, DC: American Educational Research Association. pp. 1122–1156.

Pascarella, E., and Terenzini, P. (2005) *How college affects students: Vol. 2*. San Francisco: Jossey-Bass.

Prebble, T., Hargraves, H., Leach, L., Naidoo, K., Suddaby, G., and Zepke. N. (2005) *Impact of student support services and academic development programs on student outcomes in undergraduate tertiary study: a synthesis of the research*. New Zealand Ministry of Education: Research Division. Available at: http://www.educationcounts.govt.nz/publications/tertiary_education/5519 (accessed 12 July 2009).

Richardson, J. (2005) Instruments for obtaining student feedback: a review of the literature. *Assessment and Evaluation in Higher Education* 30 (4), 387–415.

Roche, L.A., and Marsh, H.W. (2002). Teaching self-concept in higher education: reflecting on multiple dimensions of teaching effectiveness. In Hativa, N. and Goodyear, P. (eds) *Teacher thinking, beliefs and knowledge in higher education*. Dordrecht: Kluwer. pp. 179–218.

Senge, P.M. (1990) The leader's new work: building learning organizations. *Sloan Management Review* (Fall), 7–23.

Senge, P.M. (1999) *The dance of change: the challenges of sustaining momentum in learning organizations*. New York: Currency/Doubleday.

Smart, J.C., Kuh, G.D., and Tierney, W.G. (1997) The roles of institutional cultures and decision approaches in promoting organizational effectiveness in two-year colleges. *Journal of Higher Education* 68 (3), 256–282.

Smith, C. (2008) Building effectiveness in teaching through targeted evaluation and response: connecting evaluation to teaching improvement in higher education. *Assessment and Evaluation in Higher Education* 33 (5), 517–533.

Sorcinelli, M.D., Austen, A., Eddy, P., and Beach, A. (2006) *Creating the future of faculty development, learning from the past, understanding the present.* Bolton: Ankar Publishing Company.

Stake, R., and Cisneros-Cohernour, E. (2000) Situational evaluation of teaching on campus. *New Directions for Teaching and Learning No. 83.* San Francisco: Jossey-Bass. pp. 51–72.

Theall, M., and Franklin, J.L. (2001) Looking for bias in all the wrong places: a search for truth or a witch-hunt in student ratings of instruction. In Teall, M., Abrami, P.A., and Mets, L. (eds) *The student ratings debate. Are they valid? How can we best use them? New directions for institutional research: No. 109.* San Francisco: Jossey-Bass.

Yorke, M., Barnett, G., Evanson, P., Haines, C., Jenkins, D., Knight, P., Scurry, D., Stowell, M., and Woolf, H. (2005) Mining institutional datasets to support policy making and implementation. *Journal of Higher Education Policy and Management* 27 (2), 285–298.

6

Innovation and Change
Responding to a Digital Environment

CATHY GUNN

Introduction

The use of evidence gathered through focused and responsive evaluation is critical to the success of any innovation. Where new ground is being explored, how could predictions based on past experience possibly provide the guidance that is needed to keep new developments on track and moving in the right direction? The common sense of this approach seems to be lost on advocates of blue skies thinking and profit driven alternatives to established educational traditions. Unfortunately for the tertiary education sector, the voice of such advocates often proves to be louder and more influential than the voice of reason and evolving evidence-based practice. This chapter on innovation and change in the digital learning environment calls for evaluation before, during and after every venture into new terrain. Established qualitative and quantitative methods can still be applied, with studies in naturalistic environments recommended. It is the pivotal role of evaluation as a driver both of educational innovation and of organizational learning that marks the proposed approach as different from the norm. The methodology is itself an innovation developed to address practical problems faced by academic development centres.

Learning with new technology has been the focus of misleading speculation for more than a hundred years. A process that has become sadly familiar has replayed through the development of correspondence schools, radio, television, video, interactive multimedia and the internet. Unrealistic expectations of the educational impact drive strategic initiatives and high levels of investment that often yield poor returns. The current 'exciting prospects' are virtual worlds and social networking applications. Although significant educational benefits usually do result from the introduction of new technologies, they are never the radical changes or paradigm shifts that their champions would have us expect. In fact, the only consistent outcome, and therefore the only reliable forecast, seems to be that expectations will fail to be met, but unanticipated areas of application will evolve to change the way people behave and interact. Whether the focus is on the actual uses that new technologies will be put to, or the level of engagement by different target groups, forecasts never seem to get it right. The beneficial outcomes that do emerge are achieved in less than efficient ways, and this acts as a deterrent to wider acceptance by the educational community. After so many cycles of speculative investment and unexpected outcomes, it is surprising that a more grounded approach to elearning innovations has not been more widely adopted. This is particularly anomalous in a sector that relies on evidence and established research methods for virtually everything. Yet the old saying 'those who do not know history are doomed to repeat it' continues to apply.

This chapter analyses the historical context and current challenges facing academic developers working in the influential, yet unpredictable area of digital technologies in tertiary education. An evidence-based approach is proposed as the basis for a more efficient and arguably more effective way of working with elearning innovation. This kind of evaluative approach has always been applied at practice level, as teachers theorize new strategies, before developing, testing and refining them. The challenge is to forge connections that allow a similar process, if not to drive, then at least to inform, strategic and sector-wide initiatives. In common with others in this section, this chapter adopts a conceptual approach to the issue of evaluation of academic development, in other words it is not based on evaluation of a particular initiative. This is because there are no known cases that illustrate the proposal in a coherent and comprehensive manner. A combination of evidence drawn from experience and examples from the literature and different institutional contexts illustrate both principles and practical components of the evaluation framework. Evaluation is a key element at every stage from scoping and concept development to impact assessment. Scoping starts with a situational analysis, and is illustrated here through the case of the strategy for elearning professional development adopted by the Centre for Academic Development (CAD) at the University of Auckland.

Academic Development with a Twist

Professional development for elearning has much in common with other areas of teaching and learning development. The target group is largely the same and many principles of good practice are shared. Transformed practice through sustained and focused engagement with new educational methods is a common goal. Differences arise from typical patterns of engagement with new technology (Schön, 1967), the ever-changing nature of that technology, and individual and collective responses to the opportunities it opens up for learning design. The success of professional development is ultimately a question of how effectively elearning innovation is enabled and how widely successful strategies are disseminated. Another question related to desirable outcomes is how actively different institutional systems support an emergent area of practice that is marked 'strategically important'. However, cause and effect relationships in this area are complex. Context has a significant influence on levels of engagement with elearning, and many factors lie outside the scope of academic development work. At the interface between strategy and practice, professional development can play an important role in promoting greater awareness of the various ways that strategic goals play out at practice level. This role is not as widely acknowledged as it might be and outcomes depend on many extrinsic factors.

The Goals of eLearning Professional Development

eLearning reflects all the common characteristics of a case of educational innovation. Goals are ill defined because new ground is being explored. Different targets apply in various parts of the organization, and impact is different at institutional, departmental and practice levels. Responses to pressure to radically change established practice are not overwhelmingly positive, as Schön (1967) noted in an early analysis of technology-related change in organizations. Aims shift over time as institutional goals respond to new opportunities and changes in the environment. This also applies to individuals as professional contexts and priorities change. The methods employed to support achievement of strategic aims through professional development must also change to suit the particular goals in focus at a given point in time. An example from elearning shows that the skills-based approach that was useful 10 years ago to build operational capacity for use of an enterprise learning management system and basic communication tools is no longer prevalent. Most academics have become competent users of these basic facilities. The bar has been raised, so engagement with innovative pedagogies and elearning opportunities can be foregrounded. This requires a very different conceptual approach and range of activities.

Current aims for elearning professional development were defined by a cycle of reflection on the outcomes of previous activities and further formative evaluation. Alignment with a new institutional elearning strategy is also a priority. One aim is to empower academics to exploit the proven potential to transform learning and educational practice in positive ways through appropriate applications of technology. This requires strategies that cater to a wide variety of user experience levels and interests as well as consideration of various ways the new overarching strategy can be articulated at practice level. Another, more challenging, aim is to support leading practitioners in the discovery and development of new areas of potential. This highly specific area of professional development has been poorly served in recent years because of the unique nature of each initiative and the limited resources available to support these individuals or small groups of staff.

Broadly defined though, the aim of professional development is to enhance learning design within courses through the application of appropriate elearning pedagogies. Various strategies to achieve this aim are currently in use or under development by the elearning group within CAD. These are based on the findings of a New Zealand-wide research study that encompassed a local needs analysis component, and include:

- assisting teaching and support staff to translate elearning concepts and ideas into practical and workable solutions for use with students and colleagues;
- generating and disseminating a knowledge base of cases where elearning strategies and activities have been used to enhance student learning;
- promoting networks and fostering communities of professional practice where elearning experience is shared and peer support relationships are established;
- exploring and promoting awareness of the potential of elearning such that a critical mass of academics can make informed choices about how to use common tools and engage with new ones that come on stream;
- establishing responsive evaluation and reporting strategies as an integral part of the elearning development and implementation cycle so that dissemination of experience can follow;
- devising ways to actively support lead practitioners and successful elearning innovations so that their long-term maintenance and sustainability prospects are assured;
- facilitating communication and providing feedback to promote discussion around the need for new organizational systems and potential areas for organizational learning arising from implementation of elearning strategies.

Evaluation with Everything

Pursuit of these aims involves some complex challenges in the cultural context of a university. The kind of healthy scepticism that arises from observing or experiencing failed expectations of the impact of new technology is one force to contend with. Some academic development activities are themselves innovations, thus requiring formative and responsive evaluation methods to ground design, monitor progress, measure impact and define direction as circumstances evolve. The same approach is used for scoping and implementing elearning development projects. Adding accountability requirements to this evaluation process results in a considerable challenge, particularly if the predominant mindset insists on quantitative data and proof of significant difference. Some practitioners have failed to accept the central premise of a considerable body of literature challenging reliance on such methods (see e.g. Mitchell, 1997; Viadero, 2005). The important message from this body of work is that studies in education, whether formative, summative or systematic, often require a different approach from the experimental and comparative methods of the sciences.

Evaluation of capacity development initiatives is described by many authors, for example Horton (2002) and Tamas (2008). This conceptual approach offers an appropriate guiding framework for situations that are complex and where no simple formula for evaluation will work in every case. In fact, all learning design and impact evaluation work has to be crafted for the context of use. A key feature of an evaluation strategy for any innovation is the use of evidence for both formative and summative purposes. The following brief historical review of the use of new technologies in education explains why this should be treated as a non-negotiable case.

Technology and the Curse of Speculation

As noted at the beginning of this chapter, the role of elearning in university education has been the subject of much speculation. This continues in the wake of what proved to be the most recent round of failed expectations. The Y2K bug didn't end up biting; the dot.com economy quickly morphed into the dot.bomb economy; and many mega online universities became expensive, spectacular failures. It's not all bad news though. As an expanding area of professional practice, elearning has brought many beneficial changes, as well as many challenges to the way academics work and facilitate their students' learning. Few of either the challenges or the changes featured in forecasts ahead of the event. This is a strategic area of investment for institutions and governments, yet the direction of the future remains uncertain, and evidence suggests that it is dangerous to try to predict. An analysis of how such highly qualified observers could get it so wrong was presented in a report titled *Thwarted innovation: what happened to e-learning and why?* (Zemsky and Massy, 2004). During the same period, many well grounded and educationally effective elearning initiatives that did not align with the speculators' vision struggled to survive. Positive outcomes from this period are that worthy initiatives did survive and continue to grow now the speculators have moved on to the next high-stakes venture. Valuable lessons can be drawn from the experience. The tragedy is that scarce resources continue to be wasted, and a lasting sense of mistrust and cynicism is created amongst the very people who are best placed to define the real educational potential of the new technology of the moment.

It is surprising how often this cycle repeats, with experience of the past as well documented as it is (Noble, 1997). The last hundred years of the literature reveal periodic reports of failure to anticipate the effects of new technology. Some are amusing in hindsight. The head of IBM predicting single-figure demand for personal computers and Bill Gates reckoning that 64kb of RAM would be more than enough for any desktop computer are two popular examples. A more sobering case from the education sector of the 1890s (no misprint!) saw expensive advertising and sales campaigns entice thousands of distance learners enrol in 'personalized, anywhere, anytime' courses offered by leading universities.

The new technology of the time was the US mail system. The initiative failed as spectacularly as the recent virtual revival of the same ideal, and for very similar reasons. These recurrent cycles of speculation and failed investment have no more sensible explanation than a Luddite curse from the nineteenth century. The lesson is clear, though, that an evidence-based approach is needed to temper the technicolor dreams of entrepreneurs in an area where unexpected outcomes have become the norm, as well as the basis of many beneficial developments.

The Importance of Evidence

It is the nature of academic practice to seek reliable evidence of the potential of any innovation before committing to its development or implementation. Although outcomes will never be entirely predictable, new directions are generally grounded in what is already known, be it theoretically, as a result of experience or a combination of both. Two critical elements of the elearning development cycle at micro level are (1) formative evaluation drawing on literature, best practice examples and pedagogical content knowledge to inform designs; and (2) impact evaluation to assess what happens when ideas are translated into practice. Evidence is gathered by means of established and mainly, though not exclusively, qualitative methods. Data are analysed and interpreted to explain the observable impact, and to guide future steps in a teaching enhancement process. This generic process applies to teaching and professional development as much as it does to any other research area. It can also be applied at macro level if, for example, elearning strategy is the focus rather than a course-related learning activity. With so much speculation on the topic, elearning strategy development and implementation would surely benefit from this grounded approach at institutional as well as at practice level. Although the main focus of this chapter is on professional development for elearning, the institutional perspective is also worth considering because many influences on engagement arise in this broader context.

Responsive evaluation methods can help to shape the direction, as well as to assess the impact of elearning or professional development strategies. A significant missed opportunity at the present time lies in the untapped potential to apply an evidence-based approach for institutional elearning strategy development and implementation, and as a catalyst for organizational learning. The common approach at institutional level is to develop strategic ideas from principle rather than evidence-based practice. Lessons that could be learned from relevant local experience and emergent practice are overlooked, and the opportunity to foster a sense of shared ownership is lost.

The practice of drawing on the experience of early adopters and lead practitioners can represent the difference between speculation and a grounded approach. It surely makes sense to use local experience to shape strategy and guide implementation. Supporting, evaluating and learning from lead practitioner experience are certainly key activities for current professional development aims. Experience shows this to be a valuable source of evidence of potential and effectiveness, as well as a useful dissemination strategy. However, like the impact of technology on teaching and learning, the outcomes of these activities are complex and challenging to measure. The following sections present principles and a methodology designed to address that challenge.

Evaluating Complex Relationships

At a conceptual level, evaluating professional development for elearning innovation can be described as a process of assessing one of a number of influences within a complex network of relationships in the institutional environment. The recommended process involves two stages, the first to define learning objectives and determine the best available means to promote them, and the second to evaluate the impact of ideas translated into practice in authentic learning contexts. These are not separate events, but different phases of a cyclical process. The diversity of focus situations and the complex nature of causal relationships are more suited to use of a guiding philosophy and principles than to tightly defined methods, procedures and performance targets.

This contrasts with the approach of some researchers, who insist that the impact of specific activities should be isolated from, and possibly compared with, that of others. These aims are more rational than realistic, and date back to the time when educational research was an emergent discipline and the only trusted methods were experimental ones 'borrowed' from another discipline. Although these experimental methods may work for studies of compounds and organisms in the sciences, they fail to identify important factors where learning and human behaviour is the focus. Debate on the issue remains active, although in the meantime much effort has gone into development of qualitative, interpretive and critical methods fine tuned to the study of learning in naturalistic settings. The philosophical difference is worth noting, because it is the source of major criticism that eventually guided development of a responsive, evidence-based methodology suited to studies of elearning. A popular version of that methodology is design-based research.

The Aims of Design-Based Research

Over the past decade or so, design-based research has become a popular methodology for evaluating elearning initiatives at practice level (see e.g. Barab and Squire, 2004; Wang and Hannafin, 2005). The general approach draws on theory and current experience to anticipate what new ideas for learning design will work in practice. A concept development phase precedes iterative cycles of production, implementation and data gathering to assess the actual impact. Interpretation of impact factors informs redesign where data identify scope for improvement.

At various points in the cycle, areas of potential for organizational learning can also be identified. The findings from empirical studies reflect the impact of strategic plans at the level of practice, which is where a Joint Informations Systems Committee (JISC) report (2008) notes that the real impact of such initiatives is felt. So, for example, assessment policy may need adjustment to accommodate a new approach or process, or new funding sources or accountability measures may be required to reflect the strategic priority assigned to particular areas of elearning development, to name just a few of many possible examples. Although these adjustments are beyond the scope of professional development work, the opportunities to feed information back into the system are present.

The blend of theory-driven design with empirical studies of the impact of these designs on learning offers a grounded approach to evaluation and supports dissemination as well as continuous improvement of emergent elearning practices. A further aim of design-based research is to provide guidance for the application of relevant educational principles beyond the development or case study environment. Again, this guidance is based on empirical evidence, and data from multiple cases may be used to justify assumptions that principles and designs may generalize. The main difference between design-based research and other common evaluation methods is the use of a combination of theory and systematic, formative process to analyse aims and inform learning designs. This is a useful approach for any educational context. It can be used to inform the design of academic development activities, as well as the overall elearning strategy that these activities are designed to promote.

Design-Based Research in Action

Applying the principles of design-based research to elearning professional development adds an important formative element to the process. Some aspects are explicit, with literature reviews, scoping exercises and situational analyses used to ground the design of activities in current theory and good practice models. Others are implicit, drawing on the tacit knowledge and experience of elearning development practitioners. Current activities and short- to medium-term plans within the CAD at the University of Auckland are also guided by a 2007–8 review of elearning initiatives across New Zealand institutions (Gunn, 2010). Using the framework for evaluating capacity development initiatives described by Horton (2002), the study sought to identify, and devise ways to remove, barriers to achievement of strategic goals around staff engagement with elearning. Although this challenge is not unique to New Zealand, it is no less prevalent there than elsewhere. Rather than simply seeking further investment that would most likely lead to the same limited impact as many previous initiatives (e.g. Darby, 1992; Alessi, 1997; Campbell, 2003; O'Grady et al., 2010), a different approach was adopted. Findings suggested the need to create conditions to allow elearning to flourish at practice level. The following summary outlines some common barriers and includes strategies to address them over time. Design-based research is a key enabling method.

1. A lack of compelling evidence of the educational value of different elearning strategies in professional practice contexts limits levels of engagement and possible points of entry for many staff. The proposed solution is to use local design-based research studies to contribute to a broader knowledge base of successful initiatives, and to identify learning design principles that will transfer across practice contexts. A community of practice model can then be used for dissemination by means of various events, networking opportunities and collegial working relationships. Broadly defined, the role of professional development is to design and facilitate these developments.

2. eLearning orientation, awareness raising and capability development strategies on staff perceptions and engagement have a limited impact. If elearning concepts are presented as easily accessible teaching and learning enhancement strategies, along with compelling evidence of pedagogical and productivity gains, then the impact of these activities is likely to be greater. Applying formative evaluation processes and grounded educational principles to the design of professional development programmes is a fairly reliable way to achieve positive results. However, evidence also points to factors other than development opportunities affecting motivation to engage. Institutional incentives and rewards are required to address them.

3. There are limited opportunities and incentives to experiment with elearning strategies in a context where workloads are full and research productivity is the priority. These are coupled with poor continuity, diffusion and maintenance support for successful initiatives. Evidence gathering can help to identify the kind of incentives and support that would improve the situation. Effective maintenance, continuity and diffusion strategies can be devised by means of scoping exercises, analysis of successful initiatives and discussion with relevant stakeholders. However, these are essentially matters of priority and resourcing, so knowing how they might be addressed is an incomplete solution. Presenting evidence to support the case may help to generate action in the right places.

4. Lack of supportive organizational structures, ineffective communication and change management processes, and limited understanding of the vision for elearning are all identified as barriers to strategy implementation. Reflecting the vision in accountability measures at faculty and departmental levels might help to address this. A systematic approach to change management with high-profile communication strategies could also contribute. Most organizations have internal cases as models to draw on and enhance if they choose to learn from this experience. Although responsibility for these matters also lies beyond the remit of an academic

development centre, the evidence that identifies the problems is information that can be passed back to relevant parts of the organization.

5. A limited sense of shared ownership is a common barrier faced by centrally driven elearning strategy development and implementation plans. This perceived barrier also falls beyond the remit of an academic development centre, though it could possibly be addressed through the enhanced communication strategies proposed as part of the change management process with consultative processes to increase levels of engagement.

Although the 2007–8 study was designed to inform the future direction of elearning professional development, it must be noted that many of the perceived barriers require action that is beyond the scope of this kind of work. Effective networks, key relationships and appreciation of different stakeholder perspectives are all noted as critical success factors in the capacity development literature. Professional development is just one key element of the 'community of professional practice' model that this reflects in a university environment. Challenges arise where existing relationships do not involve all key players and new connections must be forged. Who is responsible for defining these new relationships, who has the power to promote them, and where do they find resources to complete the necessary tasks? The acknowledged existence of 'academic tribes and territories' (Becher and Trowler, 2001) demands skill in what Gunn and Cavallari (2007) describe as 'cross-cultural communication'. Although central service unit staff such as those in academic development centres may be well experienced in this respect, power and politics often prove to be stronger forces.

Working from this analysis of the context that elearning professional development operates within, and the competing influences it has to contend with, the remainder of this chapter focuses on the key principle of using evidence, rather than speculation or poorly grounded forecasts, to inform practice. Strategies to address the first three points listed above and some suitable evaluation methods provide the focus for the illustration. These perceived barriers fall largely, though not entirely, within the remit of academic development work, and reflect the core aims of current work. Ways to address the broader institutional issues outlined in points 4 and 5 are also considered. Although their relationship to the academic development role is debatable, they can act as deterrents as much as, and sometimes more than, even ideally designed activities can encourage engagement. There is also a common tendency to name professional development as the scapegoat when expectations fail to be met. These broader issues are rather less sharply in focus at this point in time, and they are certainly more challenging to influence and evaluate. However, the key principle of using evidence applies across the board; in this case, to test assumptions underlying investment and systems implementation; to inform elearning strategy-related decision making; and to ground assessment of the impact of new technologies. It is to some of these forms of evidence, the aims they are used to support and the methods of collection that the chapter now turns.

A Knowledge Base for eLearning

Across this institution (University of Auckland), a broad range of elearning applications has been developed and successfully integrated into educational practice over a number of years (e.g. Gunn et al., 2005; Gunn and Harper, 2007; Hamer et al., 2007; Brussino and Gunn, 2008; Denny et al., 2008). This typically involves a blend of face-to-face and computer-based activities, rather than complete online courses or stand-alone solutions. These developments are the result of a process that largely reflects the design-based research cycle undertaken by capable and creative teachers, whether or not it is explicitly identified as such. Not all such initiatives are formally evaluated and results published, although a number of significant ones are. The quality of these initiatives is reflected in the contribution this local experience makes to a growing international body of literature on elearning. This literature also contributes to the local knowledge base.

Generating and disseminating this information is one useful strategy for professional development of teachers. Although essentially an awareness-raising exercise, the preferred approach is from peer to peer. The broad aims are to raise awareness of the available options, and to encourage adaptation of ideas and resources for use in different practice contexts. Fostering the sharing of this kind of experience within a community of professional practice serves a number of useful purposes. First, it allows personal meaning to be constructed from the experience of others in similar professional roles. Second, it is often easier for teachers to relate to colleagues who are a few steps ahead in terms of elearning experience than to so called 'experts'. Third, it raises awareness of what is possible and what has already been achieved. Because the focus is on authentic cases in the same, or a similar, institutional context, this kind of evidence is a valuable aid to navigation through what can seem like an impenetrable maze of options and speculation. Evidence of where, how and why different elearning strategies have proved successful offers a reliable form of guidance for those who have less time and perhaps less inclination to experiment and take risks than some of the 'early adopters'. In a number of cases, collegial relationships that originated at showcase or seminar type events designed to disseminate experience have resulted in reuse or repurposing of elearning systems for different discipline areas, thus taking the range of potential to a new level. In one respect, this can be considered a measure of success for professional development. However, the evidence is anecdotal and the instrumental role of any event or activity cannot be isolated from other influential factors. Indeed, if asked about the origin of their 'great ideas' for elearning, staff may only vaguely recall the moment that a single event set them off on a path to greater achievement. Although evidence could be gathered in a systematic way, for example, through in-depth interviews, it would be time-consuming and almost certainly require ethics consent. At best it might reveal a causal relationship that is plausible though difficult to prove. The question is: would it be worth the investment in the light of scarce resources and competing priorities? The answer is probably not – except in accountability terms.

Criticism of this approach hinges on the unique nature of each case and the resulting inability to guarantee successful results that can be generalized. The point is valid, but can also be addressed by means of design-based research cycles, where the aim is to develop principles that transcend the unique aspects of a single case study.

The embedded nature of most elearning activities means that transfer to different contexts involves the skill to craft and fine tune systems for each new situation. Supporting development of these skills is another key professional development aim, though one that cannot be addressed by externally defined objectives, delivery of specific content or generic professional development programmes. The process typically involves collaboration between elearning design and development and teaching staff. Each party brings partial knowledge to the situation and the subject-based teacher is the one who determines what form the outcome will take. In the same way that different players in institutional elearning strategy implementation have to work across functional boundaries, Gunn and Cavallari (2007) compare this kind of cross-disciplinary collaboration to communication across academic cultures. Experience suggests that the key role elearning designers can play in this process is to facilitate knowledge sharing within a community of professional practice, while constantly evaluating and redefining what this means in the focus situation.

Orientation and Capability Building

Although much professional development work aims to disseminate a knowledge base for elearning as outlined in the previous section, orientation and capability building still have an important role. The focus of this tends to shift as new technologies come on stream and staff want to explore the potential. This purpose is well served by workshops, seminars and showcases. These are typically organized to meet demand and are often facilitated by academic development centre staff. There are opportunities to promote new technology tools such as an in-house web-based 'CourseBuilder' tool that has been designed to increase autonomy and productivity levels amongst academic and support staff. The challenge in this area is wide engagement. There tend to be a relatively small number of interested individuals and a majority who rarely or never attend elearning development workshops, perhaps because they do not consider elearning skill development as a priority or as relevant to their teaching. This is inclined to shift only when momentum gathers in a strategically important area, as it currently has for lecture recording technology. Then the challenge becomes one of scale and focus. Is it the role of professional development to train staff in operational aspects of new centrally provided technology systems or should the focus remain on the pedagogy?

Encouraging Experimentation and Providing Support

Creating a culture where experimentation and risk taking in the teaching environment is encouraged is a challenge, particularly in an institution where research is clearly the priority. There are cases where this has been achieved, most notably within course teams responsible for large classes with elearning as a key course delivery method. The results are positive, yet hard to replicate through external influence. Evidence shows that the conditions required to create this kind of culture are a supportive head of department, and a context where teaching excellence is highly valued and a collegial approach and team teaching are the norm. Professional development units can support these cultures in a number of ways, for example through customised workshops or other events, retreat facilitation and contributions to strategic planning for teaching and elearning. However, it is often the case that development activity takes place within the team and that the staff involved are invited to talk about or demonstrate what they do in professional development events arranged for the benefit of other colleagues. Support is always available on demand for these initiatives, and good working relationships are fostered.

Conclusion

The activities described in this chapter represent a significant departure from the 'professional development as training' philosophy. Although this has a useful place it is not a main driver of the transformational learning that needs to occur for innovation, in this case, elearning development and integration, to spread across the institution. The increasingly popular community of professional practice approach is recommended for that purpose. This clearly defines the role of the academic developer as skilled facilitator rather than teacher in a more traditional sense of the term; a complex and many-faceted role. Both the range of activities involved and the overall impact of the work are hard to describe in the concrete terms required for annual plans, accountability and performance appraisal. The design-based research approach may serve the purposes of formative implementation and summative evaluation for elearning initiatives well. However, it is still challenged to produce the kind of hard evidence required for reporting purposes, and sometimes even for people in the role to feel 100 per cent confident that what they are doing is having the desired effects. Perhaps the best expectation is that professional development will continue to be recognized as one important contributing factor to implementation of strategic plans for elearning. Evaluation methods will continue to evolve to address design questions, assess impact and identify other influences. The academic development community world-wide is working on the remaining challenges. It is to be hoped that this chapter and others in the book will offer some useful insights.

References

Alessi, S. (1997) *Seeking common ground: our conflicting viewpoints about learning and technology.* Available at: http://www2.gsu.edu/~wwwitr/docs/common/index.html (accessed 24 May 2010).

Barab, S. and Squire, K. (2004) Design-based research: putting a stake in the ground. *Journal of the Learning Sciences* 13 (1), 1–14.

Becher, T. and Trowler, P. (2001) *Academic tribes and territories.* Milton Keynes: Open University Press.

Brussino, G. and Gunn, C. (2008) Australasian language learners and Italian web sites: a profitable learning partnership? In Zhang, F. and Barber, F. (eds) *Handbook of research on computer enhanced language acquisition and learning.* Hershey, PA: IGI Publishing. pp. 1–19.

Campbell, L. (2003) Engaging with the learning object economy. In Littlejohn A. (ed.) *Reusing online resources: a sustainable approach to e-learning.* London: Kogan. pp. 35–45.

Darby, J. (1992) The future of computers in teaching and learning. *Computers in Education* 19 (1–2), 193–197.

Denny, P., Luxton-Reilly, A. and Hamer, J. (2008) The peerwise system of student contributed assessment questions. Proceedings of the Tenth Conference on Australasian Computing Education, Wollongong, NSW, 22–25 January.

Gunn, C. (2010) Sustainability factors for elearning initiatives. *Association for Learning Technology Journal* 18 (2), 89–103.

Gunn, C. and Cavallari, B. (2007) Instructional design, development and context expertise: a model for 'cross cultural' collaboration. In Keppell M. (ed.) *Instructional design: case studies in communities of practice.* Hershey, PA: Idea Group. pp. 127–150.

Gunn, C. and Harper, M. (2007) Using e-learning to transform large class teaching. In Bullen M. and Janes D. (eds) *Making the transition to e-learning, strategies and issues.* Hershey, PA: Information Science Publishing. pp. 139–156.

Gunn, C., Woodgate, S. and O'Grady, W. (2005) Repurposing learning objects: a sustainable alternative? *Association for Learning Technology Journal* 13 (2), 189–200.

Hamer, J., Kell, C. and Spence, F. (2007) Peer assessment using aropa. In Mann, S. and Simon (eds) Proceedings of the Ninth Australasian Computing Education Conference, Ballarat, Australia. *Conferences in Research and Practice in Information Technology* 66, 43–54.

Horton, D. (2002) *Planning, implementing and evaluating capacity development.* The Hague: International Service for National Agricultural Research. Available at: http://www.isnar. cgiar.org/publications/briefing/Bp50.htm (accessed 23 June 2009).

Joint Informations Systems Committee (JISC) (2008) *Effective practice with eportfolios: supporting 21st century learning.* Available at: http://www.jisc.ac.uk/publications/publications/effectivepracticeeportfolios.aspx (accessed 23 June 2009).

Mitchell, D. (1997) Evaluating the impact of technology on education: a radical reappraisal of education technology research. *Association for Learning Technology Journal* 5 (1), 48–54.

Noble, D.F. (1997) *Digital diploma mills: the automation of higher education.* New York: Monthly Review Press.

O'Grady, W., Rouse, P. and Gunn, C. (2010) Synthesizing management control frameworks. *Measuring Business Excellence* 14 (1), 96–108.

Schön, D.A. (1967) *Technology and change: the new Heraclitus.* London: Pergamon Press.

Tamas, A. (2008) Capacity development analysis framework. Available at: http://www.tamas.com/samples/source-docs/capdev.pdf (accessed 24 May 2010).

Viadero, D. (2005) Mixed methods' research examined. *Education Week* 24 (20). Available at: http://www.apa.org/ed/schools/cpse/publications/mix-methods.pdf (accessed 23 May 2009).

Wang, F. and Hannafin, M.J. (2005) Design-based research and technology-enhanced learning environments. *Educational Technology Research and Development* 53 (4), 5–23.

Zemsky, R. and Massy, W. (2004) *Thwarted innovation: what happened to e-learning and why?* Final report of the Weatherstation Project. University of Pennsylvania: The Learning Alliance.

II

Case Studies of Evaluative Practice

CASE STUDY 1
Whaia te pae tawhiti
Māori Academic Development at the University of Auckland

MATIU RATIMA

E kiia nei te kōrero ko te wāhi ko tā te pūkenga Māori he wero i te whare wānanga kia huri ai. He hurihanga tēnei kia whakaritea he wāhi mō te Māori, mō tōna reo me ngā tikanga, kia tipu ai ia hei Māori (Smith, 1993). Ko te tauira e whai ake nei, e whakamarama ana i ngā mahi whakapiki i ngā kaimahi Māori mai 2007–2009 kia huri. Ko te rautake hei aromatawai i ngā hua, ka whakamaramatia atu, ā, ka tāpirihia ko ētahi whakaaro hei whakapakari i taua rautake aromatawai mō ngā rā kei te tū mai.

It has been suggested that the role of the Māori academic is to effect change within the university. This change is intended to 'create space' for Māori language, culture and people and to facilitate the development of Māori as Māori (Smith, 1993). The following case describes the Māori developmental activity undertaken with staff from 2007 to 2009 with a view to instigating change. The current strategy for evaluating the impact of these activities is described and some suggestions are made for improving upon the strategy.

The Context

The purpose of this section is to provide a brief introduction for readers of the context within which Māori academic development is provided at the University of Auckland (UoA).

Like the histories of colonised peoples the world over, the Māori story is one of struggle, characterised by loss of language, disruption of culture, alienation from material resources, and subjugation through both violent and non-violent means. This is not to say that Māori have been the docile victims of the British colonial imperative. There have been plenty of examples of Māori agency and cooperation between Māori and non-Māori New Zealanders for mutual gain. However, the current positioning of Māori people within the lower societal echelons of contemporary Aotearoa (New Zealand) may be seen as a consequence of long-standing historical injustices. The UoA has been a direct beneficiary of historical injustices against Māori. Land confiscated from Ngati Awa (a Bay of Plenty tribe) in 1865 was given by the state as part of an endowment to establish the University (Sinclair and McNaughton, 1983). Although the Ngati Awa claim was settled in 2005, the reconciliation of past wrongs and the full participation of Māori within the Pākehā[1]-dominated society and institutions of contemporary Aotearoa (New Zealand) are the ongoing subject of negotiation, debate, and collaboration between the New Zealand Crown, its mandated agencies and those who represent Māori.

The Treaty of Waitangi, signed in 1840, provided a blueprint for the rules of engagement between Māori and the Crown. The UoA, like all other Aotearoa state-funded universities, is required to acknowledge the principles of the Treaty in the execution of its duties (Bishop, 1992). Objective 10 of the UoA strategic plan stipulates amongst other things a commitment to the development of Māori students and staff.[2] One of the widely acknowledged principles of the Treaty is protection of Māori language and culture as 'taonga' (treasured possession); another is the right of Māori people to develop as Māori (Durie, 2003). From the 1870s to the present day Māori have rarely had access to developmental opportunities, mediated by their language and culture. Meanwhile Pākehā New Zealanders are privileged by their status as a dominant majority and their language and culture have come to be taken for granted in every aspect of the public life of the nation. Within the Centre for Academic Development at the UoA the Māori Academic Advisor/Te Kaiwhakaako position (established in 2007) is one example of the Centre's commitment to the Treaty principles and to redressing this imbalance.

In 2007, Māori made up six per cent of the total academic staff population at UoA, and seven per cent of the general staff population. In total there were 265.5 full-time equivalent staff positions occupied by Māori. In 2008, methods of data gathering changed to record those with Māori ancestry rather than those who identify as ethnically Māori (making subsequent comparisons problematic). Those figures can be compared with the national Māori population, which is 14 per cent (by ethnicity) of the total New Zealand population, and the Auckland region's Māori population, which is approximately 10 per cent, according to the 2006 census data.[3]

Past initiatives to offer opportunities for development of Māori staff have included hui,[4] where representatives of the faculties were invited to discuss initiatives within faculties to advance Māori interests and engage Māori stake-holders. Other parties within the University who share an interest in developing Māori staff include the Māori Studies Department, the office of the Pro Vice Chancellor Māori, the Equal Opportunity Office, Human Resources and Ngā Pae o Te Māramatanga (the Māori Research Centre of Excellence, a pan-university government-funded research centre based at the UoA).

Intended Outcomes

The primary role of the Kaiwhakaako Māori/Māori Academic Advisor is to design and implement a programme of academic development for Māori staff at the UoA. If this programme is to remain true to the spirit of the University's Strategic Plan, it must reflect the principles of protection of Māori language and culture and of Māori development as Māori. Within this broader objective there are three key desired outcomes:

- to support Māori language development for staff
- to provide culturally relevant training for staff
- to develop and deliver a collaborative programme of development for Māori staff (Māori staff advancement).

In order to meet these desired outcomes for Māori staff advancement a multi-faceted strategy has been employed, centred around four core activities: support for and participation in the MANU AO (National Māori Academic Network) programme; provision of te reo Māori (Māori language) classes for all staff; development of the Māori Staff Advancement hui series; and the provision of training for the Tuakana (Māori and Pacific tutoring and mentoring programme). The following sections will summarise how the three desired outcomes have been achieved by means of various aspects of the four core activities.

Supporting Māori Language Development

The significance of this outcome is made salient in the saying 'ko te reo te hā o te māoritanga', which means 'the language is the essence of Māori culture'. If the University – or any university – seeks to become a place where the indigenous culture is authentically integrated into the fabric of the institutional life, then there must be support for language development at both the individual and institutional levels. With this in mind, an eight-week te reo Māori programme for staff (academic and general) of beginner and intermediate-level ability was developed and implemented in 2007, which attracted 30 Māori staff. A second four-week programme was offered in 2008 with a cohort of 30 staff members (beginners only) that was open to all university staff. During the first half of 2009, a monthly cohort meeting was also held with advanced Māori language speaking staff to provide support for advanced Māori language development, in the form of debates and discussions of issues relating to staff and Māori community development and te reo Māori. A cohort of approximately twelve staff participated in the monthly language development meetings.

Perhaps a more subtle but significant way of providing support for te reo Māori was bringing bilingual and bicultural skills to the fore as the Māori Academic Advisor for the facilitation of hui. The MANU AO network is a Tertiary Education

Commission (New Zealand Government)-funded initiative which aims to raise the level and breadth of Māori scholarship (research, teaching and dissemination of knowledge) in the university sector and foster greater levels of synergy with Māori professional organisations. In 2008 MANU AO provided funding for university campus-based development initiatives for Māori development across New Zealand. As the University of Auckland MANU AO co-ordinator, I facilitated two of these forums and provided cultural support for the third. Two were held on the university marae[5] and a third took the form of a writing retreat for Māori staff. The writing retreat was run off campus in collaboration with The Māori Centre for Research Excellence (Ngā Pae o te Māramatanga).

Providing Culturally Relevant Staff Training

Two examples of core activities that provide culturally relevant training for staff include the Māori language classes for beginners and the training of Tuakana tutors and mentors for Māori and Pacific students. In this context, the meaning of 'culturally relevant training' is training that is underpinned by openness to different ways of doing, knowing and expressing. At times this might include things as obvious as prayer or ceremonies of welcome and closing. A less obvious but no less significant requirement would be regular opportunities for participants to bring their personal experience to bear on the content and the training process.

The beginner Māori language class was designed with this dual concern for content and process. The first and last classes in the eight-week programme were delivered on the marae, which necessitated the inclusion of whakatau (formal welcome) and whakawātea (formal farewell). Every class began and ended with prayer. Much of the learning was task based and students were asked to prepare for an upcoming task each week. This approach was favoured as a way of allowing students to bring their own experience and preferences to bear on the task at hand.

Similarly, the training days for tutors and mentors who work with Māori and Pacific students were designed with a concern for culturally relevant content and process. For the most part the content of this programme is based on generic principles of good tutor and mentor training. However, there is a constant and regular focus on drawing out the experience of the tutors (often there is a mix of more and less experienced tutors present), especially with regard to their knowledge of Māori and Pacific peoples. Furthermore, the open discussion session entitled 'dealing with difficult situations' asks the participants to identify problems they have experienced as tutors, mentors or students and to explain how these were or might have been resolved. This session is regularly identified in evaluations as one of the most useful to both new and experienced tutors.

Designing and Delivering a Collaborative Professional Development Programme for Māori Staff

In collaboration with the Co-ordinator of the Tuakana tutoring and mentoring programme, who is based in the Equal Opportunity Office, a Māori Staff Advancement hui was convened on behalf of the Pro Vice Chancellor Māori (University of Auckland). The objective was to seek feedback from staff as to their developmental needs. This was a preliminary step towards providing a programme of Māori staff development. The programme needed to account for the diverse groups of stakeholders mentioned above with an interest in developing Māori staff for higher levels of engagement, promotion, and participation in the life of the institution. Sixty-three Māori staff members attended the hui and the feedback gathered emphasised four areas of need: Māori language development for staff; development of human resources (HR) processes of advertising, recruitment and hiring to demonstrate a greater recognition of Māori cultural competencies in all staff (not just Māori staff or specialist Māori positions); development for promotion; and development for leadership.

In response to this feedback the Māori language programmes outlined above were developed and implemented, and the issue of reviewing HR processes with a view to them becoming more responsive to Māori language and culture is ongoing. A Māori staff promotions workshop was developed and initiated and the Māori Staff Advancement (MSA) committee was formed in 2008. The MSA committee, whose key objective is to provide a programme of development for Māori staff, includes members from the Centre for Academic Development, Equal Opportunity, the Pro Vice Chancellor Māori Office and Human Resources.

At the time of writing the MSA committee was in the process of implementing a three phase programme for Māori staff. The first phase was a further hui, where Māori staff were presented with a basic statistical profile of Māori staff at the UoA. Summaries of issues for Māori development from the Māori Deans of Faculty[6] were presented. Staff were invited to give feedback on a draft programme of seminars and workshops for the phase two follow-up hui. Finally, staff were invited to participate in a follow-up peer mentoring programme to run over a period of three months. The follow-up hui was where the seminars and workshops were delivered; topics such as work/life balance, reports from the faculty Deans on faculty commitment to the Treaty and Māori engagement, promotions workshops and change management for Māori Advancement were covered. The final phase of this development programme will offer follow-up workshops and a chance to seek feedback and evaluate the overall three phase programme. Further developments for Māori staff members will flow from this initiative.

Evaluation strategy

> Ehara taku toa i te toa takitahi engari taku toa he toa takitini
> My strength is not mine alone it is the strength of many
> (Māori proverb)

One of the complicating factors in developing an evaluation strategy for the impact of the Māori development programmes outlined above is the essentially collaborative nature of the activity. The cornerstone MSA programme doesn't 'belong', in a territorial sense, to the Centre for Academic Development. In order to be effective it needs to belong to a number of stakeholders. Another complicating factor for measuring impact is that Māori staff at the UoA are relatively few and thinly spread across seven faculties and four campuses. Notwithstanding these factors, an evaluation strategy has been employed that is based on a combination of traditional methods (in the university sense) and Māori customary methods. The strategy consists of:

1. standard written participant evaluation feedback
2. critical reflections from the Māori Academic Advisor
3. observations and constructive feedback from colleagues
4. oral evaluation feedback at hui (in accordance with Māori protocols).

The final sections of this case study will consider what this evaluation strategy has delivered and how well aligned it is to the three intended outcomes, and will make some suggestions for future improvement of evaluation of the impact of future Māori academic development activity.

Discussion

Standard written participant feedback has been gathered on a regular basis for the Māori language classes, the Tuakana tutor and mentor training, and the inaugural Māori Staff Advancement workshop and seminar series. At times written feedback forms have been distributed at the conclusion of a session. At other times forms have been sent out by email one to two weeks after an activity and participants given a further one to two weeks to return feedback. There is a marked difference in the quantity and quality of feedback depending on when the feedback is sought. Feedback sought at the conclusion of a session tends to capture a high rate of responses from participants but the feedback is often superficial. When feedback is sought by email one to two weeks after the session there is a lower response rate but feedback is generally more detailed and analytical. This written feedback has revealed a high rate of participant satisfaction with the development opportunities on offer, but it has also identified a need for more follow up and collegial support as Māori staff often feel isolated when they return to their faculties and divisions (for example, not having anyone nearby who can communicate in te reo Māori or not feeling supported to implement change for better work/life balance when managers and colleagues are not 'on board').

One's own critical reflections on feedback are just as important. Participant responses should never be taken purely on face value. One participant at a session on 'engaging Māori and Pacific students' wrote on the evaluation form 'this session was a waste of taxpayer's money'. Although this comment was in no way representative of responses, nor was it accompanied by any constructive feedback, it is important. It acts as a reminder of the potentially controversial nature of offering Māori specific academic and professional development. In a sense it highlights just how important this agenda is and suggests that in order for the university to continue to acknowledge the principles outlined in the Treaty of Waitangi, there will continue to be an urgent need for developmental activities that broaden perspectives on the place of Māori academic development within universities.

Observations from colleagues who understand the context yet can provide an 'outside' eye on the design and delivery of developmental activity are always useful in improving provision. To date this strategy has been underutilised as a source of evaluative feedback. Colleagues have provided significant feedback in the form of written observation reports on general academic development activities in which I am involved (i.e. academic development activity not focused specifically on Māori). Such feedback is intended to continually enhance our delivery and the responses from participants in development activities or programmes. However, this potential source has not yet been fully taken advantage of for Māori developmental activity in this early phase and this is an area which will be capitalised on in the future.

The fourth source of evaluative feedback comes in the form of oral responses from participants at hui. It is commonplace at hui to conclude proceedings with speeches of thanks and challenge, thanks to the hosts and organisers in appreciation of their efforts to provide opportunities for dialogue and mutual learning, and challenges if and when perceived errors of judgement or omission have been made in the course of proceedings. These oral presentations will be more or less formal and more or less critical depending on the nature and tone of the hui, but they always need to be carefully recorded and included as legitimate sources of evaluative feedback. One example is the time a senior Māori academic stood to address the MSA hui. In her oratory she thanked the organisers, acknowledged how important these hui were in mediating the isolation Māori staff sometimes feel and raised the question of how the findings from the hui would have impact with the wider university community. She expressed concern that these hui often make strong statements about strategic development directions for Māori that are easily ignored by those outside of the gathering, those with the ability to instigate change.

Alignment

So how well is this evaluation strategy aligned to the three intended outcomes as stated above? The answer to this question is twofold. On the one hand, alignment is very good. There is now a well established channel of communication of evaluative feedback between participant stakeholders and the Māori Academic Advisor, utilising multiple sources and various models of gathering data, and demonstrating a high level of appreciation for the stated outcomes. On the other hand, a lot of work remains to be done. The existing strategy caters well for gathering feedback from individual stakeholders. However, the group stakeholders with interests in Māori staff development (listed above) have to date played little part in the provision of evaluative feedback. This is an area of concern and a focus for future accommodation and revision of the existing strategy. The second significant area of concern relating to the evaluation strategy is the need to include decision makers in the process and outcomes of Māori staff developmental hui. How can key decision makers across the institution be included to provide evaluative feedback and in turn to have issues pertinent to Māori development feature more prominently on the institutional list of priorities?

In summary, this case study has revealed the following strengths and weaknesses in the current approach to the evaluation of a programme of academic development for Māori staff. Strengths include:

1. multiple sources of feedback
2. multiple strategies to elicit different types of feedback
3. a high level of participant satisfaction and appreciation of the intended outcomes.

Areas for focus of future efforts to improve the evaluation strategy have been identified as:

1. inclusion of written observations from colleagues
2. gathering of feedback from interest group stakeholders as opposed to individual stakeholders
3. seeking feedback from key decision makers within the institution beyond those who attend the Māori developmental hui.

Endnotes

1. 'Pākehā' is a Māori word whose common meaning is New Zealander(s) of European ancestry.
2. See objective 10 in the University of Auckland Strategic Plan 2005–2012; available at http://www.auckland.ac.nz/webdav/site/central/shared/about/the-university/official-publications/documents/strategic-plan-2005-2012.pdf (accessed 3 June 2010).
3. See the Statistics New Zealand website: http://www.stats.govt.nz/Census/2006CensusHomePage/QuickStats/AboutAPlace/SnapShot.aspx?id=1000002&type=region&ParentID=.

4. 'Hui' is a Māori word for meeting or gathering. It is one of a number of Māori words recognised by many speakers of New Zealand English.
5. A marae is a Māori cultural meeting house, and it is a commonly understood vocabulary term in New Zealand English. There are literally hundreds of marae the length and breadth of New Zealand. Most are community owned and operated. However, some universities have their own marae as teaching facilities and for ceremonial purposes.
6. At the time of writing there were seven faculties within the UoA, of which five had Māori Deans (Business, Engineering, Law, Health, Science). The Māori Dean's role varies from faculty to faculty, but generally they provide advice and support to their faculty Dean and fellow staff on responsiveness to Māori, and they lead or support Māori development (teaching, research and knowledge dissemination) within their faculty.

References

Bishop, J. (1992) The treaty and the universities. In Oddie, G.J. and Perrett, R.W. (eds) *Justice, ethics and New Zealand society.* Auckland: Oxford University Press.

Durie, M. (2003) *Ngā kāhui pou: launching Māori futures.* Wellington: Huia.

Sinclair, K. and McNaughton, T. (1983) *A history of the University of Auckland, 1883–1983.* Auckland: Oxford University Press.

Smith, L.T. (1993) Ko tāku ko tā te Māori: the dilemma of a Māori academic. In Smith, G.H. and Hohepa, M.K. (eds) *Creating space in institutional settings for Māori.* Monograph no. 15. Auckland: Research Unit for Māori Education, University of Auckland. pp. 1–20.

CASE STUDY 2
Academic Partnership
Peer Mentoring with Early-Career Academics

BARBARA KENSINGTON-MILLER

Introduction

It can be exciting to start work in the academic world of universities. For early-career academics, however, this excitement can be dampened by the overwhelming prospect of teaching new courses, coping with large lectures and other elements of teaching while at the same time developing a research portfolio. Beginning this journey may feel lonely and solitary. Furthermore, arriving in a new city, a new country, or even a new culture, can increase this isolation. Whatever the background, the transition can be daunting. Where do early-career academics find support? How do they ask questions when they're not sure who or even what to ask?

Within the University of Auckland, there is anecdotal evidence that a lack of support for early-career academics is a systemic problem. As part of the Centre for Academic Development, my role is to provide support as new academics embark on this journey and to evaluate the effectiveness of that support. However, being an early-career academic myself, I was eager to provide a service that would not only sustain my new colleagues but also benefit me in the process. Peer mentoring therefore was offered – a variation of the traditional dyadic model. In this type of mentoring relationship, both partners have equal status and may be mentor and/or protégé at any one time. The value of this strategy is that it makes use of a resource while simultaneously addressing a need. Through peer mentoring, friendships can be made, a colleague can be supported, concerns can be addressed in a 'safe' environment, and any of the demands of academic life and a new position can be integrated more easily (Lacey, 1999).

This case study explores the dynamics of the peer mentoring strategy and the role the relationship plays in supporting early-career academics. It also examines some of the complexities around evaluating this approach and how they can be resolved.

Supporting Early-Career Academics through Peer Mentoring

In the following excerpts from participants, all names have been changed for the purpose of confidentiality but dialogue is 'real'.

Catherine was a new academic and had arrived in New Zealand with her partner a few weeks before the semester began. She was English, her partner was American, and neither had been to New Zealand before. Both had been working on post-doctorates in the United States when they met. They were keen to start a new life together in a different country from their own and both had managed to secure lecturing jobs at the same university in New Zealand. When I first met Catherine she was still finding her way around the university and trying to balance her teaching load with the demands of research. She and her partner had moved house twice in a short time since arriving. Catherine expressed that she was missing her family back in England and was feeling homesick.

Harry was another early-career academic. He had recently joined a new department as his original one was small and would not be recruiting new staff any time soon. He had been in the job three months and commented that 'when I started I had these big ambitions for my research . . . I was told that this was all crucial for making any advancements . . . having this research . . . but I have just lost the energy for it.'

Catherine was paired up with Brett, who was also English and new to New Zealand. Equally important, he had come from working in the United States as had Catherine. Brett stated that they:

> were quite well matched . . . not just because we were English but the whole situation actually . . . being English was an immediate ice breaker and common ground, which makes life quite straight forward but I think both being new arrivals, new positions, both moved from the States . . . it was helpful . . . we had a lot in common.

Catherine and Brett were in different departments and different faculties, and found that this worked well for them with the peer mentoring. Brett found:

> having a chat about things and talking with someone from a different department was good . . . if it was with someone in my own department I would certainly be more reserved . . . because the implications of what you say are sort of wider . . . the person you are talking to knows everybody . . . I would be more defensive, reserved, worried.

For an early-career academic this is often their first teaching position. The teaching might involve designing a new course, preparing lectures and writing assessments. It may involve teaching in lecture theatres with up to a thousand students, or using different technology in a lecture theatre they have never seen. There are many different aspects.

They may have to teach a number of classes every day over a defined period, or block teach, and be involved in running tutorials for the first time. Whatever the need may be, support and reassurance can help. Catherine found Brett:

> very friendly, sociable and easy to talk to . . . we had similar backgrounds so we could talk about the differences between teaching here and in the States . . . it was good to have this in common . . . we didn't talk about England as such but the fact we were away from family . . . it was nice to be able to focus on things that were different and to support each other.

There is also the expectation that academics will be involved in productive research projects and writing papers for conferences, journals or books as well as sourcing funding for them. Many early-career academics have only experienced writing a PhD and producing some papers from these. Trying to balance the demands of research with teaching and with life outside of work is difficult, and to do this successfully can be better achieved with good support. Margaret commented that with peer mentoring:

> it was definitely useful having someone to bounce ideas off and if you're at the same level it's really good because I can for example show them my writing and not feel like oh gosh I have to show it to a professor.

Evaluating the Overall Process

The process for peer mentoring was initiated either by invitation at the teaching and learning workshops for new lecturers, which our team is involved in running, or as a request from a department to support research capacity. Each new group is coordinated and monitored by myself and has a set time frame, the minimum being three months. The peer mentoring is not open ended but can be renegotiated at the end for a new period. There are specific goals and rules agreed upon by the participants who choose to be involved. Setting up this strategy was an opportunity for me to combine the evaluation process with research.

Prior to the start of peer mentoring, ethics consent was obtained to conduct research. As new groups became involved, I was able to include them by informing the ethics committee each time. From my previous work on peer mentoring (Kensington-Miller, 2007) I knew the importance of collecting information about my participants before assigning them into pairs so that there was some common ground between them when they started. This was important for establishing the relationship (Ertmer et al., 2003) so that it could develop and strengthen more easily. The literature by Zachary (2000) warns against making assumptions about the mentee, and the temptation of projecting one's own experiences and reality. There is also the danger of adopting a one-size-fits-all approach.

A simple pre-questionnaire was created, which provided information about the participant that would help with the pairing (see Appendix 1). This was handed out and collected at the first meeting, when the process was explained to a new cohort, as previously I had found that questionnaires often did not return if participants took them away. My previous experience had also taught me to make the questions short and straightforward but such that would at the same time elicit enough information for me to get some sense of who each person was and where they were going. The pre-questionnaire was modified for each cohort depending on the background of the group and the discipline. Pairs were matched as far as possible by level of seniority, level of research, cultural background, languages spoken and, if they were a parent, children's ages and so on. However, the reality of working within small cohorts of approximately ten participants has meant that it has sometimes been difficult to match pairs.

For evaluation of the peer mentoring I interviewed each participant using a semi-structured style to create a conversation (see Appendix 2). This allowed them to respond to some questions directly but gave me the opportunity to delve deeper for clarification. The interviews provided good feedback on the process informing me what worked and what did not. As the process of interviewing and transcribing is a long and time-consuming process, I am currently working on another means of evaluating the process for future use – possibly a post-questionnaire with open and closed questions.

Continuing Evaluation

The outcomes of the evaluation process of three initial groups of early-career academics have given me insights that will help to shape future management of the meetings and the peer mentoring. Each group had meetings once a month, which all participants were expected to attend. Abby stated that 'having the meetings over that three months . . . where we bring you up to date, that was essential.' It was impossible to find meeting times to suit all the participants, and the feedback they gave was to send out the dates and times for the semester to be put in their diaries in advance.

The meetings lasted for at least an hour and were divided into three parts: a sharing time, a teaching time of some new aspect with a task for the month based on this, and a collegial time. Pairs discussed how their month went, celebrated the positives, and worked together on suggestions to address the negatives. These meetings gave immediate feedback about what was (or was not) happening more easily. Evaluation of this is ongoing and for each cohort creating openness is important.

Attendance fluctuated and it was difficult to assess whether the meetings took precedence over other things. Were they priority? Did they add value? Would the plan for one cohort work for another? Alan enjoyed the meetings, saying:

> I didn't come away from any of them thinking oh maybe I shouldn't have put my time into that. Each time it was good, each time they were different . . . I thought it was spot on and I wouldn't want to change it, so more of the same.

Michael also found the meetings useful as 'you don't want to make it just a chat, you want a structure to give it some substance' but felt that 'it would have been better actually putting more pressure on us to be presenting our work.'

Once each person was assigned a peer mentor, they were encouraged to meet together at least twice between each meeting. Many of the pairs met for lunch or coffee, or at each other's offices. Some chose to meet after work. Bob and Charlie tried a variety of places. 'We met in the tea room twice, at his office or mine, and once we went to the food court downtown, and another time at the graduate lounge for lunch.' To assist them, small tasks were given that were related to the monthly meetings. The benefit of these was easily evaluated as they enjoyed sharing what happened at the monthly meetings.

Some pairs bonded easily and quickly became productive, moving on to critiquing each other's writing, or in the case of teaching, observing the other and offering suggestions. Again, the benefit of the meetings allowed me to quickly evaluate how these were going, what they were doing and whether they were finding them useful.

Zachary (2000) describes each peer mentoring relationship as unique and having no set formula. How would I evaluate the relationships if each journey is different? How much time should I allow for those peer mentoring relationships that are struggling? Anna tried to peer mentor with Kate but was:

> disappointed that it didn't work out the way that I expected it to work . . .
> I felt I was always initiating, but I didn't get the same commitment . . . you
> can work on communication, I mean I tried working on that, to get it going
> . . . but for commitment I'm not sure how you address that.

She suggested that some initial input from the coordinator might have helped. I hadn't anticipated this and realise now the importance of pastoral care as well as organisational input for future peer mentoring.

The evaluation process of peer mentoring is still in progress as new insights are gained into how individuals benefit. A much longer-term strategy is to take the evaluation to a higher level, so that it gives broader insights into the benefits for the institution.

Are the Peer Mentoring and Evaluation Strategies Transferable to Other Areas of Academic Development?

The evaluation of peer mentoring has limitations. In essence, this strategy is transferable to other academic development inputs as it is based predominantly on support. However, there are caveats that must be noted before setting it up, and the evaluation of peer mentoring long term is part of my ongoing research. For some, the short-term availability of peer mentoring is all that is required as it is immediate and helps the early-career academic to get established and feel that there is at least one person they can turn to for support on any level. For others, the long term is preferable in that it doubles as a professional working relationship and as a friendship. Becky discussed her peer mentoring relationship with Emily, saying:

> I'm not sure if we would have met other than as acquaintances as our paths are so different. I enjoy peer mentoring with Emily as we have similar backgrounds, both of us have large families and so we understand the constant demands of juggling work and family. We are both career-oriented and it is nice to have someone who understands that while we want to advance in our career we are also very family oriented and it is a struggle to do both well. We are very flexible in fitting in with each other and our meetings are usually social as well as working on our writing.

A major factor for participants in the process is time. For those meeting across disciplines this was an issue. Consequently, most of these were short-term relationships, for about three months, filling an immediate need although some have lasted longer and have re-established themselves. The demands of heavy workloads for early-career academics make it difficult for them to find the time to meet, but paradoxically those who do unanimously comment on the value of it. Spending time at each meeting discussing different issues allows the group to talk and make suggestions for alternatives. Alison valued the peer mentoring as it meant she could 'get another perspective' and her partner Zoe valued 'the opportunity to exchange ideas'. Coming from different disciplines, Zoe and Alison found their timetables constantly clashed but persevered in finding times, usually over morning tea, and usually in each other's office, to get together.

The second caveat is to have regular follow-up meetings as a large cohort. The meetings provide an environment for camaraderie while developing a community of practice. They also provide the opportunity for quick evaluation of what is happening. By sharing as a group and participating and learning together, a sense of ownership and renewed productivity develops. This role of the group dynamic appears to be key for effective peer mentoring in the initial stages. How well the group bonded reflected the ability of the coordinator(s) to facilitate discussion and present new material. It was also an important time to bond with each other and this flowed into the peer mentoring relationships.

Wenger (1998) states that communities of practice have life cycles which will evolve depending on the practice, those involved and the purpose for being. They may take a while to come into existence but are not dependent on a fixed membership or bound to each other. Olivia enjoyed coming to the meetings as:

> it is difficult for me to meet new people, so it was good to be involved . . . the topics were quite good, quite valuable. The first one you can clearly see the point of setting goals, you can see results of that. With the second meeting, it was too generic maybe . . . I didn't know what I could take out of that or how I could improve something.

The link between peer mentoring and building a community of practice is significant because of the impact they have on one another. My research is ongoing and now involves more groups, including one at a university overseas. There are still many features of the model to develop and evaluate. One of these is making sure the meetings are well structured to the needs of each cohort so that they add value. Another is exploring how these meetings can become self-sustaining. And for peer mentors, how can they ensure that their one-on-one meetings are always productive? As the number of groups increases over time and their diversity extends, the model for peer mentoring becomes more complex and the evaluation will become a challenge.

References

Ertmer, P.A., Richardson, J., Cramer, J., and Hanson, L. (2003) *Critical characteristics of professional development coaches: content expertise of interpersonal skills?* West Lafayette: Purdue University.

Kensington-Miller, B. (2007) *Peer mentoring as a professional development strategy for mathematics teachers in low socio-economic secondary schools in New Zealand.* Auckland: University of Auckland.

Lacey, K. (1999) *Making mentoring happen: a simple and effective guide to implementing a successful mentoring program.* Warriewood, NSW: Business and Professional Publishing Pty Ltd.

Wenger, E. (1998) *Communities of practice: learning, meaning, and identity.* Cambridge: Cambridge University Press.

Zachary, L.J. (2000) *The mentor's guide: facilitating effective learning relationships.* 1st edn. San Francisco, CA: Jossey-Bass Publishers.

Appendix 1   Peer Mentoring Pre-Questionnaire

As part of your academic career development supported by the …. department, I would like to give you the opportunity to become involved in an ongoing peer mentoring programme for an initial period of three months. This would involve meeting with your peer mentoring partner (who we will organise for you) on a regular basis and working on a task together. It will also involve coming together once a month as a group to network, share ideas and learn about developing research goals, work/life balance, time management, and more.

If you would like to be involved in a peer mentoring programme could you please answer the following questions to assist:

1. Name: .... Male/Female
2. Department: ....
3. Email: ....
4. Academic Rank: (please circle one)
    Lecturer   Senior Lecturer   Senior Tutor   Other ....
5. a) Are you full-time or part-time with the university?
    b) If part-time with the university, what is your load and what days do you usually work?
    c) Do you work elsewhere and if so where?
6. Is this your first academic position at tertiary level? (you may like to expand)
7. Have you studied at different universities or polytechnics? Please indicate which ones and what you studied at each. ....
8. a) Are you currently enrolled in a higher degree? [Name]
    b) What stage are you at with your study (e.g. writing a thesis, doing papers, writing a proposal, thinking about further study, other)?
9. Are you new to New Zealand? If so, when did you arrive and from where?
10. Are you a working parent? If so, how old are your children? ....
11. What else can you tell us that would be helpful in pairing you? (Hobbies, interests)

Appendix 2   Semi-Structured Interview Questions

Lead in questions/prompts for interviewing

1. You were peer mentoring with................Can you tell me how this went?
2. How were practical issues such as time and venue arranged for meetings? Were they easy to organise? Were you successful in getting together as planned? What would have made it easier?
3. How did you feel working with your partner? How similar in terms of background did you feel your partner was to you at the beginning of the relationship? Was it easy/difficult to work together? Did one partner tend to lead the relationship? Who decided what you would do?
4. What qualities did you have to offer that were significant for peer mentoring? What qualities did you think you lacked?
5. How did you think your partner felt working with you? What qualities did your partner have to offer and/or lack that were significant for peer mentoring?
6. What did you like best about working in a peer mentoring relationship? What made it so positive/negative for you? Or, if unsuccessful, what did you hope would be good about working in a peer mentoring relationship?
7. What would you change/do differently if you were in a peer mentoring relationship again?
8. How did you feel having someone choose a partner for you?
9. At the monthly meetings, did you get to all of them? Were they useful? What about the time of the day and the length? Did you like the structure of the meetings? Some time for networking, some teaching, some collegiality?
10. If you were offered this again do you think you would be interested?
11. Any advice you would offer me to make the meetings or the peer mentoring more successful?

CASE STUDY 3
Tending the Secret Garden
Evaluating a Doctoral Skills Programme

FRANCES KELLY, IAN BRAILSFORD AND SUSAN CARTER

Developing a Doctoral Skills Programme

Doctoral study was, until recently, the least visible facet of university teaching and research. Typically, the lone candidate slaved away on a research project guided by a single supervisor. Out of view, this student–supervisor relationship has been likened to a secret garden (Park, 2007). Although the mythology of the isolated student coming to grips with the vagaries of their supervisor's personality quirks persists, the reality in most parts of the world is that the cloistered existence of the doctoral candidate has come to an end (Powell and Green, 2007). More and more people tend the PhD garden. We are three such people. This case study evaluates the impact of academic development initiatives at the University of Auckland seeking to assist the growing ranks of doctoral candidates at our institution.

What began as an ad hoc 'PhD Network' support programme in the mid 1990s was enhanced by the University's decision to appoint a full-time doctoral skills lecturer in 2003 (the first appointment of its kind in New Zealand). The increased capacity to support doctoral candidates coincided with the University of Auckland's rapid increase in doctoral enrolments. In 2005 this university set itself the ambitious goal of 500 annual completions by 2012; in part, this growth is achieved through targeted recruitment of PhD students from beyond New Zealand. The target of 500 annual completions, if achieved, would mean a doubling in the number of doctorates in the space of a decade. Doctoral enrolment reached 1,600 in 2008 from 1,000 in 2000. This growth, coupled with national changes to university financing that shifted funding from enrolments to completions, underscored discussions in 2006 around creating a 'generic capabilities programme' for PhD students, leading to the establishment of the Doctoral Skills Program (DSP) in early 2007. This initiative brought together academic and support staff from the Centre for Academic Development (CAD), the Library and the Careers Centre under the auspices of the School of

Graduate Studies. With the assistance of current doctoral students and experienced doctoral supervisors, the DSP aims to help the doctoral student's research blossom – and be ready for harvest before the season has passed.

Our first comment on evaluation of the DSP is that it meets the criterion of being 'informed by research'. In the planning stages we paid attention to global discussions about the nature and future of the doctorate so that the DSP is in line with initiatives elsewhere (Bologna Process Stocktaking, 2007; Powell and Green, 2007). Recent discussions in Australia (Gilbert et al., 2004) and in the United Kingdom (Park, 2007) raised the issue of the *purpose* of the PhD, highlighting two potential outcomes: the person (researcher, potential academic or employee) and the product (the thesis, the contribution to knowledge). Although the traditional secret garden may once have been a nursery for future academics, many candidates enrolling in doctoral degrees have no intention of pursuing academic careers (Park, 2007). Employers outside of the tertiary environment value the acquisition of other skills over the acquisition of the specialist knowledge that is the primary attribute of a PhD graduate in the University of Auckland's terms. Submissions to the University of Auckland's Curriculum Commission (University of Auckland, 2002) by university stakeholders, who include potential employers of students, indicated that the acquisition of communication skills, oral presentation skills, information skills and the ability to relate theory to current practice were highly valuable attributes in research graduates (p. 16). Universities increasingly offer doctoral support programmes that are additional to the assistance and guidance given by supervisors (Bologna Process Stocktaking, 2007; Powell and Green, 2007) and which aim to assist in the development of these other skills. World-wide there are many more fingers in the PhD pie.

The DSP was designed to fit a shifting doctoral landscape. In establishing the DSP, we were clear that our aims were to support doctoral students to completion, to help them meet the significant milestones of the degree and complete in a timely fashion. At the same time, we had a mandate to assist in preparing them for their future careers, within or outside academia. The discussions in the planning stages of the DSP about whether 'generic doctoral skills' referred to workplace-related skills or to the skills which enable students to successfully complete their research projects determined that in fact we needed to do both. Publicity materials given to new candidates define the DSP's goals as helping students to acquire the skills to complete their doctorate successfully *and* to plan their career and undertake professional development during their degree, thus equipping themselves for life after the doctorate.

The design of the programme also took account of the shifting needs of students over the doctoral process. Conceptually the DSP is divided longitudinally into three phases – early, middle and final – and vertically by eighteen core 'highly recommended' workshops and twenty-two 'additional' ones. Doctoral candidates availing themselves of the core DSP workshops (such as completing the literature review, developing a research proposal, presentation skills and career planning) would be committing themselves to approximately 30 hours of voluntary skills development during their four years or so of candidature. The most well attended non-compulsory courses in the DSP are the core courses aimed at students in the 'early phase', or provisional year.

Historically, student evaluations were typically favourable. However, in the past attendance was always optional: students participated by choice. The key-stone to the DSP is a *compulsory* induction day which all new doctoral students are required to attend in their first year, preferably within the first three months. Evaluation therefore became more crucial and, for us, more fraught. Would mandated attendants be more critical? Our intrusion into the secret garden felt less safe, our contribution to ideas of 'best practice' – problematic as that term is – less happily Edenic.

During 2007 and 2008, 625 doctoral candidates attended an induction; for some of these doctoral students the induction day *is* the DSP. Induction days, held approximately once per month to follow the pattern of registration over the year, randomly bring together about thirty new candidates each time. We attempt to mitigate feelings of resentment about the compulsory element by making the day informal, with a catered lunch shared by current doctoral students, and with a celebratory and welcoming tone. The Dean of Graduate Studies begins the day with an impromptu question and answer session; students are grouped together on the comfortable sofas of the postgraduate lounge in fives and sixes so that they can get to know each other and are given 10 minutes to formulate questions: anything about the doctorate is permissible and questions range from the minutiae of doctoral life (parking one's car) to the question 'what *is* a thesis?' The day includes workshops on supervision and the first year goals from CAD's learning and academic advisors, and an information literacy session with the University librarians. Aiming to give a realistic expectation of the first year within this institution's culture, we show candidates relevant guidelines and regulations. Students briefly self-audit their research skills and are directed to the support offered, including our own.

The day is evaluated electronically and anonymously by all attending students. This chapter scrutinises the evaluation plan for the first two years of the pro-gramme's operation (2007 and 2008) and considers what the evaluation has so far revealed, concluding with a framework for evaluating the DSP in the longer term. What emerges is that we are seeking to evaluate multiple variables (productivity, satisfaction levels and completion rates); some of these are quantifiable but there are others (such as thesis quality, career development and personal development) which remain tantalisingly out of reach.

Evaluating the Doctoral Skills Program

At the establishment of the DSP all contributing service providers agreed to an initial trial period of two years, commencing in March 2007 and concluding in

March 2009. During this time almost every individual session and induction day were evaluated by means of a standard evaluation form, based largely on the existing evaluation form used by the University Library. The Library's practice is to evaluate all sessions, whereas academic practice is to evaluate much less often, with allowance for more frequency when formative data are sought. The evaluation has been of use to the fine tuning of the DSP and of our session design within it, but has also given us fuller summative data than are usually available under the institution's student survey policy (namely, 'don't over survey'). Because evaluation is generally positive, it has been useful for our professional development as teaching academics and to feed back to our line manager and the Board of Graduate Studies, comprising principally senior faculty representatives, who also have some governance over the DSP.

Evaluation is fairly basic. The students are asked to indicate whether they 'strongly agree', 'agree', are 'neutral', 'disagree' or 'strongly disagree' with two statements ('the course content is useful' and 'the course was taught effectively'). There are spaces for open-ended comment in response to the prompts 'what I liked about this course' and 'how could the course be improved?' The evaluation form is generated automatically for every session by the bookings database and can be completed either electronically by the student, or in paper form, then loaded into the database. Presenters can download summaries of any course evaluation and frequently do so, adapting elements of the course in response to the student comments. At the end of each year, the evaluations and attendance figures for every course were analysed and presented in the form of a summary report to the Board of Graduate Studies.

The bookings database also invites facilitators of each session to comment on aspects of the course, including use of teaching material, responsiveness to activities and so on; this tool has benefits for enabling a reflective teaching practice, and also enables teams of teachers to share notes on teaching developments. The CAD teaching staff have also organised peer observation of their teaching in the induction days: peers from outside the DSP have attended for a full day and presented us with a written review of our teaching. Peer evaluation has encouraged us to rely less on PowerPoint, but crucially it has prompted us to become more interactive.

Summary of Evaluation Findings

Being anonymous, and with almost a 100 per cent response rate due to evaluation being the final act of the induction day, the student evaluations of the 2007 and 2008 inductions were extremely positive: expectations of the day were largely met or exceeded in the view of most students. Comments indicated that all sessions were useful to students and that the fairly informal and 'relaxed' style of presentation was favourably received. There was a clear indication that the induction day is most useful if done early in the candidature. Students commented on there being opportunities to learn things they didn't know (and, in several cases, didn't know they didn't know). Illumination metaphors used by the candidates indicate that the sessions 'shed light' on issues that had been obscure or hidden: 'It's a revelation'; the facilitators 'enlightened me' and 'offered insight into studying methods and faculty resources'; and 'shed light in a very dark cave'. Respondents also used travel metaphors, including comments that the day 'help[ed] me to stay on track', 'gave me . . . a sense of where I should be at this particular moment of my PhD' and 'confirmed what I have been doing is on the right track'. A relatively high number appreciated the opportunities to meet other students, to network over the lunch and tea breaks and to develop a sense of the cohort. Setting out with others 'experiencing [the] same challenges' has been consistently noted as valuable. Providing opportunities for doctoral candidates to meet with others, even to form intellectual communities, is one of the core functions of a programme such as the DSP: it helps to guard against the isolation endemic in doctoral study and fosters opportunities for research collaboration across disciplines.

The non-compulsory programme consisting of early, mid and final phase courses were also regarded favourably. Thirty-four of the thirty-eight courses offered during 2007 and 2008 received 80–100 per cent responses of 'strongly agree' and 'agree' to the statements that the course content is useful and the course is taught effectively. Suggested improvements to the courses have led to adjustments in teaching activities. One recurring comment in the first year was that certain courses were too generic and could be tailored more to the individual disciplines. Some students enrolled in courses on preparing thesis proposals and in researching and writing literature reviews stated that the course 'needs more discipline specific examples' and could be 'more specific to specific field'. Although we are limited in what we can do – it is a generic programme – we have split these two courses into two groups: one that is aimed broadly at arts/humanities students and one that is geared towards science/engineering. We are also developing other ways of meeting students' needs that are additional to the generic DSP by tailoring sessions for departments and faculties.

Reflecting on Evaluation: Other Ways of Measuring the Impact of the DSP

The DSP evaluation has thus far been instructive. It indicates that the course content of the programme is 'useful' and that the courses are taught effectively. The frequency of evaluation has enabled the programme to be responsive and adjust (where possible) to student comment. Given that the programme is new, these have been valuable lessons. Furthermore, this system of evaluation enables the DSP to be accountable to the group that oversees the governance of the programme, and to the School of Graduate Studies: we have statistical evidence that demonstrates that the DSP is largely successful at attracting student numbers and providing courses that are considered useful, and qualitative data (comments from students) that indicate that it is impacting positively on the student experience.

The DSP evaluation is also limited. We have no gauge on *how* students deem what is useful. Significantly, it doesn't tell us anything about what we don't do – for instance other course topics that the students (or their supervisors) might want to see included in the DSP. Discussion with students has informed our decisions but also made us aware that, given the range and wide variation of disciplines, the diversity of the doctoral population and the different phases of the doctoral process, we would need to have a great many student viewpoints before we could feel we had a rigorous overview of student needs.

Evaluation is demanding on students, who are asked to evaluate every single session that they attend in contrast to less thorough evaluation elsewhere on campus. In addition, other than at their instigation, there is no opportunity for them to comment on the evaluation of the DSP – whether or not they find the evaluation onerous or time-consuming. Nor is there any feedback to students on the results of the evaluations or whether their suggestions for improvement have been taken into account. The evaluation doesn't tell us if or how the courses have actually had an impact on the student's work; for example, whether or not a core course on the thesis proposal actually assists the student in submitting a thesis that is of a high standard (and on time). There have been no follow-up evaluations down the track, such as at the end of the provisional year, that enable the student to comment on how the milestones of this year have been handled and whether or not the DSP had an impact on facilitating this rite of passage.

To sum up, at present, the evaluation plan does not give us any indication if the average time to completion is impacted upon in any way by students' attendance at the DSP, if their experience while completing is enhanced or if they feel better prepared for the jobs that they will take up on completion.

Future Direction

If the DSP is adding value to the doctoral experience then the fruits of students' labour – and ours – should manifest themselves as they approach completion. At the end of 2009, the cohort of doctoral candidates whose candidature commenced after the DSP was launched will be approaching their completion phase. According to the PhD statute at the University of Auckland, the PhD takes 36 months; most scholarships fund doctoral study for this period, with several allowing further funding for an additional six months. Candidates who complete within 48 months are also entitled to a monetary completion award. According to current completion statistics, most candidates complete at between 48 and 54 months; so the 2007–8 cohort are likely to finish late 2010–11. Currently, work is being done on an institutional exit survey which could include questions that ask doctoral students to indicate which DSP courses they attended and to comment on their effect. If there is a demonstrable difference in completion time for 'our' cohort, then the DSP could be, perhaps, one of the contributors to this positive change.

Although a core function of the DSP is to assist students to complete doctoral projects, preferably within the desired four years, we are assisting doctoral candidates in developing 'doctoral skills' (e.g. project management, creativity, lateral thinking) that will also benefit them in their future careers, after completion. Once doctoral candidates have left, how has their experience impacted on their journey out of the doctoral garden? If we want to learn more about our impact down the road we will need to establish a longitudinal study, tracking the careers of the 2007–8 cohort on completion. In the more immediate future we intend to survey candidates at the end of the first year to establish whether they perceive that the compulsory induction day has helped them to meet this milestone.

Conclusion

Our task is to improve doctoral retention and completion times. We serve the institution's need to compete successfully in a 'knowledge economy', a problematic concept for some who fear that quality is compromised by the quantity of research rolling out of the doctoral plantation. In addition, we are keen to contribute to a vibrant doctoral community.

Our challenges in measuring effectiveness are common to academic development: the lack of a clear framework for evaluating what we do, coupled with a need to be accountable, to be able to *show* that we add value. This is not easy: other factors such as the completion awards and increased attention to supervisory practice (including compulsory training for all new supervisors) make the link between our teaching and retention or timely completion more tenuous. The eternal dilemma of correlation versus causality is even more critical because the DSP is part of a raft of improvements to the doctoral process. Implementing the measures described above, such as a survey at the one-year mark, would be formative in the development of the programme's content, but would also give us summative information that we can use for our own growth: the evaluation of our teaching effectiveness.

References

Bologna Process Stocktaking (2007) London: Department for Education and Skills. Available at: http://www.dcsf.gov.uk.londonbologna/uploads/documents/6909-BolognaProcessST.pdf (accessed 25 October 2008).

Gilbert, R., Balatti, J., Turner, P. and Whitehous, H. (2004) The generic skills debate in research higher degrees. *Higher Education Research and Development* 23 (3), 375–388.

Park, C. (2007) *Redefining the doctorate: discussion paper*. York: The Higher Education Academy. Available at: http://www.grad.ac.uk/downloads/documents/Reports/HEA/RedefiningTheDoctorate.pdf (accessed 7 December 2009).

Powell, S. and Green, H. (eds) (2007) *The doctorate worldwide*. Maidenhead: Society for Research into Higher Education and Open University Press.

University of Auckland (2002) *Report of the Curriculum Commission*. Auckland: University of Auckland.

CASE STUDY 4
Evaluation as Bricolage
Cobbling Together a Strategy for Appraising Supervision Development

BARBARA M. GRANT

Introduction

Doctoral supervisors are targets for significant institutional angst. Several revisions of the University of Auckland's (UoA) guidelines for supervision have proliferated the responsibilities of the supervisor, whereas those of the student have remained virtually static. Perhaps more significantly, supervision 'training' was the first development program to become mandatory for target groups of academic staff. In this case study, I describe a bricolage-style[1] programme comprising several evaluation tactics cobbled together from available resources.

However, first we will look at the bigger picture. Formal professional development for supervision is relatively well established in many countries: most universities in Aotearoa/New Zealand, Australia, and the UK have offered such programmes for around two decades. More recently, attendance at some kind of introductory 'training' has become mandatory for new supervisors. Prior to the emergence of formal programmes, the main mode of preparation for supervision was the experience of being supervised plus, if you were lucky, some informal mentoring or apprenticeship from a more experienced colleague. Although many institutions had an expectation that a new supervisor would pair up with an experienced one for their first supervision or two, in practice this pairing was often a non-event (Graham, 1996).

Exactly what constitutes adequate and effective preparation for graduate research supervision is unclear. The literature reports diverse programmes: from week-long intensive programmes to single workshops and seminars, learning circles (Manathunga, 2005), reading groups, narrative-based group work (McCormack and Pamphilon, 2004), programmes that blend face to face with online elements (Brew and Peseta, 2004), action research projects involving supervisors and doctoral students (McMorland et al., 2003), supervision observations and mentoring where new supervisors observe experienced supervisors at work, and (more rarely) formal supervision of new supervisors (Melin Emilsson and Johnsson, 2007). In addition, there is a raft of self-access technologies such as the Reflective Supervision Questionnaire (Pearson and Kayrooz, 2004), the Supervisor Student Alignment Tool Kit (Gurr, 2001), the suite of tools developed for supervisors and students at the UoA and those found on the Australian fIRST site (http://www.first.edu.au/). Although benefits are reported for most of these approaches, there has been little systematic evaluation of their impact over time – probably because such evaluation is difficult to carry out, as will be depicted in this case study.

At the UoA, the mandatory supervision training programme has two parts: (1) a two-hour seminar on local policies and processes governing doctoral education that all new academics no matter how experienced must attend and (2) a half-day pedagogy workshop that introduces those who have 'not yet supervised a doctoral student to completion' to some theory and practice for supervision. The programme is a modest one, an important consideration when thinking about its evaluation. It is complemented by a series of refresher seminars across the year (e.g. on working with a co-supervisor, examining doctoral theses, supervising interdisciplinary projects), although these seminars are not the focus of this discussion.

Assorted Hopes for Supervision Development

Supervision workshops had featured in the University's academic development programme for about a decade before the 2002 decision to make them mandatory. The exact hopes underpinning the decision were not clear, although there were growing concerns about supervision 'problems' and pending changes in government funding to reward completions. When the decision was made, it was agreed that the new programme would add to the existing pedagogy-focused workshop, The Art of Supervision, by 'creating a new module that provides information on UoA policies and practices in supervision' (email from DVC Academic, 7 Nov 2002). If the institution's hopes for the programme were not explicit, they can be deduced from its ambitions to significantly increase the number of postgraduate research students and to 'ensure that all [supervisors] are appropriately prepared . . . in ways designed to maximise the quality of supervision and probability of student success' (UoA Strategic Plan 2005–2012, p. 4; http://www.auckland. ac.nz/uoa/strategic-plan-2005-2012). Such hopes can also be inferred from the Dean of Graduate Studies' regular restatement of the importance of 'good supervision' and its link to timely completions. Concrete information about the nature of good supervision is given in the document *Senate Guidelines on Thesis Supervision* (http://www.auckland.ac.nz/webdav/site/central/shared/for/current-students/academic-information/pg-policies-guidelines/doctoral/senate-guidelines-thesis-supervision.pdf).

The academics who attend the programme also have hopes for it (expressed through comments in pre- or post-event questionnaires or unsolicited emails). They want to know about their university's aspirations, they want information about relevant regulations and policies, they want to feel as if their time has been well spent and they definitely don't want to be patronised by trivial content or process. New supervisors in particular hope to feel more confident as a result of attending and want to explore some quite basic issues such as whether or not they can refuse a student's (or, more problematically, a head of department's) request for supervision.

Finally, as the key provider of the programme, I too have hopes of it. In particular, I hope to light my colleagues' fire for this demanding but pleasurable mode of practice by:

- quickening their intellectual engagement with the work of supervision;
- kindling their confidence in being a 'good enough' supervisor;
- fuelling a sense of commitment towards the work of supervision, especially a problem-solving attitude towards the dilemmas inevitably entailed;
- inflaming respect for the complexities of experience and the diverse possibilities for 'good practice';
- sparking collegial conversations about supervision.

I aim to do this by providing an invigorating 'academic development' programme that successfully balances theory and practice, experience and reflection, and challenge and enjoyment. I also hope that those who attend will want to come back for more, despite the potentially prickly encounter of a *mandatory* full-day programme.

A Bricoleur's Approach to Evaluation

Where there are hopes, there are grounds to frame the question, 'Did you succeed?' To date my evaluation of this programme has been constructed out of what comes to hand: the regular use of convenient and conventional processes interlaced with occasional chances to grab an interesting opportunity. At a deeper level, however, it is anchored to some values that I hold about the practice of evaluation itself.

In a workshop for new academic developers (co-presented with Alison Kirkness, a HERDSA Fellow from nearby AUT University), I proposed the following GEM, or 'good evaluation method', rubric for guiding evaluation practice:

1. A GEM is modest: it knows what it is trying to do and it is focused.
2. A GEM is ethical: it attends to issues of consent, anonymity and power.
3. A GEM is economical: it is the right size for the purpose and does not collect gratuitous data that can't or won't be used.

This rubric challenges a proliferating and anxiety-ridden evaluation practice in universities that sometimes produces very little of value for *any* of the three purposes of evaluation identified by David Baume (2003): accountability (typically summative), improvement (typically formative) and understanding (typically scholarly and academic). The underlying intention of the GEM approach is that, as academics and professionals, we take control of our evaluation practices and use them more like the surgeon's knife than the soldier's machine gun.

In what follows, I describe the evaluation 'strategy' that I cobbled together for the mandatory supervision programme and reflect a little on each element.

How Did Participants Experience the Event?

The most common kind of evaluation has been the post-event questionnaire to find out how the event struck those who participated, how it might have fulfilled, or not, their hopes and mine. From the beginning, I approached the two parts of the programme separately; partly because there were quite different intentions attached to each, as I will explain, but also, because whereas the two-hour policy and process seminar was completely new and team taught, the pedagogy workshop was closely modelled on an existing, regularly evaluated workshop that I taught alone.

The policy and process seminar sought to give new academics an overview of the University's current position and future hopes for postgraduate research education, especially at the doctoral level. I carefully planned the content and pace with the inaugural Postgraduate Dean, who was the main presenter. Most of what we presented was already available in a plethora of institutional policies and guidelines but we wanted to short-circuit the reading process and draw attention to the crucial issues. We also wanted these new colleagues to meet some of the key resource people in the University. We made it clear that the seminar was a fast-paced, information-sharing event rather than an interactive one. To evaluate it, I drew on past practice to prepare a compact, customised questionnaire with six Likert scale and three open-ended questions:

1. How useful was the coverage of issues?
2. How logical was the sequence of material?
3. How clear were the presentations?
4. How helpful were the materials given out?
5. Overall, how useful did you find the seminar?
6. Overall, how well was the seminar presented?
7. Main things you liked about the seminar?
8. Main suggestions for improvements?
9. Any other comments?

The questionnaire was given to everyone at the end of the first two iterations

of the seminar. Subsequently I collated the feedback (60 responses) and the Dean and I reviewed the seminar in response. Since then I have repeated the end-of-seminar questionnaire process about once every 12–18 months and the responses inform ongoing, usually minor, changes to the event.

Targeted at new supervisors, the pedagogy workshop was a longer, more interactive event that sought to achieve a small number of practice-related 'outcomes'. Past experience has made me quite confident of participant reception to this workshop so I 'borrow' my Centre's standard evaluation questionnaire about once a year (perhaps more frequently if I have an upcoming bid for promotion on my mind). The questionnaire had two Likert scale and two open-ended questions:

1. Overall, how useful did you find this course?
2. How well was the course facilitated?
3. What did you like best about this course?
4. How do you think this course could be best improved?

The forms are posted out to all participants the day after the workshop, and have a return rate of 30–40 per cent. (Requiring the questionnaire to be completed at the end of the workshop might give a higher return rate but I am reluctant to use time in a short workshop for this activity, which is largely for my benefit.) Again I collate the open-ended feedback and draw on it to make changes to the workshop content and process.

Both evaluation tactics are modest, ethical and economical: they simply address the participants' experience of the event and invite constructive criticism in order to show accountability and to make improvements.

Did It Have Any Impact on their Practice?

After the programme had been running for 18 months, the Director of the Quality Office (DQO) and I collaborated on an 'impact evaluation project'. The DQO was keen to find ways to explore the medium- and longer-term consequences of professional development activities at the University; I saw an opportunity to gather novel evaluative information about my work.

The DQO and I designed the three-part survey questionnaire together. The first part asked workshop participants to indicate if they were currently supervising masters or doctoral research students. The second asked them to indicate a level of agreement (from strongly disagree to strongly agree) with eight statements that directly addressed the 'outcomes' posted at the beginning of the workshop:

1. I have a better understanding of my supervisory skills and strengths.
2. My interest was stimulated in practising supervision more effectively.
3. I have a better understanding of areas where I wish to improve my supervision skills.

4. My approach to supervision has changed.
5. I feel able to make better decisions about whether to accept a new research student.
6. I have a sufficient understanding of University policies and expectations concerning supervision.
7. I reflect upon and evaluate my supervision approaches and practices more often.
8. I feel I am overall a more effective supervisor.

The third part asked them to respond to four open-ended items related to changes to their supervision (Q9), other effects on them or their departments (Q10), workshop features that could be improved (Q11) and aspects of the survey process that could be improved (Q12).

The DQO invited those who had attended two separate workshops approximately six months previously to fill out the survey: from a pool of sixty-four, a total of twenty-one replied. When I received the Quality Office's summary of the findings, I wrote a considered rejoinder in which I responded to several suggestions that had been made. In some instances, I explained a change I would make to the workshop; in others, I offered alternative 'solutions' (e.g. things I could do through an ongoing seminar series). The rejoinder was sent to the original sixty-four workshop attendees.

I learned several things from the survey, some unexpected. Generally, the findings suggested that the workshop was successful: respondents thought it had made a difference to them as supervisors on all matters except one, 'my approach to supervision has changed'. More unexpectedly, I found that only half the respondents were actually supervising at the time they filled out the questionnaire (and this may account for the response to the approach to supervision item). On reflection, this is not so surprising because most of the supervision in the University is done by a subset of academics and also many workshop participants were academics in the first year or so of their career or new to this particular university.

Several respondents suggested that the survey should have been carried out sooner as either they found the specifics of the workshop hard to remember or other things had happened to muddy any cause–effect link. This strikes me as a significant problem for evaluating much academic development – it is one I came across when trying to evaluate the impact of attending academic writing retreats on writing output (Grant, 2006). In that research I asked retreat attendees to quantify the writing outputs that could be attributed to attending retreats, but mostly they couldn't, as particular retreats were hard to remember (especially for those who had attended several) and the effects of the retreats, although powerful, were often diffuse.

The survey was also modest, mostly ethical and economical: the goal was to explore the medium-term effects of professional development on supervisors.

In the survey development stage, the DQO and I negotiated quite hard over the questions. I insisted, for example, that they reflect the workshop outcomes and I wanted to keep the number down. The invitation letter said we wanted to find out if the pedagogy workshop had 'an impact upon subsequent thinking and practice'. In fact, we could not do this in the confined resources of such a project (hence the caveat of 'mostly ethical'): in the end, we only gathered data about thinking.

How Does my Practice Look to an Expert Observer?

Another opportunity for evaluation of the mandatory programme arose when a long-time colleague and collaborator (Adele Graham), now with a similar portfolio but in an overseas university, asked to audit the programme for her own purposes. Once again I grabbed an opportunity: I invited Adele, as an expert academic developer in the field, to undertake a peer observation of my teaching.

Prior to the observation, we met to discuss the issues I wanted to receive particular attention. For the policy and process seminar (and with consent from my fellow presenter), I asked her to keep this question to the fore:

- How sufficient might this workshop be to a newly appointed member of staff (new-to-the-University and possibly new-to-supervision)?

For the pedagogy workshop, I asked her to observe several dimensions of the teaching:

- Does the session meet the intended learning outcomes?
- If I were new to supervision, would attending it give me a boost and a sense of achievement?
- How effective was the (new) metaphor activity?
- How effective was the (new) use of the document camera?

Adele not only observed both events but also talked informally to participants during and after. Afterwards, she wrote a six-page report detailing 'perceived strengths/what seemed to work' and 'considerations/suggestions', focusing on the issues I had raised and also offering other observations. We met for an hour and a half to discuss her commentary and think together about how I might respond to any suggestions.

The expert review was also modest, ethical and economical: the goal was to see my practice through the eyes of an expert colleague so that I could find ways to improve it. The process required little, if any, participant time (although Adele talked informally to individuals during the sessions) but significant commitment from the reviewer (about three days in total). Later I wrote a reflective account of the experience (for my annual performance review) outlining the changes I would make to the programme for the following year. At the time I wrote:

I enjoyed the privilege of a deeply engaged conversation that focused on my work. The effect has been to refresh my energy for these two events in particular (which I have been teaching at least three times a year for several years) but also more generally to remind me of the kind of questions I need to ask myself about my teaching in an ongoing way. (30 November 2006)

Closing: the Bounds of Evaluation-as-Bricolage

Looking back across my evaluation practice in relation to the mandatory supervision programme, I have found it to be a bricolage of convenient, often borrowed, tools and fortuitous opportunities. Each evaluation event, however, is anchored to an enduring personal value base or philosophy expressed, albeit incompletely, in accordance with the GEM principles. I continue to experience real tensions around this practice: I know in my bones the value of keeping an eye on the quality of my teaching and have many informal methods of doing this beyond the end-of-workshop questionnaires. I also understand the symbolic importance of the mandatory status of the supervision programme: it says to supervisors that the institution takes their performance in this area seriously. Yet I feel a defensive anticipation towards being called to account for the value of my work (or indeed *my* value or the Centre's) to the institution when some hoped-for accounts are difficult to provide, such as evidence of the clear effects of the programme on the practices of supervisors, or its effects on the experience of individual supervised students or their persistence and completion rates. At the same time I keep careful accounts of programme frequency and the number of participants who attend each part; I also (ambivalently) assist the University to keep accurate records of who actually attends.

What might I do differently in the future? I am a researcher (as well as a supervisor–practitioner) in the area of graduate supervision: to date I have not trained my research eye on the thorny matter of evaluating the mandatory programme. Doing the research myself would raise some tricky ethical issues. Still, my interest is piqued in exploring what further questions could be asked about the effects of the programme, how those questions might be pursued (for example, in a longitudinal study), and by whom. Unsettling these 'possibilities' and a desire to pursue them, though, is my understanding of what it means to be an academic advisor: my role is to persuade supervisors to *care* about their supervision practice; it is also to deepen their *understanding* of what might be involved and what the institution expects. The practical task of supervising well is theirs – and the reasons for pursuing or succeeding at such a task are usually more complex than whether or not they attended a one-day mandatory supervision development programme.

Endnote

1. Bricolage: a do-it-yourself approach to making something, using any materials at hand.

References

Baume, D. (2003) Monitoring and evaluating staff and educational development. In Baume, D. and Kahn, P. (eds) *A guide to staff and educational development*. London: Kogan Page.

Brew, A. and Peseta, T. (2004) Changing postgraduate supervision practice: a program to encourage learning through reflection and feedback. *Innovations in Education and Teaching International* 41 (1), 5–22.

Graham, A. (1996) Developing research supervision skills by apprenticeship: a hit or myth affair? University of Auckland: unpublished paper.

Grant, B.M. (2006) Writing in the company of other women: exceeding the boundaries. *Studies in Higher Education* 31 (4), 483–495.

Gurr, G. (2001) Negotiating the 'rackety bridge': a dynamic model for aligning supervisory style with research student development. *Higher Education Research and Development* 20 (1), 81–92.

McCormack, C. and Pamphilon, B. (2004) More than a confessional: postmodern groupwork to support postgraduate supervisors' professional development. *Innovations in Education and Teaching International* 41 (1), 23–37.

McMorland, J., Carroll, B., Copas, S., and Pringle, J. (2003) Enhancing the practice of PhD supervisory relationships through first- and second-person action research/peer partnership inquiry. *Forum: Qualitative Social Research* 4 (2), article 37. Available at: www.qualitative-research.net/fqs/ (accessed 7 December 2009).

Manathunga, C. (2005) The development of research supervision: 'turning the light on a private space'. *International Journal of Academic Development* 10 (1), 17–30.

Melin Emilsson, U. and Johnsson, E. (2007) Supervision of supervisors: on developing supervision in postgraduate education. *Higher Education Research and Development* 26 (2), 163–179.

Pearson, M. and Kayrooz, C. (2004) Enabling critical reflection on research supervisory practice. *International Journal of Academic Development* 9 (1), 99–116.

CASE STUDY 5
Archiving for the Future
A Longitudinal Approach to Evaluating a Postgraduate Certificate Programme

HELEN SWORD

Introduction

The University of Auckland has recently joined the ranks of international research-led universities that offer their academic staff a formal qualification in higher education teaching. Launched in 2006, our Postgraduate Certificate in Academic Practice provides early-career lecturers and other university staff with the tools to become successful teachers, research scholars, and citizens of the academy. Through an emphasis not only on teaching, learning and assessment but on 'academic practice' writ large, the Certificate programme seeks to address the particular challenges faced by academics who must constantly juggle the competing demands of teaching, research and professional service.

The fact that our university has decided to offer a qualification that includes tertiary teaching affirms, at least symbolically, our institutional commitment to the continuing professional development of our academic staff and to the educational needs of our students. But how do we go about evaluating the effectiveness of such a programme? Do we monitor self-defined shifts in the participants' thinking? Changes to their behaviour? Improvements in their students' exam results? Future career trajectories? Declarations of personal well-being? Academic developers have thus far failed to 'prove' the direct impact of such initiatives on undergraduate education (Prebble et al., 2004). Indeed, no single empirical research strategy can adequately measure the long-term personal and institutional effects that the Certificate in Academic Practice aims to bring about. These effects are by no means nebulous, but they are extremely difficult to quantify, as our programme emphasises values, skills and outcomes that vary according to each individual's academic profile and are designed to unfold slowly over time.

This case study describes a novel research methodology, dubbed 'longitudinal archiving', that our teaching team has formulated in response to these practical and pedagogical dilemmas. 'Longitudinal' designates a study 'concerned with the development of persons or groups over time', whereas 'archive' signifies 'a place in which public records or other important historic documents are kept' (*Oxford Dictionary of English*, 2003) – a physical designation both expanded upon and challenged by cultural theorists such as Derrida (1995) and Foucault (2002). A 'longitudinal archive', then, houses a body of materials (in this case, electronic as well as physical) that have been collected with the express purpose of documenting institutional change over a relatively long period of time.

Assembling the Archive

Building for the future without knowing exactly who will use our archive, or how, or why, our teaching team has begun systematically collecting and preserving an array of materials related to the Certificate in Academic Practice, including curriculum development notes, administrative records, syllabi, evaluation feedback, transcripts of online discussions and copies of student assignments and final projects, with names, grades and comments removed. Alumni of the programme will periodically be invited to contribute, on a voluntary basis, new artefacts to the archive: updated copies of their teaching portfolios, materials relating to innovative course developments, reflective accounts of academic citizenship initiatives in which they have taken part, and so forth. We will also ask our alumni soon after they complete the programme, and then again every two or three years, to fill out a questionnaire and/or take part in a structured interview in which they will reflect on how (or if) the programme has influenced their subsequent academic career. Inevitably, the resulting archive will contain some data gaps; for example, we cannot preserve items from former participants who have declined to sign a consent form, and we are unlikely to have the resources to follow up on alumni who have moved to new positions in universities overseas.

We believe that, to gauge the long-term impact of our programme on the academic staff who pass through it and the institution where they ply their trade, we need to move beyond the kinds of survey questions we are used to asking at the end of each semester, such as 'What did you find most helpful about this course?' and 'How could it have been improved?' Instead, we must try to anticipate the kinds of questions we might want to ask in five, 10 or even 20 years' time. For example:

- Will the special focus of our programme on 'academic citizenship' and work–life balance help alumni successfully negotiate the competing demands of teaching, research and service? (How do we define and measure such success?)
- Will the participants' exposure to research-based principles of teaching, learning and assessment lead them to become more innovative, energetic

and successful teachers than colleagues who receive no explicit pedagogical training? (Again, how do we define, measure and compare such success?)

- Will our current participants eventually take on academic leadership roles within their respective departments, as we implicitly expect them to do?
- Can we trace any trajectories of influence – direct or indirect – between our programme and improved student learning?
- How will the programme itself change over time, and in response to what institutional factors and pressures?

Our ability to answer such questions – some of which may well prove unanswerable, especially where cause-and-effect relationships prove murky – will depend on the richness and robustness of our archive. Indeed, the questions we ask today might not be the same ones that future analysts of the archive will want answered.

Problems and Silver Linings

Inevitably, a number of thorny ethical issues have come into play in the assembly of our archive – issues that can either be regarded as impediments or, more optimistically, appropriated as teaching and learning tools.

Power Plays

The Problem Potential contributors to any longitudinal archive must always receive assurance that their names and other identifying information will be removed from the public part of the archive, along with grades and instructors' comments. (Programme administrators may, of course, continue to maintain such information in a secure private archive, just as they would do for any other academic programme; but they may not use grades as research data except in aggregate form.) In particular, if the curators of the longitudinal archive operate in a differential power relationship with any of its potential contributors – for example, as teachers who will be issuing marks to students or as permanent staff who give feedback to probationary staff – they must take special care to avoid even the slightest hint of coercion when asking for informed consent.

The Silver Lining A forum such as a tertiary certificate programme offers an ideal platform for discussing such ethical issues in detail with academics who might at some stage face the same dilemmas from the other side of the desk. For example, our Certificate in Academic Practice includes a module on classroom-based research, and a number of our programme participants must consequently draft ethics consent applications as part of their coursework. It therefore makes sense for us to use our own consent procedure as a practical example of the ethical issues involved in collecting research data from students.

Self-Fulfilling Prophecies

The Problem Participation in any longitudinal study can lead to the so-called 'Hawthorne effect', whereby the subjects of a study alter their behaviours because they know they are under observation, and/or the 'Pygmalion effect', whereby students unconsciously live up to their teachers' expectations. Thus the process itself risks generating a kind of self-fulfilling prophecy that can potentially skew the study results – a phenomenon parodied in a 2007 episode of *The Simpsons* entitled 'Springfield Up', where the Simpsons dress up in polo-playing gear in an attempt to persuade the producer of a longitudinal documentary (à la director Michael Apted's famous *Up* series) that Homer has finally risen in the world (Warburton and Sheetz, 2007).

The Silver Lining In the case of a longitudinal teaching archive, the self-fulfilling prophecy effect need not cause undue concern. The purpose of the archive, after all, is educational as well as empirical. Rather than ignoring the Hawthorne effect or trying to wish it away, researchers can use it both as an immediate teaching tool (yet another occasion to discuss the ethics of educational research with current course participants) and as a long-term means of improving the programme being studied. If the periodic follow-up interviews inspire alumni to try out new teaching techniques or undertake new service initiatives shortly before each interview takes place, why complain? Anticipatory behaviour modification can be regarded – in a salutary rather than a cynical light – as yet another form of reflective practice.

Archival Teleologies

The Problem A different kind of teleological effect can arise when the researchers studying the long-term effects of a given academic programme are the very same people who teach on that programme. Teachers, one might object, can never serve as unbiased researchers of their own teaching; human nature dictates that most of us will hastily bury, rather than carefully preserve for posterity, any document that presents us in an unflattering light. Indeed, as the philosopher Jacques Derrida notes, no archival project can entirely escape accusations of personal or political bias. Archiving itself is always a political act, and whoever controls the archive controls historical truth, or at least perceptions of that truth (Derrida, 1995).

The Silver Lining The longitudinal archive responds to such objections by bringing programme-related materials, including student assignments and evaluation comments, into the public realm, where any interested researcher – an external auditor, a representative of the university's quality assurance office or a colleague investigating tertiary teaching certificates world-wide, or a current participant completing an assignment on classroom-based research – can have access to them. At the same time, the archive offers teachers and programme coordinators an opportunity to model for their students reflective practice in action. For example, if the teachers on a tertiary certificate receive lukewarm student evaluations, damning alumni interview reports or other potentially damaging data, they can set an example for their current and future students (who are also, of course, their colleagues) by placing those data in the public archive and, equally crucially, by responding to negative feedback with positive change. Later, when processing and analysing the accumulated data, they can demonstrate how negative and positive evidence can be braided together into a complex critical narrative.

The Future of the Archive

Already our teaching team has discerned hints of the ways in which our nascent longitudinal archive might lend itself to such 'complex critical narratives' in the future. For example, we recently facilitated a class session focused on 'signature pedagogies', a phrase coined by Lee Shulman (2005) to describe the distinctive teaching methodologies found in different academic disciplines. Shulman interrogates the underlying assumptions behind those methodologies and suggests ways in which teachers might profitably borrow from the signature pedagogies of other disciplines. Responses to the seminar were mixed. One of our course participants (an engineer) commented during the class discussion, 'All this talk about "signature pedagogies" is just a fancy way of saying that engineers teach like engineers and lawyers teach like lawyers; as far as I'm concerned, that's common sense wrapped up in convoluted pedagogical jargon.' Another class member later complained in a mid-term evaluation that the session on signature pedagogies was interesting, but it didn't have any practical application. However, a third participant on the same course became so interested in signature pedagogies, and so fired up at the prospect of investigating and expanding the signature pedagogies of her own discipline, that she applied for and was awarded a teaching improvement grant based around the topic. Thus a single class session yielded three very different participant responses.

How can we evaluate the long-term effects of such a complex teaching situation except through dialogical narrative, attention to verbal nuance, and, significantly, the gathering of longitudinal data? The session was initially judged a failure (or, worse, a waste of time) by two out of three participants. Yet it sparked a response in the third that could lead to real changes in student learning – changes, incidentally, that the lecturer plans to measure and document as part of her teaching improvement grant, in which case her data will, we hope, eventually enter our archive. Over time, moreover, having witnessed the results of their colleague's more enthusiastic and proactive response, the two resistant course participants might well change their views – in which case our follow-up interviews a few years from now will capture their change of heart. Alternatively, the interviews could reconfirm our current perception that, in two cases out of three, the seeds of change fell on inhospitable soil. In either case, only by assembling a capacious, 'messy' archive – one that deliberately captures dissenting voices and apparently contradictory data – can we later tell stories that will capture the frustrating yet fertile messiness of higher education research and teaching.

Acknowledgement

This case study has been adapted from Sword, H. (2008) The longitudinal archive. *International Journal of Academic Development* 13 (2), 87–96.

References

Derrida, J. (1995) Archive fever: a Freudian impression. Trans. E. Prenowitz. *Diacritics* 25 (2), 9–63.
Foucault, M. (2002) *Archaeology of knowledge*. Trans. A.M. Sheridan Smith. London: Routledge.
Oxford Dictionary of English (2003) Oxford: Oxford University Press.
Prebble, T., Hargreaves, H., Leach, L., Naidoo, K., Suddaby, G., and Zepke, N. (2004) *Impact of student support services and academic development programs on student outcomes in undergraduate tertiary study: a synthesis of the research*. Wellington: Ministry of Education.
Shulman, L. (2005) Signature pedagogies in the professions. *Dedalus* (Summer), 52–59.
Warburton, M. (Writer), and Sheetz, C. (Director). (2007) Springfield Up [Television series episode]. In Groening, M. and Brooks, J.L. (Producers) *The Simpsons* [television series]. Beverly Hills, CA: Fox Broadcasting Company.

CASE STUDY 6
Tracking the Invisible
An eLearning Group's Approach to Evaluation

CATHY GUNN AND CLAIRE DONALD

Introduction

This case study describes the design-based research approach to evaluation of professional development for elearning taken by the eLearning Design and Development Group (eLDDG) within the Centre for Academic Development (CAD) at the University of Auckland (UoA).

Evaluation permeates all aspects of the eLDDG's work. It is a systematic process with a significant formative element. These deceptively simple statements mask what is actually a very challenging task spanning a range of elearning design and professional development activities.

Professional development for elearning falls into two categories that can be roughly described as 'overt' and 'covert' operations. Overt activities take the conventional form of seminars, symposia and workshops, whereas covert ones occur in the context of working relationships formed around elearning development projects. Evaluating overt activities is reasonably straightforward, as established methods can be used to collect feedback from participants in events. Difficulties arise with long-term impact measurement, as professional development cannot be separated from many other influences on teacher development. However, the standard measures are enough to meet accountability requirements, so the problem is not a pressing one. Covert activities are a different matter and require a crafted approach for each situation. These activities tend to render the underpinning academic development input invisible. The unique nature of covert elearning academic development activities adds a layer of complexity to elearning design and development, as well as to impact evaluation. Although this invisibility makes no difference in some respects, it constantly challenges the professional judgement of learning designers and makes reporting on impact an almost impossible task.

Another major strand of evaluation activity occurs in the context of elearning

133

projects. An intensive, formative process examines the objectives of subject-based activities or courses through a learning design lens. Summative evaluation is more reflective to focus on the impact of completed learning designs in practice contexts. Cycles of design, development, review and refinement are ongoing throughout these projects.

A note of caution comes with the description of evaluation strategies and methods in this case study. All types of professional development of university teachers occur in a complex practice context with many competing influences. The relationship between institutional strategy, professional development and teaching practice is complex, and evaluation must account for this on many levels. The following sections present a brief overview, with examples, of how the CAD's elearning group currently meets the challenge of evaluating activities designed to promote effective elearning practice across the institution.

Evaluation as Learning Design

A key area of activity for the eLDDG is, as the name suggests, contributing to design and development of elearning courses and resources. This work is framed within a project process that involves flexible relationships with staff from teaching departments and central service units. Evaluation is a critical element of the project process that serves a different purpose at each stage. As a general rule, evaluation starts at the beginning and continues as an iterative process throughout the lifecycle of a project, as illustrated in Figure CS6.1.

Many models and methods are available to guide this process (e.g. Reeves and Hedberg, 2003), and the importance of evaluation cannot be underplayed. It guides design and offers the means to monitor impact, as well as evidence to support future revisions of courses and activities. Areas of focus for evaluation at different stages are summarised in Table CS6.1, although, as already noted, each project has its own unique set of requirements.

Evaluation starts with a feasibility check of project proposals submitted by staff. Availability of resources and development requirements are also assessed. Some elearning concepts are already well developed at this stage, whereas others come in the form of a great idea with little practical sense of how they might

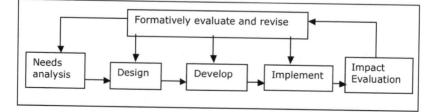

Figure CS6.1 The Iterative Development and Evaluation Process Used in Learning Design Projects.

Table CS6.1 Types of Evaluation Activity at Different Development Stages of eLearning Projects

Stage of elearning development project	Type of evaluation activity and sources of data
Initial inquiry and planning	Literature reviews, examination of related initiatives, evidence of learning principles and assumptions, analysis of course and discipline-specific pedagogy, review of previous evaluation findings
Learning design specification	Analysis of fitness for purpose, assumptions about users, media selection, interaction design, alignment with objectives and other courses, assessment components, time on tasks, content selection, analysis of professional development needs. Prototypes may be developed and tested for initial feedback on proof of concept
Production	Ongoing prototyping and usability testing of design and functionality
Teaching	Presentation to learners, performance of tasks, interim measures of learning outcomes, measures of motivation, evidence of relevance of initial assumptions, ideas for revisions or refinements, impact on teachers and teaching strategies, invited feedback from learners
Summative review	Assessment of learning, acceptance and attitude surveys, peer review, recommended revision or further development, comparison with previous iterations of courses or activities, reference to literature for new developments, reflection on experience, publication, presentation and discussion of evaluation findings

be articulated or what is involved in the process. In the latter case, an intensive, formative process is used to examine the objectives of subject-based activities or courses and learning design considerations. This takes the form of a conversation between learning designers, professional staff and subject teachers, during which various forms of evidence are examined. The aims are to develop a shared understanding of what is proposed; to align theories of teaching and learning in the discipline with the best available elearning options; and to agree what it is practical to develop in the circumstances. This phase concludes when realistic expectations are established and a project plan is produced. Although scoping can be a lengthy process, it is a critical phase that makes sure everyone gains a sense of ownership and is expecting the same outcomes. The project plan defines roles and responsibilities, as well as key attributes of the learning design that will be applied. Data collection methods that may be used at this stage include student surveys, observation of classes, focus groups and literature reviews. Scoping sometimes extends to a larger needs analysis phase, as illustrated in Case 1.

Case 1 Needs Analysis for Enhancements to an Existing Online Course

The teaching team of a large, undergraduate, online course approach the eLDDG with a project proposal that has two main goals. They plan to develop more interactive learning resources for the course, in order to (a) increase participation in the class discussions, both online and during weekly tutorials on campus, and (b) support earlier and deeper student engagement with the course content. The materials for the course are available online and in print, for students to purchase as a course handbook. Other online components are weekly quizzes, discussion forums and multimedia tutorials with high quality graphics and animations. Optional face-to-face tutorials and workshops are offered, which a third of the students attend.

Learning designers undertake a needs analysis (with ethics approval) prior to preparation of the project blueprint. This includes a review of the course materials, observing the weekly tutorials and workshops, interviews with students and staff, collecting student demographic data, monitoring students' use of online components and administering a student questionnaire. A report is compiled for the teaching team, with recommendations for the elearning project blueprint as well as for other course-related activities and assessment strategies.

Some of the recommendations are trialled by the teaching team during the next course delivery. The trials are monitored and the learning designers gather additional evaluation data. The data are used to inform further developments for the next delivery of the course.

Two aspects can make this phase particularly challenging: (1) University policy requiring research ethics approval for this data collection activity; and (2) the need to elicit teachers' tacit knowledge about the pedagogy of the discipline. In the first case, discussion with members of the University's Ethics Committee, coupled with similar requests from faculties, resulted in development and current trialling of a streamlined process for 'low-risk' applications. In the second case, eLDDG learning designers are in the early stages of developing and trialling a learning design support strategy to make explicit teacher-designers' pedagogical beliefs that underpin design decisions (Donald et al., 2009). This strategy also aims to assist in learning design conversations with teaching staff during project and course design work.

An appropriate conceptual approach for this kind of work is design-based research. Wang and Hannafin (2005, p. 6) describe this as 'a systematic but flexible methodology to improve educational practice through iterative analysis, design, development, and implementation.' This is 'based on collaboration among researchers and practitioners in real-world settings, and leads to contextually-sensitive design principles and theories.' Similar in many respects to action research, design-based research blends theory and empirical evidence to derive principles of good elearning practice that generalize beyond individual case studies.

eLearning Impact Evaluation

Strategies to evaluate the impact of learning designs after implementation are a key area of activity that needs to be further developed. Once the processes of scoping, design and development are complete, and the products are integrated into learning environments, the priorities of teachers often diverge from those of the eLDDG. Our project process ideally involves formal evaluation of the impact of the design on student learning. How else can we learn from the experience and share this knowledge with others? Yet the locus of control reverts to the teacher, and access to students, other teachers or tutors as evaluation activity has to be negotiated. Although it is easy to say that evaluation is a condition of eLDDG project support, which we do at the acceptance stage, calling in this commitment can be problematic for a number of reasons, usually related to time constraints and priorities.

Where access is available, impact evaluation strategies can be quite straightforward, although custom design for each case is still required. It is least intrusive to include questions about new activities or resources in standard course evaluation questionnaires. However, this runs the risk of low return rates or students not taking the process seriously as a result of being oversurveyed – although there is a policy in place to ensure that this doesn't happen. At best, the data collected are high-level, Likert scale ratings, with additional scope to include a small number of open-ended questions with free-text responses.

From a research perspective, something more detailed and specific on the subjective side for triangulation with objective measures would be preferred. Various techniques have been applied as circumstances permit, including analysis of learner performance on particular tasks, classroom observations, system log data, interviews and focus groups. Another strategy that could be used more widely involves interviews with teaching staff, heads of departments and other stakeholders a year or so after project work has been completed. Learning designs would then have been in use long enough for the impact to be realistically assessed, and for further developments to have been considered or undertaken. Many evaluations happen too early to reveal long-term effects of elearning integration, so longitudinal studies may be considered.

Serving the Master

Evaluation of elearning projects is a key area of the eLDDG's professional practice that counts as part of our teaching role. There is also a bigger picture perspective, within which our group's performance is measured for its contribution to institutional goals. The current elearning professional development strategy relates to the institutional elearning strategy and has five aims:

1. *To align with the aims and targets defined by the University's elearning strategy.* This forward-looking strategy was developed by a working group

reporting to the UoA's Teaching and Learning Technology Committee and was approved in April 2009. Implementation is now in progress and the eLDDG has a key role to play. The strategic vision is for widespread use of a range of emergent technology tools to support innovative pedagogies, including Web 2.0, virtual worlds and various collaborative applications supported on the technical side by a service-oriented architecture model. Fostering greater collaboration between the institutional IT Services, the Library, academic support staff and faculties will help to achieve this.

2. *To systematically apply scoping, user needs analysis and evaluation processes to all new technology systems.* Various trials of emergent technologies take place prior to investment and installation. The current focus is on enterprise-wide installation of lecture recording technology. Ideally, service providers, support staff and users collaborate to ensure timely, well informed decisions. Formative evaluation of the sort that learning designers already use for project scoping could offer a formula for success (see Case 2).

3. *To apply formal processes to document, evaluate and disseminate cases of elearning design, development and integration into teaching practice.* This is essentially a knowledge management process designed to support the sharing of experience within the university community, and across the national and international tertiary sectors. The aim is to create a degree of structure and process around elearning developments to overcome what is known as the 'silo effect', a common phenomenon that limits the spread of information about innovations beyond the immediate development environment.

4. *To promote a community of professional practice approach* to accommodate different levels of engagement, types of support and practitioner contributions. This reflects current beliefs about effective forms of professional development, and highlights the value of shared experience and mutual support. eLearning has long since passed the stage where competence with basic skills and tools (or 'IT training') is a necessary focus for professional development. Experience shows that learning from peers, experience and sustained engagement with new pedagogies, systems and ideas are appropriate means to achieve current transformational aims.

5. *To provide a range of professional development activities* designed for different purposes, levels of prior knowledge and user needs, as outlined in Table CS6.2.

Table CS6.2 Types of Professional Development

Level	Nature of professional development activities/aims	Outcomes
Introductory	Short term, voluntary, workshop, showcase, seminar and discussion; introduce concepts, teaching and learning strategies, elearning tools, options and support provision	Concept development and plans for elearning enhancements for specific teaching environments
Intermediate	Sustained, situated, supported; varied according to discipline, prior knowledge level and teaching context (this is the type of professional development currently incorporated into elearning projects)	Transformed practice, fluent use of elearning systems and strategies, course-specific and reusable resources, evidence of effectiveness
Advanced	Networking and Code of Professional Practice promotion; dissemination; measures to ensure long-term sustainability; integration of elearning tools, systems and strategies into departmental practice	Sustainable, integrated elearning systems; transformed practice; relevant policies; rewards for innovation; opportunities to share experience; return on investment; organizational learning

Case 2 Evaluation of a Pilot Project on Lecture Theatre Recording (LTR)

A working group, which reports to the Teaching and Learning Technologies Committee, is conducting a pilot project to trial and implement LTR systems and processes. The pilot involves members of the eLDDG in three ways: compiling student and teacher guidelines on how to use LTR, attending staff meetings in different faculties to provide information on pedagogical aspects of LTR, and conducting a small, formative evaluation study. Initial rollout of LTR has been limited to a small number of large lecture theatres, and uptake by lecturers who have agreed to participate has been relatively low. The purpose of this evaluation exercise is not to make any recommendations on the ultimate value of LTR at the university, as the technology, support mechanisms and services are still evolving. The formative evaluation is intended to supply feedback on pedagogical aspects of LTR, to supplement extensive logistical and technical data that will be gathered by other members of the working group.

The evaluation will involve getting feedback from a small number of staff and students by means of questionnaires and interviews. A more extensive, summative evaluation will be undertaken after the pilot study, to compare outcomes with other more established LTR systems already being used in schools and faculties.

Three overarching aims of this professional development strategy are: production of acceptable evidence of effectiveness of different elearning strategies; support, dissemination and sharing of experience for practitioners within and beyond the institution; and developing appropriate ways to promote long-term sustainability of successful initiatives. These aims present further challenges related to impact evaluation, as the outcomes are hard to quantify.

Evaluating Professional Development

On one level, evaluation of elearning professional development is a relatively simple process of setting objectives, conducting a needs analysis, designing activities or products, collecting data and then reflecting on outcomes with a view to making beneficial changes. Data can be collected through a range of established methods including feedback from event participants, observation, interviews, focus groups, performance on task and informal feedback. Many of these processes are in use by the elearning group, whereas others are in the planning stages. A CAD-wide teaching evaluation plan is under development (where 'teaching' refers to both covert and overt professional development as described above). The aim is to develop a shared portfolio of evaluative practice for teaching activities, as outlined in Case 3.

Case 3 eLDDG Teaching Evaluation Plan

eLDDG staff contribute to programmes run by the Academic Practice Group (APG), as well as teaching workshops and seminars independently. In both cases, evaluation mechanisms similar to those used by other functional groups within the CAD, such as standard questionnaires, will be used to gather evidence of teaching effectiveness: individuals will gather feedback on their teaching two or three times each year. A variety of methods (e.g. questionnaires, focus groups, observations, case studies, usability testing, rapid prototyping, peer observation, formative, summative and/or impact evaluation, user tracking) will be used to gather diverse perspectives (from current and past 'students', CAD colleagues, external colleagues and ourselves) at different points in time. Evaluation reports will include an analysis of data, what was learned from the experience and changes that were made to teaching as a result.

We will seek to gather data about each kind of work we do (consultancies, invited seminars and workshops, teaching on the Postgraduate Certificate Program) at least once every three years, using a broad mix of tools and drawing on a range of perspectives. Team-taught events such as the PostGraduate Certificate and the mandatory UoA three-day

University Teaching and Learning Program will be evaluated at least once every three years, taking into account (a) modelling appropriate use of UoA student feedback forms (where the classes are small and/or the teaching is shared); and (b) modelling good alternative methods. From time to time, we may engage in research that attempts to measure the impact of our teaching.

These methods cover most evaluation requirements for conventional (overt) professional development activities, and for assessing the impact of learning designs on educational practice. Covert elements, and long-term impact of activities designed to transform practice are not so easily measured. Many factors affect the outcomes and causal relationships are hard to identify in complex situations. Furthermore, the priorities of the elearning group are not fully aligned with those of lecturers and academic support staff in our target group. For example, eLDDG goals to evaluate impact or disseminate experience may be less important to a discipline-based academic with a full workload. Evaluation of contributions to elearning strategy implementation is even more complex as a broader range of influences is at play.

Conclusion

Taking into account the various aims and outcomes, which can all be hard to measure, there can be no generic formula for evaluation of professional development for elearning. The ideal approach to institutional elearning strategy implementation reflects the ideal way to evaluate elearning design and professional development activities: by drawing on evidence from various sources, involving people with relevant interests and experience, and using a range of methods to present the most reliable and valid evidence. The principle applies equally well to strategy and practice. The difference lies at the point of application.

Like all new methodologies, design-based research has evolved to address questions left unanswered by other means. Now it is established, the challenge is to find channels to feed significant findings back to the elearning community and into strategy implementation and policy review processes at institutional level. An advantage, as well as a challenge, arises from the multi-level and cross-disciplinary working relationships involved in elearning (Gunn and Cavallari, 2007). These relationships foster development of the networks needed to transform practice by extending the range of inputs as well as the breadth of influence.

In the current context, formative and responsive evaluation methods may be the best remedy to our proven inability to predict or control the future of institutional elearning landscapes (Zemsky and Massy, 2004). The best way to manage uncertainty is to be open to new ideas, work collaboratively across roles and disciplines, be responsive to changing circumstances and base decisions on existing evidence from authentic cases. Design-based research is a structured approach to elearning design and integration at both practice and institutional levels. It can also become a catalyst for organizational learning if institutional systems are open enough to respond to the impact data thus revealed.

References

Donald, C., Blake, A., Girault, I., Datt, A., and Ramsay, E. (2009) Approaches to learning design: past the head and the hands to the HEART of the matter. *Distance Education* 30 (2), 179–199.

Gunn, C. and Cavallari, B. (2007) Instructional design, development and context expertise: a model for 'cross cultural' collaboration. In Keppell, M. (ed.) *Instructional design: case studies in communities of practice.* Hershey, PA: Idea Group. pp. 127–150.

Reeves, T.C. and Hedberg, J. (2003) *Interactive learning systems evaluation.* Englewood Cliffs, NJ: Educational Technology Publications.

Wang, F. and Hannafin, M. (2005) Design-based research and technology-enhanced learning environments. *Educational Technology Research and Development* 53 (4), 5–23.

Zemsky, R. and Massy, W. (2004). *Thwarted innovation: what happened to e-learning and why?* Final report of the Weatherstation Project, The Learning Alliance, University of Pennsylvania.

CASE STUDY 7
Continuous Improvement Projects
Whose Evaluation Matters?

LORRAINE STEFANI

Introduction

One of many facets of the work of the Centre for Academic Development (CAD) at the University of Auckland is supporting departments in their drive for continuous improvement of learning, teaching, research and service endeavours. An efficient means of doing this is to work with a whole department, including academic and related staff and the administrative team in the context of facilitation of a Strategic Planning Day Retreat. 'Efficient' in this context is taken to mean working with a critical mass of staff from a single discipline.

This style of working has taken place with many different departments including Art History, Pacific Studies, Geography, Geology and Environmental Science, Political Science, Audiology, General Practice and Primary Health Care, and many others. The last of these named departments is the subject of this case study.

Academic developers from the CAD work with staff from all disciplines, and thus part of our remit is to develop an understanding of the contexts within which we operate. This is often stated as the attraction of asking CAD staff to facilitate departmental Retreats.

The Process

The request for facilitation of a Planning Retreat is made by the head of the department in question. Generally the preparation for the Retreat entails initial meetings between a CAD staff member and the Head of Department (HoD), and often one or two other staff members from the department such as the learning and teaching and research coordinators. The purpose of these meetings is to share information on key issues to be resolved in the department, to identify any major problems or concerns and to discern the hoped-for outcomes of the Strategic Planning Retreat. The initial role of the facilitator is to work with the

HoD and other staff from the department to formulate a working plan for the day that the HoD then shares with the staff in the department.

Behind the scenes, the facilitator does much more than this. It is important to gain as much information about the department as possible: numbers of staff, main research areas, how the department presents itself on its website, the nature of the courses offered and so on. The purpose of this background work is to gain an understanding of the culture of the department. As academic developers, it is expected that we have a wide knowledge and understanding of the institutional context within which departments operate, depth and breadth of knowledge of learning and teaching issues, an understanding of research pressures and recognition of the important role of administrative staff in the smooth running of a department. The facilitation role itself must not appear to be the primary focus of the day. The important matter at hand is to lead the department to the point of being in a position to draw up an action plan at the end of the Retreat day. The more prepared the facilitator is, the more chance there is of enabling the department to achieve positive outcomes.

The scholarly input of the academic developer lies in their ability to gain very quickly an understanding of the culture of the discipline (Becher and Trowler, 2001) and the ethos and philosophy of the department. Input on issues related to teaching, research, service and administration needs to be subtle, well timed and meaningful to the staff of the department. In other words, part of enabling a department to move forward with its agenda is about transforming our generic understandings of academic and related matters into pragmatic suggestions which will fit with the nature of the department.

The CAD is in the fortunate position of sitting outside of any faculty and therefore the staff of the CAD carry no 'emotional baggage' with respect to the departments with which we work. Staff of the CAD are highly aware of the institutional hierarchy, but the hierarchy of the department is not of any interest to the facilitator carrying out this work. For this event, all staff are equally important and encouraged to participate and to bring up difficult or sensitive issues.

The Case Study

The model department for this case study is the Department of General Practice and Primary Health Care. The department sits within the School of Population Health in the Faculty of Medical and Health Sciences. In early 2006, I was approached by the HoD to set a date for and have preliminary discussions about the planned Strategic Planning Retreat. The focus of this Retreat would be on enhancing the research endeavours of the department. It was clear that the Department is highly productive in research terms but that there is a desire for continuous enhancement to move from 'excellent' to 'outstanding'. The 'problem' for the department was that, at this time, existing staff were working at or very near capacity and there was a strong sense of a need to protect and increase the number of research active staff. The overarching long-term goal was for the department to compare favourably with its benchmark department at the University of Melbourne.

The first action I take as a facilitator arriving at the Retreat venue is to introduce myself to everyone over the pre-meeting coffee to 'break the ice' and attempt to make everyone feel at ease. Generally, more formal introductions are made at the start of the meeting. Part of the 'art' of good facilitation is to be present and highly alert to the nuances of the department or organization you are working with and how it operates (Schwarz, 2002, p. 37), but at the same time to be almost 'invisible', very much the 'guide on the side' orchestrating the processes of the day, and certainly not the 'sage on the stage'. The staff need to feel that they own the process and the proceedings.

In this case, as with many other Retreats, the first activity that I suggested was a brainstorming session on issues impacting on the department. This is an opportunity to involve everyone from the start of the day. No point raised is more or less important than any other; they all get listed on a flip chart.

The issues raised in this instance were:

- the infrastructure for research in the department;
- nuts and bolts issues, such as obtaining physical resources, office space, desks, email accounts, etc. for new staff
- whom do you contact to get basic things done?;
- a sense of 'dinosaur' processes (e.g. human resources processes);
- how can administrative processes be enhanced at both departmental level and School level?;
- how can research capacity be increased?;
- how can an increase in people engaged in research be effected?;
- some people working at capacity, which raises issues of sustainability;
- lack of research support;
- the need for an ethos of 'can do' and celebration of success;
- demographic and retention issues relating to PhD students and postgraduates;
- enhancing career pathways for above groups;
- part-time staff – an untapped resource in terms of engagement in research; how can the disengaged be encouraged to engage?;
- assessing potential graduates and postgraduates from overseas;
- marketing the department;
- relationships with the University Research Office.

The issues being raised are quite wide ranging and not particularly unusual. They give a sense of the broad range of factors essential to the development of a positive research environment. The nub of the matter seemed to be that many issues were being dealt with on an ad hoc basis in the department, particularly the 'nuts and bolts issues', and this was seen as a matter for concern for an aspirational department.

The next activity was a general discussion around the departmental infrastructure, with a particular emphasis on 'nuts and bolts' and administrative issues. At this point it seemed appropriate to contribute some ideas for ways forward on the basis of my knowledge of institutional infrastructure and ideas from other departments.

Within the general discussion, it was recognized and acknowledged that relations between academic staff/researchers and administrative staff at the School level could be improved. There was recognition too that the general and administrative staff are crucial to the success of the department but that they are generally not included in celebration of success or acknowledged for the role they play.

Out of this general discussion with the large group arose three important points. It was decided that there should be a one-stop shop for organization of 'nuts and bolts' matters; that a key person would be empowered to manage the one-stop shop; and that there should be more effort devoted to better liaison between the administrative and academic staff.

At this stage we engaged in a brainstorming session and, as an immediate follow up, started to address some of the points that arose from the brainstorming session. That is not to say that all the points were done and dusted, but it was the start of building the action plan to move the department forward.

In order to vary the activities and maintain the momentum of high levels of engagement, the general discussion was followed by a small group work session. We went back to the initial notes on the flip chart to pick out themes for the small group discussion and staff divided themselves into three groups, each taking one theme from the following list:

- increasing departmental Performance-Based Research Fund (PBRF) outcomes [PBRF in New Zealand is equivalent to Research Assessment Exercise (RAE) in the United Kingdom];
- retention of PhD and other postgraduate students and promoting research career pathways;
- the untapped resource – part-timers, addressing the matter of disengagement.

These themes arose from the initial brainstorming session and were pointed out by me as the facilitator but actively chosen by the departmental staff. A part of my role is to cluster the points raised during brainstorming into 'themes' that can be worked through.

Time was given over for the small groups to work without any input or interference by me, but a key stipulation was that a note-taker would be appointed in each small group and that someone would present back to the wider group during a plenary session.

There was no shortage of discussion within the groups and this in turn led to a final distillation of issues that could be actioned. The group working on the theme of boosting PBRF outcomes suggested:

- getting more staff onto editorial boards of highly rated journals;
- promoting broad authorship of papers and grant proposals to support early-career academics;
- building research clusters;
- enhancing international orientation.

Regarding retention and research career pathways, the ideas generated included:

- provision of mentors for early-career academics and postgraduate students;
- attention to the potential sense of isolation amongst postgraduate students;
- encouraging journal clubs and presentations for postgraduate students;
- engaging the support of the Student Learning Centre and the Library for appropriate professional development for postgraduate students;
- encouraging refresher sessions for postgraduate supervisors.

The group considering the untapped resource of part-time staff and issues of disengagement considered a number of ideas including:

- reviewing the job descriptions prepared for part-time staff and discussing research in the context of annual performance review;
- involving part-timers in different aspects of research projects;
- developing a culture of celebration within the department to acknowledge the successes of individuals;
- setting up a Publications Notice Board to showcase publications from all staff;
- encouraging staff to write editorials for well respected journals.

It was agreed that a wealth of ideas had been presented in a short space of time and that all of the suggestions were tangible and could be acted upon. It was also time to congratulate the staff on covering so much ground and to acknowledge the high level of commitment being shown. University staff are very busy on a day-to-day basis and too often there is a lack of a congratulatory culture simply because we are too busy.

To capitalize on the ideas from the small group work, the next session of the day was a large group discussion capturing some of the ideas, and starting to consider what would need to happen to action these ideas and to appoint, by asking for people to volunteer, staff who would move the ideas forward. Again this was part of developing the action plan to be worked through over a period of time within the department.

The final activity of the day was to ask each individual to reflect on and write down what they would do to progress the ideas and issues that had arisen from the day's session.

Some of the actions presented are as follows:

- prepare an inventory of the skills of the individual staff members;
- prepare an inventory of staff's professional development needs;
- take steps to bridge the gap between academic and administrative staff;
- find out what postgraduates need or want to support them and action that;
- work on research proposals with postdoctoral staff;
- have conversations with all part-time staff to help make them feel part of the department;
- set up a database of international contacts;
- work towards setting up the Publications Notice Board;
- review induction processes for new staff;
- organize twice-yearly presentation sessions for the postgraduate students.

Many other ideas flowed from the group of staff and it was clear that there was genuine commitment to following up the matters discussed throughout the different sessions of the day. In completing my facilitation role I took all flip chart materials and the handwritten notes of small group sessions and shaped these into a report which was then sent back to the HoD. I also let the departmental staff know that CAD staff would be happy to work with them on any aspects of their action plan.

It is generally possible to gauge whether or not a Retreat has gone well. If a coherent action plan can be drawn up from the day's proceedings with which all staff feel happy, the Retreat is considered a success. In this case, as with many other departments, individual staff members, including the HoD, sent emails thanking me for my input and telling me how much had been gained from the Retreat. This is useful feedback, if not formal evaluation.

I often met the HoD at committee meetings and he would tell me how the department was progressing after the Retreat. It is helpful to know that staff are engaging with the action plan to achieve the enhancement goals. This type of input is also a useful indicator of 'effectiveness' of my work as a facilitator.

The Follow Up

In late summer of 2008 the HoD approached me again and asked if I would facilitate a follow-up Strategic Planning Day to which I duly agreed.

For the second Retreat, the venue was the same as for the first. We did not need to spend a lot of time on preliminaries as we all felt comfortable and had a good idea as to how the day would progress.

The first session of the day was this time given over to the HoD. It was important to start the day with feedback on progress made since the previous Retreat. The HoD's presentation detailed the enhancement activities and the successes for the department, covering increased research outputs in highly rated peer-reviewed journals; factors adding to the peer esteem component of the PBRF, such as an invitation to a staff member to talk about research writing at the University of Melbourne; keynote presentations at prestigious conferences delivered by three individual academics; a Research Program Award; a Best Presentation Award; and an increase in research grants obtained.

Positive steps had been taken to bridge the gap between academic and administrative staff; there was a strong sense of enhanced cooperation within the faculty and a better streamlining of the 'nuts and bolts' infrastructure. The meetings with part-time staff had occurred with some of them showing interest in carrying out research for a Master's level qualification – one research project with a part-time staff member was under way – and overall, efforts had been made to enable people to become more engaged with the department. The strategies used had been very successful in departmental terms.

Many other actions had been taken to enhance the research environment, the overall culture of the department and the research profile, which were also considered successful. The HoD also talked about some of the points that were more difficult to achieve. One of these was the fact that it is problematic to set up research teams or clusters because of the widely distributed research interests of the departmental staff. However, there was the issue of the department being 'General Practice', with a strength actually being its 'generalism'. This suggested to staff that the idea of research teams in some ways militated against 'generalism' and that this was perhaps a philosophical matter for the department to discuss.

The general discussion around the HoD's report indicated that all of the staff present were in agreement with the achievements presented.

The rest of the second Strategic Planning Retreat followed a similar pattern to that detailed above, with the emphasis being on resources, workload models, training for research assistants and succession planning. There were some overlaps with the first Retreat, with strategies and actions being more refined and detailed, and there were new issues to consider.

It is quite likely that the department will have a further Retreat at some point and will show positive progress in delivering on their latest action plan.

Evaluation Issues

This work is strenuous, time consuming and problematic to evaluate. Heads of Departments consider it important enough to timetable a day when as many staff as possible can free their diary to attend a Strategic Planning Retreat. The cost can be said, on the one hand, to be relatively modest for a large department. The main expense is the booking fee for the venue and catering. On the other hand, an entire department giving over a full day is a substantial cost.

To 'measure' the effectiveness of a Strategic Planning Retreat as a site of academic development input, the issues to be addressed are: what were the benefits to the department and all of the staff members in the department of working together in a focused manner, concentrating their energies on contributing to the strategic direction of the department; of working in a truly collaborative and collegial way for the betterment of their own research environment and reputation; and of putting aside hierarchy and all taking an equal share of the tasks to be carried out to achieve their goal of becoming an 'outstanding' department?

Another question could relate to the role of the 'facilitator' in this scenario. The actions taking place are 'situated' and contextualized to the needs of the department. In my experience of facilitating such Retreats, much of the ambience hinges on the facilitator quickly establishing academic credibility with everyone present. The next most important matter is to move quickly into the departmental agenda and establish that the 'ownership' of the actions and activities lies with the 'participants', the departmental staff.

My workload in this area informs me that HoDs value having a facilitator from the CAD. Informal feedback from many departments indicates that HoDs and other staff members value our knowledge and understanding of academic matters, of institutional policy and context, and of the institutional teaching and research infrastructures.

As an academic developer I am not a 'neutral' individual. Throughout the sessions I am steering the department in particular directions because of my knowledge of shortcomings that exist across the institution, such as poor induction processes for new staff, lack of knowledge of the support that is available for supervisors, for postgraduate and doctoral students, and the entrenched separateness within the institution between academic and general staff.

I consider that part of my role as an academic developer carrying out this work with departments is to 'nudge' these departments towards recognizing, acknowledging and reconciling the sorts of matters outlined above. I am also not neutral with respect to how best to provide an excellent learning experience for all students, nor with respect to enabling staff to enhance their research profile, because of the institutional goals.

I am fully engaged in my role as an academic developer when facilitating departmental Strategic Planning Retreats. Much of what I do is at a subliminal, some might say subversive, level but always within the framework of institutional strategic goals. There is no model to evaluate how effective my work has been.

The real issue of effectiveness lies with the department and what staff feel was achieved as a result of their input to the Retreat. An evaluation of effectiveness would be multifarious; some aspects would be 'buried' within the day-to-day operations of the department, and some could possibly be measured in tangible research outputs, but it is not possible to suggest 'cause and effect'. This would be to suggest that the baseline from which the department started at the time of the Retreat had no bearing on the subsequent successes that were achieved by working through the action plan. Also, the research environment, the ambitions of staff members, the collegiality, the relations between academic and administrative staff and many, many other factors also have a bearing on the research success of a department.

On a political level, if units such as the CAD are required to show accountability by means of, for example, key performance indicators (KPIs) for all of the different types of work we carry out, we would need to ask the question – if we can't define KPIs, do we stop doing work which benefits the staff and the department (otherwise HoDs would not countenance the activity) and ultimately the institution because it is not amenable to being 'measured' by means of simplistic KPIs?

As more of the departments that have requested the CAD's support in facilitating Strategic Planning Retreats for the purposes of 'continuous improvement' are now planning follow-up Retreats, and other departments are gaining an understanding of the benefits of a Retreat and having CAD staff as facilitators, does this in itself give a measure of 'effectiveness'?

References

Becher, T. and Trowler, P. (2001) *Academic tribes and territories: intellectual enquiry and the cultures of discipline.* Buckingham: Open University Press/SRHE.

Schwarz, R. (2002) *The skilled facilitator: a comprehensive resource for consultants, facilitators, managers, trainers and coaches.* 2nd edn. San Francisco: Jossey-Bass.

CASE STUDY 8
Leadership Programmes
Evaluation as a Way Forward

LINDA McLAIN

Introduction

The mandate to provide leadership programmes for both academic and general staff at the University of Auckland is the responsibility of the Staff and Organisational Development Unit based within Human Resources (HR/SODU). The SODU was established in 2006 after a restructure which separated the responsibilities to provide professional development between two major providers, HR/SODU and the Centre for Academic Development (CAD).

Within the SODU team there is a Leadership Program Manager and a Project Manager for the Future Research Leaders Program, who between them have responsibility for the leadership programmes and their evaluation. The Organisational Development Manager ensures that these programmes fit with the strategic priorities of the institution.

This case study documents the opportunities that still exist at the University of Auckland to improve academic development in research, leadership and management by using evaluation as a way forward. Leadership development programmes carry with them the inherent difficulty of measuring success. The question of how and what to evaluate is complex and multi-faceted.

Evaluation of Leadership Programmes – the Possible and the Potential

At some universities where I have previously worked there was no formal evaluation of leadership programmes except for use of the ubiquitous 'happy sheet' which (sometimes) included a link back to the objectives of the learning opportunity – and also generally asked about the level of catering and the venue. These 'domestic' issues are a consideration in that the overall learning environment should be conducive to learning, but the 'happy sheets' in general rather gloss over the real point of the learning opportunities.

Although evaluations are often carried out as a necessary 'add on', it is important to consider the question of why programmes should be evaluated in the first place; what is to be gained by evaluating a leadership programme?

According to the Centre for Creative Leadership (2009), there are many reasons for evaluating leadership development programmes, including:

- the ability to demonstrate the benefit of the programme;
- to use the evaluation as a mechanism to improve the initiatives;
- to demonstrate the impact on the specific goals;
- to promote learning-centred reflection (e.g. by means of follow-up evalua-tion, contacting participants in the leadership development programme sometime after the programme has been completed and asking how it has affected or changed their working practice);
- to link with accepted contextually important leadership capabilities within the organisation;
- to be used as a catalyst to discuss what works and why.

In short, evaluation enables organisations to track behavioural change, and measure the value of these programmes and their contribution to the organisa-tion's goals and objectives: 'when evaluating development programs and whole systems of programs, the real goal is to find a causal link between initiative objectives and behaviour change or development' (Allen 2009, p. 1).

In my practice, I have designed the evaluation methodology and instrument concurrently with the development of the leadership programme. This evaluation has been linked clearly to the objectives of the programme, which themselves link clearly to the strategic objectives of the University. This seeks to enhance organisational learning and to demonstrate the link between leadership develop-ment and evaluation in achieving organisational goals.

This process is shown in Figure CS8.1, which illustrates an integrated model and approach for the design and assessment of effective leadership development programmes.

Evaluation should be developed at steps 4 and 5 of the model so that there is a clear link between the aims and objectives of the programme and the evalu-ation. The evaluation strategy is then integral to the entire process of planning leadership development.

The remainder of this case study articulates the nature of the leadership programmes currently offered at the University of Auckland and the means of gathering information to determine whether they achieve the stated objectives.

Leadership Programmes at the University of Auckland

There are a number of leadership programmes offered to staff at the University of Auckland. The governance of all of the programmes offered by HR/SODU is

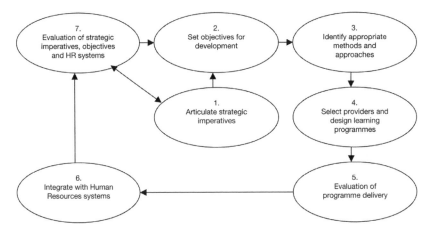

Figure CS8.1 An Integrated Approach to Planning Leadership Development.

carried out by a number of senior-level committees, for example the Staff and Professional Development Committee (SPDC), the Academic Heads Advisory Group (AHAG) and the Women in Leadership Working Party. These bodies provide advice and guidance and have high-level status within the University committee and policy structure, indicating to staff that the University takes leadership capacity building seriously.

Table CS8.1 provides extensive details of the range of leadership programmes on offer, and outlined below is a snapshot of the evaluation strategies deployed for each of the programmes.

Academic Heads Leadership Programme

The major academic leadership programme offered to staff is the HeadsUp Program for disciplinary-based academics who aspire to, or who have been encouraged by their Head of Department to consider, a future leadership role such as head of department. This programme has three subprogrammes, as detailed below.

Future Heads Evaluation is used to inform the design of content and delivery for the following year's programme. Feedback is shared with facilitators, and improvements or changes are agreed where applicable and cross-checked during implementation of the programme.

The on-course evaluation is undertaken by acquiring verbal feedback from participants and debriefs with facilitators during the programme and after the sessions, with the content, format and style being adjusted if necessary.

There is also a shadowing component as part of this programme which provides an opportunity for observation and interaction with a senior staff member to enhance the understandings of the leadership role in practice. This

Table CS8.1 University of Auckland Leadership Programmes

Programme	Audience	Purpose	Duration	Other	Evaluation
HeadsUp – Leadership Development and Support Program for Academic Heads					
Future Heads	Academic staff who are likely to be heads of department in the next one to two years	Leadership development. Understand scope and responsibility of headship. Stimulate thinking about broader University and external environments	Eight days of interactive workshops spread across seven months. Action learning project work	Combined with the Leadership Development Program for four out of eight days. Work in small teams with Leadership Development Program participants on a University-wide project	Core programme evaluated yearly, assessing: • programme aims against achievement • facilitator impact • programme components • overall satisfaction with programme. Evaluation used to inform design of content and delivery for following year's programme. Feedback shared with facilitators; improvements/changes agreed upon where applicable and cross-checked during implementation. On-course evaluation with verbal cross-checks with participants and debriefs with facilitators during and post sessions. Content/format/style adjusted if necessary. Shadowing component includes evaluation feedback from both shadow and shadowee. Observation sessions evaluated by participants
New Heads	Newly appointed Academic Heads	Induction to the role. Leadership development	Half-day induction plus Two-day leadership workshop	Mentoring is offered to all participants on this programme in addition to the workshops. All new Heads can also attend the Academic Heads Program	Mentoring programme feedback is provided by the mentors and mentees. Feedback sought from previous year's new Heads: 'What would you want/need to know but weren't told at the beginning of your Headship?' Used to inform Induction workshop and information folder in subsequent year

Programme	Audience	Purpose	Duration	Other	Evaluation
Academic Heads	Current Academic Heads	Networking and information sharing Leadership development Skills development (various)	Two three-hour Forums, one half-day Retreat and Dinner and a variety of optional workshops throughout the year	Forums and Retreat are core Optional workshops: • Managing change • Managing and motivating performance • HR clinic • Priority management • Leadership in Promotions • Media training • Financial management • Strategic planning • Performance reviews • Leadership in Research • Leadership in Teaching and Learning	Currently each workshop is evaluated by participants and facilitators two weeks after delivery and this information is used to inform programme planning for the following year. Vice-Chancellor's HeadsUp Retreat evaluated separately HeadsUp Program (future, new and current) substantially reviewed by external consultant in 2005. Concluded there was no evidence that any part of programme should be dropped or altered significantly. Recommendation made not to 'over evaluate' for next few years Quality Leadership Profile 360 feedback process evaluated

Continued . . .

Table CS8.1 continued

Programme	Audience	Purpose	Duration	Other	Evaluation
Women in Leadership					
Women in Leadership	Academic and General female staff who want to pursue career development and leadership opportunities	Increasing the number of women in senior positions Enhancing recruitment and retention of women in non-traditional areas Career development	A WIL two-day Retreat is held at the beginning of the year Three core days plus various workshops spread across a 10-month period	Includes mentoring by a senior person Won the EEO Trust Manaaki Tangata Innovation Award in 2006	Retreat evaluated separately using feedback from participants which they share from their Reflective Journal writing All participants keep a Reflective Journal to enhance the evaluation process at end of year. Workshops, mentoring and achievement of personal goals and programme expectations evaluated Both quantitative and qualitative data used to inform design of following year's programme. Narrative feedback from evaluation shared with next year's participants, e.g. 'What is your best advice to new participants on the programme?' Feedback loop to new participants incorporated into Retreat and to facilitators when designing new workshops Mentee and mentor feedback sought halfway through programme to ascertain mentoring on track
Senior Women in Leadership	Senior Academic and General staff women	Networking and information sharing Building relationships across the University Building understanding of strategic issues Skills development (various)	Eight fora, workshops, guest speakers throughout the year		There was a 'whole-of-programme' evaluation undertaken in 2004, with smaller evaluations completed in subsequent years. These evaluation results are used to inform programme planning

Programme	Audience	Purpose	Duration	Other	Evaluation
Leadership Development for General Staff					
Leadership Development Programe	General staff currently in middle–senior leadership roles	Leadership development Network development Increase understanding of higher education environment and UoAs positioning within that environment	Eight days spread across six months, plus project work	Combined with Future Heads Program for four of the eight days Work in small teams with Future Heads participants on a University-wide project	Core programme evaluated yearly, assessing: • programme aims against achievement • facilitator impact • programme components • overall satisfaction with programme Evaluation used to inform design of content and delivery for following year's programme. Feedback shared with facilitators, improvements/changes agreed upon where applicable and cross-checked during implementation On-course evaluation with verbal cross-checks with participants and debriefs with facilitators during and post sessions. Content/format/style adjusted if necessary Shadowing component includes evaluation feedback from both shadow and shadowee Observation sessions evaluated by participants

includes evaluation feedback from both the participant (shadow) and the senior staff member. There are plans to enhance this component of the programme on the basis of the feedback which indicates the value of shadowing.

Observation sessions are also offered and are evaluated by participants. For example, these observation sessions can include an opportunity to learn about various aspects of governance within the University, such as observing a University Council meeting.

The annual programme evaluation assesses:

- programme aims and achievements;
- facilitator impact;
- programme components; and
- overall participant satisfaction with the programme.

New Heads The New Heads Program is a natural extension of the HeadsUp Program. New Heads can access any of the workshops and seminars they may have missed in the HeadsUp series, they have a mentor and they are encouraged to attend induction sessions and leadership workshops.

Feedback is sought from newly appointed Academic Heads after one year in their role. Questions include 'what would you want/need to know but weren't told at the beginning of your Headship?' This information is used to inform the Induction Workshop and is logged in an information folder for the purposes of planning development opportunities for the following year.

Academic Heads As can be seen from Table CS8.1, the Academic Heads Program comprises primarily a series of workshops or seminars and a Vice Chancellor's Retreat. Currently each workshop is evaluated two weeks after delivery, and the results are used to inform programme planning for the following year.

The Vice-Chancellor's HeadsUp Retreat is evaluated separately and suggestions for improvement are taken into consideration for the following year. The HeadsUp Program (future, new and current) was substantially reviewed by an external consultant in 2005. The review did not recommend that any part of the programme should be dropped or altered and, significantly, it did recommend that the programme should not be 'over evaluated'.

The issue of overevaluation is important. On the one hand, there is, at institutional level, a need to know that the resource being directed to leadership capacity building is worthwhile, and on the other hand, too much evaluation tends not to yield fruitful information.

Leadership Programmes for Women

Two highly significant leadership programmes offered at the University of Auckland are the Women in Leadership (WIL) and the Senior Women in Leadership (SWIL) Programs.

The WIL Program has undergone extensive evaluation since its inception and this attention to the value of the programme to women who have participated has been invaluable in terms of constantly updating the programming and ensuring that it is meeting the needs of women academic and general staff members in terms of enabling them to enhance their career development.

As can be seen from Table CS8.1, participants attend a residential Retreat and this major event is evaluated separately from the rest of the programme. However, the Reflective Journal is a popular and important aspect of the entire programme. Participants must set their own goals in alignment with what the programme can offer and a significant aspect of the evaluation is to pose the following questions: did the programme meet expectations and did the participant meet their own goals? The feedback provided to the programme facilitators enables further development.

This programme won a major award, the Equal Employment Opportunities (EEO) Trust Manaaki Tangata Innovation Award, in 2006, adding to its already high level of credibility within the institution.

The SWIL Program is intended as a positive networking forum. The most popular aspect of it is the programme of guest speakers, some of whom are the most senior level staff in the University giving an update on current issues impacting on the university as a learning organisation. Many of the speakers are highly successful women leaders from a range of professions and occupations in both the public and private sectors and from other higher education institutions.

This programme is evaluated both formally and informally, and qualitative and quantitative data are collected and used for future planning.

Leadership Development Program

The Leadership Development Program (LDP) is designed specifically for general staff to build knowledge, skills and capabilities to enhance the effectiveness of participants in their roles as leaders. It is also designed to broaden the networks of participants and to increase their understanding of the higher education environment and the University of Auckland's strategic position in this environment.

There are similarities between the design of this programme and that of the HeadsUp Program; the evaluation strategies used are also similar and are detailed in Table CS8.1.

A further leadership programme currently being piloted is the Future Research Leaders Program (FRLP). The University of Auckland is a research-led institution and hopes to maintain its high standing in current league tables. In order to build research leadership capability the University is piloting the FRLP, which was developed by the Australian Group of Eight (top performing universities; Go8).

Evaluation Theory and Practice – Increasing Organisational Performance

In order to know if leadership programmes are meeting their objectives in helping the organisation to achieve its goals, there needs to be a structured framework for evaluating the impact.

One way to do this is to use Kirkpatrick's levels of impact tool, which outlines the hierarchy of change in a useful framework for leadership programme evaluation.

At present, the leadership programmes at the University of Auckland are evaluated at Level 1 and, sporadically and unsystematically, at Levels 2 and 3.

Kirkpatrick proposes four levels of impact:

- Results (Level 4 and the Return on Investment);
- Transfer (Level 3 and behavioural change);
- Learning (Level 2);
- Reactions (Level 1) (Kirkpatrick, 1998).

Table CS8.2 provides a chart of Kirkpatrick's levels of impact mapped against potential methodologies and metrics for determining training effectiveness combined with DeSimone et al.'s (2002) expansion of this model for measuring training effectiveness (see column 4). What this shows is the increasing effort and complexity of the evaluative measures required in order to show increasing organisational effectiveness – in this context – of the leadership capacity building programmes being offered. The crux of the matter is that in-depth evaluation requires considerable resources.

The 'So What?' of Evaluation

An alternative view, taking account of the many variables in evaluating, is that a 'snapshot' is not easily taken. People are changing all the time, and the demands on them and the effect of these demands influence how they act and react; how they learn; how they transfer these learnings; and, therefore, the bottom line of how we measure the results or the 'return on investment' with respect to offering leadership capacity building professional development programmes.

The 'five-way bottom line', as described by Vaill (1998), supports the premise that the organisation is a five-dimensional, intertwined stream whose energy comes from the individual and joint actions of people as they work out their sense of what is important, for example organisational goals.

Table CS8.2 Kirkpatrick's Levels Mapped against a Methodology of Common Metrics for Measurement

← Increasing effort and complexity

Kirkpatrick level	Method	Common metrics	Measuring training effectiveness
4. Business results	360 assessment Participant impact survey Interviews Business metrics analysis	Amount or percentage of change reported for key competencies The leading edge in the field of leadership development evaluation is the linkage of programme evaluation data with independent business metrics. This includes not only gathering participant perceptions of business impact within the work group, but also analysing business metrics over time in relation to the programme evaluation data	'Is the organisation more profitable as a result of the learning program?' (DeSimone et al., 2002, p. 232). This level is seen as the most attractive to those organisations whose sole focus is on 'the bottom line'
3. Behaviour change	360 assessment Participant impact survey Interviews	Percentage who report that the programme outcomes were achieved Behaviour change in targeted competencies (amount or degree of change) Percentage who receive high levels of supervisory support Percentage who experience common challenges in changing behaviour in targeted areas	This level of evaluation is seen as the most powerful indicator of learning effectiveness. Has the participant changed their behaviours? Are they now performing to a higher level? Just how much more competent are they becoming? Often the course participant and the line manager are best placed to evaluate changes in behaviour
2. Attainment of knowledge	End-of-programme survey Participant impact survey	Percentage who report successfully learning the models and content presented during the programme Percentage of participants who report using specific programme content and finding it valuable	While an increase in knowledge will not guarantee changes in behaviour in the workplace, it is often the foundation of any future changes. By measuring knowledge attainment, we are able to ascertain the ability of an individual to take the next step and apply the learning
1. Participant reaction	End-of-programme survey	Participant satisfaction Achievement of programme outcomes Intent to use content Ratings of facilitator knowledge and skill	The 'course feedback' sheets handed out at the completion of a workshop. Commonly we are asked questions around appropriateness of the course content, the competency of the facilitator and so on

← Increasing organisational performance

This means that measuring any of Kirkpatrick's levels of impact is difficult and we can only do our best to access, report on and improve each level.

To purport to be able to evaluate leadership programmes accurately is very difficult. We do the best we can, realising that this is a complex issue with many dimensions, relationships, actions and complexities.

Leadership Program Review

In trying to do the best and to measure good practice, in 2009 I commissioned a review of all of the HR/SODU leadership programmes. The purpose was to identify and celebrate what we were doing well; to identify and to improve some areas; and to identify any gaps in the programme content and delivery mode(s) and the evaluation framework.

Early reports from the review show that the content of the programmes is relevant. This is in line with the findings of the Learning Leaders research carried out in Australia (Scott et al., 2008). The evaluation processes in place for the programmes ensure that they are tailored towards their participants. As successful as they are, there are opportunities where the SODU can further improve upon the excellent standard of leadership development at the University of Auckland. The implementation of stated learning outcomes is an area where the Australian universities currently hold an advantage.

The Leadership Program Review is close to completion and has identified the following general issues for improvement:

- Evaluations are mostly carried out at Level 1 of Kirkpatrick's levels of impact.
- There is ad hoc and anecdotal evidence that the programmes are helping the University of Auckland to achieve its strategic goals.
- The evaluations are weakly linked to objectives and learning outcomes.
- There is a need for a clearer systematic process for the evaluations, and for outcomes from previous programmes to be reviewed and incorporated into the programme improvements.
- There is no long-term impact measure;
- There are no key performance indicators.

An efficient framework could include a variety of options for evaluation which would be dependent upon the aims and objectives of the programmes and which would clearly link back to these:

- tracking inputs (Level 1);
- measuring satisfaction (Level 1);
- assessing knowledge/skill acquisition (Level 2);
- monitoring behaviour and performance changes (Level 3);

- determining results (Level 4);
- tracking goal achievement (Levels 3 and 4) (Centre for Creative Leadership, 2009).

There is a need to determine which level or combination of levels would be appropriate for which leadership development programme and/or learning opportunity. For example, it may not be necessary to evaluate at Level 4 at all. For some programmes, Level 3 is the most critical level for evaluating the movement to, and alignment with, the organisation's goals and objectives. Evaluating at Level 1, however, may be sufficient for some learning opportunities.

A Way Forward

The way forward is to develop an 'evaluation framework' which outlines systematic use at specific levels and times during leadership development programmes, is easy to administer and use, and is clear in its goals.

This could be done in a variety of ways but, most importantly, it needs to be clear not only to the programme developers, but also to the participants of the programme, that there are a number of identified outcomes that will be evaluated and reported upon. Past participants could be involved in the evaluation development.

The way forward could also include a 'feedback loop' that would help to communicate the outcomes of the programme to the wider university community. These methods could include at the 'ground level' an 'Example of good leadership' column in the institutional weekly newsletter, *University News*; information on the institutional website which could include a similar story; blogs/Twitter or

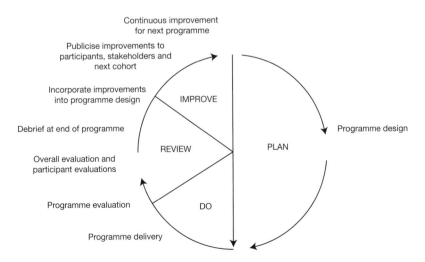

Figure CS8.2 Evaluation Feedback Loop with a Quality Cycle Overlay.

Facebook space; or other ideas to let the university community know that the programmes are worthwhile and that there are measurable University results. I have developed a feedback loop to illustrate this point (Figure CS8.2).

This will be considered as part of the overall HR/SODU Leadership Program Review, and will help to get the right information to the right people at the right time.

References

Allen, S. (2009) An exploration of theories of action in leadership development: a case study. *Organization Development Journal* (Summer), 1–6.

Centre for Creative Leadership (2009) *Developing a leadership strategy: a critical ingredient for organizational success.* Available at: http://www.ccl.org/leadership/pdf/research/LeadershipStrategy.pdf (accessed 20 November 2009).

DeSimone, R.L., Werner, J.M. and Harris, D.M. (2002) *Human resources development.* 3rd edn. Orlando, FL: Harcourt College Publishers.

Kirkpatrick, D.L. (1998) *Evaluating training programs: the four levels.* 2nd edn. San Francisco, CA: Berrett-Koehler Publishing Inc.

Scott, G., Coates, H. and Anderson, M. (2008) *Learning leaders in times of change: academic leadership capabilities in Australian higher education.* Strawberry Hills, NSW: Australian Learning and Teaching Council.

Vaill, P.B. (1998) *Spirited leading and learning: process wisdom for a new age.* San Francisco, CA: Jossey-Bass Inc.

III
Evaluation of Large-Scale Development Projects

7

Accreditation, Accountability and Assessment
Addressing Multiple Agendas

CLAUDIA J. STANNY AND JANE S. HALONEN

Introduction

To: Faculty
From: The Dean
Re: Status of Assessment

With our regional accreditation review looming, I grow increasingly concerned that somehow we are collectively missing the mark of what will be required in producing evidence of program quality. Accountability practices have become standard operating procedure in higher education. Simply offering a grade distribution does not constitute evidence that high caliber learning is taking place in any classroom. Although I have every confidence we are doing exemplary work based on testimonials from students, I am concerned that we are falling short of developing a repository of solid evidence to support that claim. I'm asking all faculty in the college to dedicate a portion of your next program meeting to determining where your program stands in its accountability practices.

Although the specifics of this imaginary note may not directly apply to your own institution, the underlying concerns tapped by the Dean's memo constitute familiar ground. Regardless of disciplinary background, most contemporary faculties have encountered unprecedented demands to accommodate teaching practices to a changing academic environment, answer questions about accountability, and document the quality of their academic performance. They must craft meaningful and complex syllabi, make their expectations of student performance explicit, and measure the impact of the learning experiences they design and deliver. Although some faculties feel at home in this complex environment,

169

others question the necessity of the administrative layers that now accompany the design, delivery, and evaluation of college courses.

Higher education has demonstrated a growing commitment to the principle of continuous improvement; the current accreditation environment demands that departments and institutions engage in program review and evaluation to maintain their competitive position as high-quality academic programs (Banta et al., 1996; Suskie, 2004). In the United States, regulation of higher education occurs at multiple levels: the Federal government, State governments, regional accreditation bodies, and discipline-specific accreditation bodies. Ewell (2007) argues that accrediting bodies in the United States represent "the major external driver of assessment for the past decade." The Federal government has established regulations for regional and discipline-specific accreditation bodies that now dictate that institutions must document the regular collection and use of direct evidence of student learning and other mission-related institutional goals (Suskie, 2004). By 1997, all regional accrediting bodies had enacted accreditation standards related to the assessment of student learning and 75 per cent of agencies that regulate education in individual states had adopted policies mandating assessment of student learning (Banta, 1997). Many discipline-specific accrediting bodies (e.g. AACSB, ABET, CCNE, CEPH, NCATE[1]) now require systematic assessment of student learning as a standard of accreditation (Suskie, 2004). The recent work of the Spellings Commission on the Future of Higher Education (U.S. Department of Education, 2006) created a sense of urgency and focused greater attention on the need to engage in credible assessment of student learning (Miller, 2006; Eaton, 2008).

Higher education administrators frequently solicit help from faculty development centers to design and implement strategies to improve effective institutional assessment practices. Faculty development in assessment typically entails an explicit agenda that supports institutional claims for high quality; however, the agenda may also include implicit goals for promoting broader institutional change. As a consequence, faculty developers serve as institutional change agents for the promotion of a variety of goals: adoption of new instructional strategies, use of new technologies for teaching, and faculty engagement in the assessment of student learning for improvement of the curriculum.

Faculty developers are keenly aware that their efforts to enhance institutional assessment must also generate evidence of effectiveness of those efforts. Indicators of successful faculty development efforts can include both direct and indirect measures. These can entail the creation and implementation of more efficient and effective policies and procedures; peer-reported or self-reported changes in faculty behavior; improvements in the protocols used to produce institutional decisions regarding curricular changes, tenure and promotion practices; and more targeted criteria used for recognition of faculty achievement in teaching and advising. Faculty developers might also lay claim, if somewhat indirectly, to the success of their efforts by invoking more traditional measures of student performance, including student retention trends, graduation rates, self-reported successes of alumni, and placement of graduates in advanced degree programs, professional schools, and employment. Determining how best to evaluate the success of an assessment program is a relatively new but necessary facet of the assessment question. We devote the rest of the chapter to two questions: What strategies can we use to develop a culture of assessment? What strategies can we use to measure success in implementing a change in the culture of assessment?

Evolving a Culture of Assessment

To respond effectively to contemporary quality assurance demands, institutions must move beyond recognition that assessment is a required activity to the development of a "culture of assessment" (Dill, 1999; Lakos and Phipps, 2004; Wehlburg, 2006). Fully committed assessment cultures have important advantages in today's competitive higher education environment (Magruder et al., 1997). Such cultures express courage about collecting, examining, and interpreting the data that reflect their success. They foster and reward good assessment practice and regard assessment as essential tools for crafting their most persuasive arguments regarding the achievement of high quality.

Institutional change is notorious for moving at a glacial pace, especially in academia. Individuals who are deep in the process of promoting institutional change may find it hard to stay the course and fulfill their assignments if they sense that a change initiative has stalled. Deliberate evaluation of progress enables faculty developers and other change agents to develop a realistic picture of what has actually been accomplished. Although there can be a fair degree of excitement about developing institutional assessment strategies that show promise for program improvement and provide positive motivations to accomplish the task at hand, faculty developers' attention can be easily diverted by the obstacles and sources of resistance that inevitably accompany serious institutional change. Faculty can be ingenious in the strategies they adopt to protest assessment practices. Typically, they invoke infringement of academic freedom as a starting point; however, the conversation can quickly deteriorate into rejection of a business model applied to higher education and an assortment of other charges. Such arguments discourage the adoption of sound assessment practice and increase the difficulty in perceiving that any progress has been made in the arena of accountability. These actions forestall the development of an institutional culture of assessment and review.

When considering the creation of a culture of assessment at an institution, faculty developers must learn to size up the degree of opposition to develop strategies that will be effective in the long term. Faculty receptivity to assessment practices within an institution will be variable; in our experience, individual faculty members can be categorized as "assessment resistant," "assessment neutral," or "assessment enthused." From the outset of assessment planning, strategies for working with faculty will need to differ depending on the mix of faculty within the culture. For example, every institution will serve as host to some individuals for whom assessment is anathema. If resistance is the dominant response from faculty, then developers need more targeted strategies to create a positive change even among the least enthusiastic. Although the mix is important at the institutional level, it also plays an important role at the programmatic level. For example, a department that hosts one faculty member who embraces assessment and critical review may be able to get through institutional reporting requirements by letting that sole individual carry the burden of the assignment. However, it is unlikely the program itself will thrive in its assessment practices without broader acceptance and participation.

We isolated several important dimensions that influence whether a culture of assessment can thrive in any institution. These include faculty (and administrative) receptivity, the design and implementation of assessment practices, the nature of faculty response to assessment data, the use of those data in fine tuning program offerings, and faculty and institutional friendliness toward the scholarship of teaching and learning (SoTL). We summarize these approaches in a matrix (presented in Table 7.1) that can serve as a rubric for assessment of institutional change and as a guide for selecting the appropriate strategy to advocate ongoing improvement in assessment practices. In the following paragraphs, we describe how these dimensions play out in the taxonomy of assessment we have proposed.

Assessment Resistant

Institutions with an ample supply of assessment resistant faculty face serious problems in meeting contemporary standards for providing evidence of quality. Assessment resistant faculty might view the entire assessment movement as a blight on the noble enterprise of higher education. They claim that assessment distracts faculty from the serious business of delivering high-quality lectures and nostalgically long for the days when administrators kept their noses out of their classrooms. They actively avoid taking on any assessment assignments in the department and may make fun of those who "get stuck" with such an unrewarding assignment. For example, they are happy to see responsibility for departmental assessment work consigned to a junior faculty member. Their hostility to the goal of making teaching more public may extend to criticism of discipline-based standards. Resistant faculty may either reject these standards as unnecessary or be blissfully unaware of their existence.

In designing and implementing an assessment strategy, the resistant faculty member may engage in assessment activities if they perceive there is no escape, but the planning they conduct will be distinguished by uninspired design. They express a strong preference for an institutional organization in which some other entity or central office conducts assessment and related activities. Such faculty may struggle to identify or articulate a meaningful assessment question to

Table 7.1 Rubric for Assessment of Institutional Culture of Assessment

	Assessment enthused	**Assessment neutral**	**Assessment resistant**
Motivation	Shows eagerness to examine new assessment questions	Shows willingness to examine new assessment questions	Shows reluctance to examine new assessment questions
Design of viable strategies	Pursues well tailored assessment strategies as legitimate means of answering questions about how well students are learning	Implements minimalist or unsystematic approaches that may not be clearly linked to key assessment questions	Demonstrates sluggishness to engage with data collection around curricular matters
Response to data	Embraces findings as confirmation of high quality or key to making changes that will lead to higher quality	Acknowledges assessment findings but attributes poor results to measurement artifacts or other external factors	Tends to be satisfied with status quo so no data confirmation is deemed as necessary or helpful
Closing feedback loop	Makes regular review of assessment findings to direct program decisions and refinements	Uses assessment data more haphazardly in making program refinements	Makes program refinements based on whim, fad, or personal objectives
Reliance on disciplinary standards	Integrates prevailing national standards for relevant discipline in assessment planning	Recognizes national standards as offering a helpful framework to guide assessment planning	Shows no awareness of or disengages from external judgments about disciplinary quality
Role of discipline-based teaching and learning scholarship	Engages in teaching and learning scholarship to disseminate ideas for personal and institutional gains	Completes assessment requirements but does not translate work to publishable caliber	Dismisses teaching and learning scholarship as inferior to traditional disciplinary scholarship

initiate the process. Instead, faculty tend to settle on a general learning outcome (e.g. critical thinking) that is measured by an existing instrument. Although the expedience of using an existing measure rather than designing a novel instrument to address a specific effectiveness question appeals to resistant faculty, these global measures seldom answer specific questions about student learning that can be translated into recommended actions for improvement. Alternatively, resistant faculty might select a measure because they suspect the findings produced by this measure will be consistent with their preconceptions about student performance. As such, these faculty engage in the reasoning strategy psychologists refer to as "confirmation bias," the unintentional selective search for information that supports an existing hypothesis or worldview (Koriat et al., 1980; McKenzie, 2004). Thus, faculty in a resistant department might attempt to use the assessment process to confirm an existing belief that all is well with current instructional strategies and argue that no changes or improvements to the curriculum are needed.

Both of these strategies produce an assessment design that is faulty from the start and likely to promote continuance of the status quo. The first strategy might identify problem areas but will provide no guidance for the critical last step of using assessment evidence to implement change for improvement. The second strategy will provide no reason to embark on any program refinement because the data will suggest that the curriculum is already working optimally. Resistant departments are often committed to traditional "talk and chalk" teacher-centered instructional strategies and protest suggestions to adopt more learner-centered strategies.

A final telling distinction that may be manifested in resistant departments is reflected in attitudes toward the scholarship of teaching and learning in their discipline. Resistant faculty members frequently argue that scholarship of this type is inferior to traditional scholarship in the discipline and may actively advocate that such efforts should be discounted in consideration of personnel decisions (e.g. tenure and promotion evaluation). Obviously, vocal critics from the assessment resistant camp can create significant obstacles in helping institutions create healthy assessment cultures.

Assessment Neutral

Faculty who are basically neutral to assessment tend not to see assessment strategies as a set of helpful tools, but instead regard them as obligations that must be accomplished in the same way that faculty are obligated to report to class on time. They may not have seriously entertained the question of whether or not there are steps that they could take to improve student learning, but they may not actively oppose beginning to ask such questions. In general, the characteristic that permeates their assessment activity is compliance with an external demand for accountability. These faculty tend to foster a culture of compliance (Dill, 1999) rather than a culture of assessment, critical review and monitoring of student learning.

Assessment neutral faculty may not be informed about relevant disciplinary or accreditation standards, but they recognize these structures as potential solutions to concerns about the quality of academic work. Because assessment is seen largely in terms of complying with institutional mandates, these faculty tend to conceptualize assessment plans and procedures in terms of archiving and reporting relevant metrics. Amassing quantities of data may substitute for systematic reflection on and use of data for curriculum improvement. Having discovered an acceptable measure for a learning outcome that meets reporting requirements, these departments are less likely to pose new questions or think about developing additional assessment measures to ask new questions about student learning. In addition, unflattering data tend to be handled defensively. Assessment neutral faculty may speculate that negative data suggest they chose the wrong measure or the students were not motivated rather than entertain the notion that the assessment data suggest they might have work to do to improve

program quality. Assessment neutral faculty have not made the important connection between negative data and the need for a discussion about program improvement. As a result, these departments may not be motivated to take any action to refine their curriculum or explore alternative instructional practices.

Although assessment neutral faculty may be less critical about the value of the scholarship of teaching and learning, they don't typically volunteer to pursue SoTL activities as part of their own research agenda. In part, it simply may not occur to them that their accountability activities have a legitimate life beyond the original institutional mandate and might inform disciplinary instructional practices. Many demonstrate surprise when they understand that publishing data about teaching effectiveness can improve their standing for a favorable tenure or promotion decision in the future when the larger institutional culture accepts the validity of SoTL work.

Assessment Enthused

Faculty who embrace assessment as a viable way to monitor the quality of their own work more naturally generate assessment questions that will lead to good strategies. For example, a professor might question whether a group assignment is a preferred strategy for teaching a particular set of concepts. The enthused faculty entertains a variety of ways to measure the impact of the teaching strategy to determine whether the approach should be maintained, enhanced, or sacked.

Typically, assessment enthused faculty are aware of relevant disciplinary standards. They can articulate the value of having performance benchmarks established by experts in the field. In addition, they actively incorporate disciplinary standards in their own curriculum planning. For example, the standards might serve as an essential framework for the construction of the syllabus, reflecting outcomes that have been deemed essential by national experts. These faculty are engaged in the conversation about assessment and continuous improvement.

Because assessment enthused faculty regard assessment as a useful tool for gathering meaningful information about a question they have about student learning, they are likely to have a specific question that motivates and guides the choice of assessment methods. The evidence gathered will be clearly aligned with instructional practices. Using an evidence base to inform curriculum change and/or experimentation with innovative instructional strategies becomes a surprisingly simple and relatively seamless transition.

Assessment enthused faculty are likely to engage in research on student learning as a form of scholarship of teaching and learning. These faculty regard enhancement of student learning as an iterative process in which new questions naturally arise after they implement changes in the curriculum or adopt new instructional strategies. Like disciplinary research, the assessment process is conceptualized as a continuous search for new and better understanding. The object of study is now student learning. Faculty who are assessment enthused are curious about new instructional strategies and eager to adopt changes such as the migration to a learning-centered approach to teaching (Barr and Tagg, 1995; Weimer, 2002).

Planning Faculty Development Activities

Faculty development activities should be targeted to address specific needs associated with a dimension that needs improvement with the goal of transforming *resistant* faculty to *neutral* and *neutral* faculty to *enthused*. Progress in establishing cultural change at an institution might be evaluated by describing the percentage of faculty who fall into each cell of the matrix (see Table 7.1) and determining where the "critical mass" of faculty reside on each dimension. In any institution or department, some faculty will be enthused, others will be neutral, and (ideally) only a few, if any, will be resistant.

After evaluating institutional culture, activities to promote faculty development should be selected to target dimensions of cultural change that are in greatest need of change. The following list suggests some basic strategies in relation to the dimensions we have articulated. If the greatest area of need is:

- *Motivation:* A variety of venues can be used to encourage faculty receptivity to assessment, including mini-conferences, faculty interest groups (or faculty learning communities), newsletters, and web resources that describe and provide practice with innovative instructional strategies. Attendance at these events might be evidence for progress, although the proof of change in the culture of teaching ultimately depends on the adoption of effective instructional methods.
- *Design of viable strategies:* Faculty may require training in basic assessment-related skills, which can be developed through workshops on writing measurable student outcomes, mapping the curriculum, and developing and using rubrics for embedded assessments (examples of these practices are described in Maki, 2004). Evidence of progress on this dimension can be gathered from departmental materials (student learning outcomes identified in curriculum change requests and included on course syllabi, departmental descriptions of assessment methods and use of assessment evidence for decision making reported in annual reports).
- *Response to data:* To facilitate the healthiest responses to assessment evidence, faculty developers can recommend setting the stage by encouraging formal goal-setting in which faculty are obliged to declare interesting questions as a prerequisite to embarking on assessment. Wise counsel identifies assessment strategies that are likely to be fruitful and strategies that might not yield solid answers to those questions. This approach can help avoid the emergence of faculty hostility should the student data be difficult to interpret or, worse, produce unflattering results without suggesting possible means for remedying any problems revealed in student learning.

- *Closing the feedback loop:* At minimum, institutional annual reports should hold faculty accountable for explaining that curricular changes are driven by data-based decisions. Programs might be encouraged to conduct a partner exchange with an allied department in which they describe their work and justify their interpretations.
- *Relying on disciplinary standards:* Development activities might consist of workshops and meetings that inform faculty about external standards and expectations. Progress in achieving cultural change on this dimension could be evaluated by monitoring outcomes of program reviews and disciplinary accreditation decisions. Increasingly, program reviews now include an explicit evaluation of the quality of assessment work and evidence that assessment data are used for programmatic decision making.
- *Role of discipline-based teaching and learning research:* Institutional support that encourages faculty to use assessment methodology to evaluate new teaching strategies and promote the scholarship of teaching and learning will entail guidance in the design of classroom research and selection, use, and analysis of evidence generated by embedded assessments (Cross and Steadman, 1996; Weimer, 2006; McKinney, 2007). Progress in this domain can be evaluated by monitoring the number of faculty who engage in conference presentations, publish, or obtain grants that involve SoTL work.

Working with Individual Faculties

The strategies adopted for development of faculty skill with assessment of student learning outcomes depend upon the attitude and level of resistance manifested by faculty. Faculty in each category tend to pose different kinds of challenges to faculty developers. We offer a sampling of suggestions for optimizing gains when working with faculty in each group.

Strategies for the Assessment Resistant

1. Use external experts and consultants to reinforce the reality of cultural change in the larger academic community and increase commitment to locally developed plans. National authorities with effective presentation styles will go a long way toward persuading resistant faculty that change can be undertaken without sacrificing academic integrity.
2. Reduce assessment jargon. Precise, institutionally shared meetings related to assessment activities will reduce misunderstandings. The language of assessment is notorious for its ambiguity and variation across disciplines. This ambiguity generates frustration and miscommunication among parties that need to cooperate to achieve their common goal of improving student learning.
3. Provide a formal role for devil's advocates. This practice ensures that the final plans can ultimately be effective and accepted because all voices – both

positive and negative, enthused and resistant – had a role in shaping the final strategies.

4. Limit the impact of dysfunctional or hostile faculty members. Assign these individuals to institutional responsibilities that are in keeping with their professed values, but do not allow these individuals to sabotage the institutional work of assessment. Be clear that the alternate assignment is not a marginalization but an opportunity to contribute from the area of the Faculty's greatest strengths.

Strategies for the Assessment Neutral

1. Provide workshops and consultations with internal and external experts to support the development of specific skill sets needed to deal with assessment needs. Assess faculty interests and needs to determine the topics and issues that have the greatest appeal and facilitate the broadest participation.

2. Strive to create the simplest solutions possible to practical problems associated with the mechanics of collecting, using, and documenting assessment processes and findings. Implement strategies that ennoble good-faith efforts to collect and use assessment evidence to improve student learning.

3. Establish a conversation with faculty about the standards for student learning established by their discipline. Clarify connections between the language used in the discipline with the language used in the world of assessment. Public conversations about how disciplines are responding to assessment demands can be very enlightening.

4. Promote the scholarship of teaching and learning as an added value for the effective pursuit of assessment questions. Assessment will gain traction when faculty discover that SoTL functions as an additional line of scholarly work, publication, and recognition within the institution, the discipline, and the larger domain of higher education.

Strategies for the Assessment Enthused

1. Encourage the most enthusiastic faculty to take formal and informal leadership roles in assessment planning for programs and the institution. Be certain that assessment contributions are duly noted as areas of important contribution in tenure and promotion proceedings.

2. Provide resources for effective assessment practices (release time, travel to conferences and workshops for professional development) and protect those resources in times of budget reductions. Otherwise, administrators mistakenly send a signal that assessment is a dispensable activity.

3. Generate rewards for effective examples of assessment (travel for presentation of SoTL findings, resources allocated to departments that achieve measurable improvements in student learning).

4. Guard against overambitious assessment plans. Good programs can be overwhelmed by attempting too grand a solution to address the fundamental question of whether the program is succeeding in delivering a good education. Make sure that assessment plans are sustainable over the long term. It is unwise to develop overambitious plans to enhance assessment. To do so risks faculty burn-out and can provide excuses for non-engagement to resistant faculty.

Strategies for Evaluating the Impact of a Teaching Center on Institutional Culture

One challenge that faculty developers and other change agents in an institution face is determining whether any progress has been made toward producing cultural change. Strategies range from relatively simple to rather ambitious.

1. Formally evaluate all faculty development activities. Providing a simple measurement of client satisfaction with suggestions for ways to improve future events will provide a wealth of data that a teaching center can identify as evidence of effectiveness. The data are likely to be supportive because most development activities appeal primarily to faculty in the *neutral* and *enthused* categories. In addition, modeling a fearless attitude about assessment can help faculty embrace their own role.

2. Develop a website as a repository of assessment data and monitor its use. Numbers of visitors, numbers of unique visitors, frequency of document downloads, hit rates on specific pages, and information about the origin of visitors (internal versus external) provide tangible evidence of the use of the website by others. These data can provide a sense of reliance by the institutional members and recognition of quality by enthusiasts outside of the institution.

3. Conduct a syllabus alignment study. Reviewing syllabi before significant development work gets under way can provide a baseline measure of faculty expertise. Revisiting the syllabi after sufficient time has passed as a post-test can produce powerful evidence about institutional change. The focus of such research can include representation of student learning outcomes or evidence of assignments that entail active learning or student engagement.

4. Provide an overarching review of gains reported in student learning outcomes. Institutional practice often entails some version of an annual report. Faculty, especially resistant faculty, believe these reports languish unread on administrators' bookshelves. However, developing a meta-strategy for synthesizing and reporting change can document that assessment data have life beyond documentation in the annual report. This approach might specifically focus on gains targeted by the institution's quality enhancement plan.

5. Validate quality through academic program reviews. Institutions are changing the charge to external program reviewers to include requests that the reviewers evaluate the quality of assessment methods and evidence that a program uses assessment evidence for decisions about curriculum improvement or adoption of new instructional strategies. In such cases, academic program reviewers need to be screened regarding their assessment fitness or they can inadvertently reinforce the perspective of resistant faculty.

6. Conduct a needs analysis to drive planning for the following year. Changes in the overall pattern of faculty response can provide direction about where progress is being made.

7. Employ respected national measures [e.g. National Survey of Student Engagement (NSSE), Faculty Survey of Student Engagement (FSSE)] annually. Improvements reported in this regular assessment can be correlated with the targeted efforts of faculty development plans. Institutions can mine these data to answer questions about student engagement on campus over time and identify colleges or departments that serve as examples for best practices in engaging students. Institutions can also identify peer institutions and other groups of institutions to create meaningful comparisons of level of student engagement.

In particular, the FSSE is a companion national survey of self-reported behaviors by faculty about active learning and engaging instructional practices. Pairing the information from the NSSE and the FSSE can shed light on gaps between faculty perceptions of the degree of engagement and challenge created in their classes with the perceptions of engagement and challenge reported by students.

Conclusion

Faculty development centers are well positioned to assist institutions in facing up to the new accountability demands and make decisions that can motivate desired institutional change. As such, they must be fearless in the measurement of their own evolution, modeling the importance of generating meaningful assessment questions, collecting and interpreting the data, and making relevant changes to improve service delivery. Although the journey for faculty developers can be a hazard-filled one, the rewards for facilitating the growth of a culture of assessment make the journey worth taking.

Endnote

1. The Association to Advance Collegiate Schools of Business, Accreditation Board for Engineering and Technology, Commission on Collegiate Nursing Education, Council on Education for Public Health, National Council for Accreditation of Teacher Education.

References

Banta, T.W. (1997) Moving assessment forward: enabling conditions and stumbling blocks. *New Directions for Higher Education* 100, 79–91.

Banta, T.W., Lund, J.P., Black, K.E., and Oblander, F.W. (1996) *Assessment in practice: putting principles to work on college campuses.* San Francisco, CA: Jossey-Bass.

Barr, R.B. and Tagg, J. (1995) From teaching to learning – a new paradigm for undergraduate education. *Change* 27, 13–25.

Cross, K.P. and Steadman, M.H. (1996) *Classroom research: implementing the scholarship of teaching.* San Francisco, CA: Jossey-Bass.

Dill, D.D. (1999) Academic accountability and university adaptation: the architecture of an academic learning organization. *Higher Education* 38 (2), 127–154.

Eaton, J.S. (2008) Accreditation after the 2008 reauthorization of the Higher Education Act. General Session address at the annual meeting of the Commission on Colleges, Southern Association of Colleges and Schools (SACS), San Antonio, TX.

Ewell, P.T. (2007) Accreditation in the hot seat [From the States column]. *Assessment Update* 19, 11–13.

Koriat, A., Lichtenstein, S., and Fischoff, B. (1980) Reasons for confidence. *Journal of Experimental Psychology: Human Learning and Memory* 6, 107–118.

Lakos, A. and Phipps, S. (2004) Creating a culture of assessment: a catalyst for organizational change. *Libraries and the Academy* 4 (3), 345–361.

McKenzie, C.R.M. (2004) Hypothesis testing and evaluation. In Koehler, D.K. and Harvey, N. (eds) *Blackwell handbook of judgment and decision making.* Malden, MA: Blackwell. pp. 200–219.

McKinney, K. (2007) *Enhancing learning through the scholarship of teaching and learning: the challenges and joys of juggling.* Bolton, MA: Anker.

Magruder, J., McManis, M.A., and Young, C.C. (1997) The right idea at the right time: development of a transformational assessment culture. *New Directions for Higher Education* 97 (100), 17–29.

Maki, P.L. (2004) *Assessing for learning: building a sustainable commitment across the institution.* Sterling, VA: Stylus.

Miller, M.A. (2006). The legitimacy of assessment. *Chronicle of Higher Education* 53 (5), B24. Available at: http://chronicle.com/weekly/v53/i05/05b02401.htm (accessed 28 May 2009).

Suskie, L. (2004) *Assessing student learning: a common sense guide.* Bolton, MA: Anker.

U.S. Department of Education (2006) *A test of leadership: charting the future of U.S. higher education.* Washington, DC: Education Publications Center, U.S. Department of Education.

Wehlburg, C.M. (2006) *Meaningful course revision: enhancing academic engagement using student learning data.* Bolton, MA: Anker.

Weimer, M. (2002) *Learner-centered teaching: five key changes to practice.* San Francisco, CA: Jossey-Bass.

Weimer, M. (2006) *Enhancing scholarly work on teaching and learning: professional literature that makes a difference.* San Francisco, CA: Jossey-Bass.

8

An Institutional Programme
A National Model for Evaluation?

RONI BAMBER

Introduction

Until recently, there was little published evaluation of Lecturer Development Programmes (LDPs), and little research on their effects (Coffey and Gibbs, 2001). In fact, educational development activities generally suffer from a lack of systematic evaluation (Gosling, 2008). A survey of ninety-three UK higher education institutions (Bamber, 2002) found that evidence of the effects of LDPs was usually anecdotal. In this case provision cannot be justified or defended, beyond that it *seems* like a good thing. Perhaps more importantly, the existing literature on links between learning and teaching could be enriched if educational developers took a research-informed approach to evaluating their programmes, and published their findings. In the absence of such approaches, educational development may, indeed, be the 'precarious business' described by Gibbs and Coffey (2000).

This chapter asks to what extent institutions should be evaluating their LDPs independently, or whether they could be helped by a national model of evaluation. There are several agencies that could sponsor a national approach to evaluating LDPs in the UK. These include the Quality Assurance Agency for Higher Education, which could play a role in leading the evaluation not only of institutional quality and standards, but of the LDPs which are part of that quality enhancement environment; the General Teaching Council, which accredits initial and continuing teacher education programmes for school teachers and could, in theory, play a similar role for higher education; and the Higher Education Academy, which accredits the LDPs of most higher education institutions and could, perhaps, use the broad outline of the Professional Standards Framework (HEA, 2006) for evaluation purposes. However, none of these agencies claim LDP evaluation as a remit, and the creation of such a remit seems unlikely in a national higher education context which is leaning towards enhancement rather than assurance, in which resources are increasingly constrained, and in which the facilitative (rather than judgemental) nature of national agencies is being increasingly emphasised.

Given these conditions, this chapter suggests that, whereas large-scale, national evaluations can help inform policy and provide helpful benchmark data, evaluations need to be developed within their local context because the aims and mission of each institution and of their corresponding LDPs are different; just as quality standards are assessed within the frame of an institution's own objectives, so must evaluations be set within the particular objectives and context of each programme.

A key element in this type of local evaluation is establishing what the theory of change (Connell and Kubisch, 1999) is behind the programme, and focusing the evaluation on the extent to which that change has happened. A theory of change articulates the links between a programme and expected outcomes, clarifying why/how the change will happen. This process is then repeated during the different stages of evaluation, taking into account stakeholder views. The real challenge posed by the theory of change approach, however, is not to analyse why an intended objective did or did not materialise – it is easy to look back and work this out post hoc. The opportunity offered by the theory of change approach is to discuss and negotiate these issues in *advance* of the evaluation. This is especially challenging for LDPs, since they are often contested territory in which the values and priorities of different stakeholders don't coincide. Stakeholders are not simply consulted, therefore; ideally, they are involved in designing and undertaking the evaluation, making explicit the diverse values of interested parties. Context is a key aspect, with continuous analysis of how the dynamic nature of context influences the evaluation, and of how the programme adapts over time in response to contextual change, such as policy development or national initiatives (Sullivan et al., 2002).

The theory of change approach is not method-specific, but an approach which uses a range of methodologies, which may be quantitative or qualitative, impact- or process-oriented, traditional or non-traditional (Connell and Kubisch, 1999), but respecting the three-stage approach of:

- surfacing and articulating a theory of change;
- measuring the programme activities and intended outcomes;
- analysing and interpreting the evaluation results (Connell and Kubisch, 1999).

Similar steps might be taken in any evaluation process, but the difference here is recognition of complexity: theories of change actively work with the multiple strands (economic, political and social) which operate at multiple levels (macro, meso and micro) (Connell and Kubisch, 1999; Saunders, 2000; Trowler, 2002). This complexity recognises and reconciles the different stakeholders' theories of change, that is, why the programme is happening and what results they expect.

It might be assumed that the theories of change behind LDPs are obvious and shared, since most (although not all) UK courses were initiated following the UK Dearing Report recommendation that lecturing staff should be trained, to promote better student learning (NCIHE, 1997, para 70). In spite of this common policy directive, the goals and approaches of courses vary and are often multifaceted (Gibbs and Coffey, 2000), and institutional programmes have their own characteristics (Bamber et al., 2006). Theories of change, therefore, are unlikely to be straightforward or shared for context-rich programmes such as LDPs. The educational developers who deliver LDPs are well aware that LDP evaluation is far more complex than the commonly used 'happy sheet' form of workshop feedback might suggest, and that there is no straightforward link between a change initiative and its outcomes (Trowler and Bamber, 2005). As preceding chapters have indicated, it is notoriously difficult to find meaningful measures for improvements in lecturer development: the concept of 'measurement' may not even be appropriate.

In the next part of this chapter, I will outline some large-scale national-level evaluations, and ask what we can learn from them and whether they could provide a national model. In the third section, more local, institution-specific case examples are considered. Finally, I will address the question of whether these evaluations lead to a national approach to evaluating LDPs.

Examples of National-Level Evaluations

In their ground-breaking supra-national project, Gibbs and Coffey (2000) gathered data from trainee lecturers and their students in twenty-two universities in eight countries, following a research-informed methodology. This evaluation was underpinned by the theory of change that good teaching can positively affect student outcomes, that higher education teachers can be helped to improve the quality of their teaching, and that student-focused teachers contribute to better student learning. To test the theory, they administered questionnaires – the Approaches to Teaching Inventory (ATI) (Prosser and Trigwell, 1999) and the Teaching Methods Inventory (TMI) (Coffey and Gibbs, 2002) – on the lecturers' entry into and exit from the LDPs. As Gibbs and Coffey (2000) sought correlations between lecturer development and student learning, the lecturers' students were also surveyed, using the Student Educational Experience Questionnaire (Marsh, 1982) and the Module Experience Questionnaire (Gibbs and Coffey, 2004). Although Gibbs and Coffey were unsure about the full methodological validity of the research, their approach demonstrated how a theory of change, theoretical underpinning and empirical data could be married together.

The UK Higher Education Academy (HEA) also undertook a multi-institution project, evaluating programmes in thirty-two institutions (Prosser and Trigwell, 2006). The approach was both quantitative [online questionnaire and the ATI (Prosser and Trigwell, 1999)] and qualitative (focus groups with course participants and senior staff), and was underpinned by the same theory of change as the Gibbs and Coffey (2000) study. Despite some questionable methodological techniques, such as asking programme participants to complete the ATI as they recalled their ideas at the start of the programme (usually two years earlier), the evaluation went some way to filling a gap, providing comparative data across institutions and individualised data for the universities involved. For example, broad findings about the effect of institutional, subject discipline and gender differences on individuals' perceptions of their LDP could be valuable when framing institution-specific evaluations.

However, a note of caution must be struck. Just as LDPs have a theory of change, so do evaluations. This means that each evaluation will take a particular philosophical and theoretical position. Although the theory of change under-pinning the HEA and Gibbs and Coffey evaluations suggested that student-focused teaching would bring deeper learning, Knight's (2006) evaluation, in another large-scale evaluation project (questionnaire data from 171 respondents and a sample of interviews), started from a different theoretical and philosophical position: it focused on the nature of professional learning. Knight's theory of change stemmed from the writings of a different school from the previously mentioned studies, underpinned by the idea that LDPs did not lend themselves to professional learning. He supported Blackler's (1995) suggestion that, if professional knowledge is largely implicit, and implicit knowledge tends to be acquired unintentionally while doing a job, then learning to teach in higher education is best done in the workplace, not on formal courses. A caution is then, that, whereas evaluation should be informed by a theory of change, it needs to be understood that the evaluators' convictions and philosophies create a lens through which data are viewed, collected and interpreted. The lens may distort findings. For example, any change initiative has unintended consequences, and LDPs certainly do. If these consequences are not visible through the particular lens of the evaluation, then some effects may be obscured. The starting point for the Knight study was critical discussion of LDPs in the press, and testing to see if LDP graduates shared these views. Could this critical starting point indicate the researchers' philosophical opposition to LDPs? Equally, does the position of Coffey and Gibbs, and of Prosser and Trigwell, lead them to an inevitable set of findings, conditioned by their own starting points?

Despite this note of caution, it is clear that such large-scale evaluations have value in that they provide a useful backdrop for the local evaluations which, as the author asserts below, are more directly useful for individual institutions. Multi-institutional studies provide tentative benchmark data, and make important links between LDP participants' experiences and theoretical constructs. They draw the broad brush strokes of key issues, such as the nature of professional learning in the higher education context (Knight, 2006); the question of balancing generic teaching and learning with discipline-specific development (Prosser et al., 2006); and the important focus on student learning (Gibbs and Coffey, 2000).

However, since large studies lack institutional contextualisation, they need to be viewed through the filter of local theories of change and contexts; hence Prosser et al.'s (2006) finding that participants in post-1992 institutions,[1] which are more teaching focused, perceived the programmes more positively than participants in the more research-focused pre-1992 institutions, alerts developers to the need to design their evaluation within their local institutional context. In other words, evaluations that ignore the theories of change of the particular institution may be skewed.

Examples of Small-Scale, Local Evaluations

Institution-specific evaluations can offer some of the benefits of the larger-scale studies if they are theory informed and structured in approach, but with the major advantage of institutional relevance.

Angela Ho (2000) wrote about a programme which also had the theory of change that changes in participants' conceptions of teaching towards a student focus would benefit student learning. The evaluation methodology was designed to cover the effects of the programme on participants' conceptions, their teaching practices, and their students' approaches to study. This involved a longitudinal study, with semi-structured interviews at different stages. Students responded to the Course Experience Questionnaire (Ramsden, 1991) and the Approaches to Studying Inventory (Entwistle et al., 1979). Unusually, Ho was able to establish a control group, with which the programme participants compared positively. A useful lesson from Ho is the value of multi-stage evaluation, to chart participants' development over a period of time. This is more achievable within a single institution, which does not need to muster the resources for a large-scale initiative.

Another institution which based its LDP on a conceptual change/student-focused approach is the University of Bangor. Lawson et al.'s (2006) evaluation administered two questionnaires, the Discipline Focus Epistemological Beliefs Questionnaire and the ATI, at the beginning and end of the programme. Student data were also included, again using the Discipline Focus Epistemological Beliefs Questionnaire, to assess the relationship between teachers' beliefs and approach and students' approaches to study. A strength of this evaluation was the commitment to year-on-year collection of data, so that even relatively small initiatives might show some statistically significant results over time. Again, this would be difficult to achieve within a national setting.

The LDP at Oxford Brookes University was predicated on a reflective practitioner model, with other, associated theories of change, such as the need for behavioural and conceptual development. Rust (1998) described two small-scale evaluation studies, using an in-house end of course questionnaire, and externally led interviews and focus groups. Although the evaluation did not link lecturer development to evaluations of improvement in student learning, as Gibbs and Coffey, and Ho, had done, it elicited lecturers' responses to the programme, using questions and statements designed to test their perception of whether better student learning had ensued. The learning from this evaluation is that one of the potential weaknesses of local evaluation – lack of objectivity in backyard research (Creswell, 2003) – can be compensated by external facilitation, and that mixed methods can triangulate data.

The course described by Stefani and Elton (2002) had a different approach and theory of change: that adults learn best if involved in their learning, and if they see it as relevant to their needs. The distance learning programme aimed to convince teachers that university teaching was a problematic and researchable activity, and that a reflective, problem-based learning approach could aid development (Stefani and Elton, 2002). In consonance with their theory of change, the evaluation approach used case studies to reflect on the course experience, together with data from the institution's internal quality audit. This had the clear benefit of alignment between the philosophy of the LDP and the philosophy of the evaluation approach.

In a Queensland University of Technology study, the theory of change behind their LDP emphasised structured reflection as a cognitive tool for enhancing teaching effectiveness, and structured reflection was the evaluation method, with a theoretical framework to explicate the meaning of 'reflection' (Diezmann and Watters, 2006). The reflective evaluation process was divided into its various components and scope (quick reading, zooming in, zooming out). This involved gathering data from a range of stakeholders, by means of open-ended surveys and through assignment work and unsolicited commentary, and these data were used to zoom in on the course experience. Zooming out involved strategic reflection within the institutional context, leading to general conjectures. The benefit of this approach was, again, alignment between evaluation and LDP approaches, and the use of reflective tools to avoid the causal simplicity of linking lecturer development directly with effective teaching and student learning.

These small-scale evaluations are examples of locally designed studies which are predicated on the theory of change of the particular course and, as such, are more likely to be relevant to the institution. The advantage is that these contextualised data can be understood and acted upon within the local situation, and evaluators can take a longer-term, iterative approach. Another strength which the above studies share with the large-scale evaluations is the use of theoretical underpinning, related to a theory of change. The evaluations are, therefore, likely to be focused through the appropriate lens: what is this programme trying to do, to what extent has it been implemented, and why? The danger is that local evaluation can lack externality, and careful triangulation is required to increase confidence in findings and cross-validate data (Jacobs, 2000).

The following example of an LDP evaluation conducted by the author will illustrate parallels with other published evaluations. The additional ingredient that may make this case study a helpful illustration for others is a structured evaluation framework which has been vital in framing the institution's longer-term evaluation strategy. This framework may be helpful when considering the idea of a national evaluation model. The LDP involved is the Postgraduate Certificate in Academic Practice (PG CAP), a two-year, part-time, Masters-level qualification, which is a probationary requirement for all new, inexperienced lecturing staff in a small, research-intensive university.

The starting point for the evaluation was a framework which requires evaluators to identify in advance the reasons and purposes of the evaluation, its uses, foci, data and evidence, audience, timing and agency (RUFDATA) (Reynolds and Saunders, 1987). To emphasise the importance of context and theories of change, these factors were added to the framework by the PG CAP evaluators, and thus the tool became RUFDATACT (Table 8.1). This tool was then used iteratively to review and update the evaluation approach over time. For example, the Teaching Methods Inventory (Coffey and Gibbs, 2002) was used and then dropped when it was found not to produce reliable data.

Focusing on the context helped decide whether the evaluation should concentrate on a quantitative or a qualitative approach. In a research-led university specialising in science, engineering and technology subjects, the technical–scientific orientation meant that quantitative evaluation data would be well regarded. However, whereas quantitative methods seemed appropriate in this institutional context, and can help to answer questions which hypothesise relationships between variables, the sample size (fifteen to twenty participants per year) would not give immediately significant results – if, indeed, significant results were obtainable. A longer-term approach was necessary, in combination with qualitative methods which might better answer questions of meaning, interpretation and socially constructed realities (Newman et al., 2003). Many social science researchers (e.g. Jacobs, 2000) advocate mixed methods, especially for complex environments such as universities, with their pluralistic, contested cultures (Becher and Kogan, 1980). The PG CAP evaluation adopted a mixed methods approach, with a combination of quantitative instruments (longitudinal questionnaires) alongside qualitative methods (interviews, open questions and reflective writing). However, the ontological and epistemological assumptions which underpin quantitative and qualitative methods are at variance (Bailey and Littlechild, 2001), and so mixed methods evaluators need to clarify their assumptions. This is, in fact, helpful, rather than problematic, as a reminder to articulate the theories of change of both the course and the evaluation. There were four theories of change underpinning the PG CAP programme, and each one was tested by different means.

The first theory of change (found also in most of the previously mentioned evaluations) derives from the extensive literature which links lecturers' conceptual frameworks to student outcomes (e.g. Trigwell and Prosser, 1996; Trigwell et al., 1999; Kember and Kwan, 2000). The theory is that student-focused teachers can lead to better student learning. The quantitative tool used to test this change was the ATI (Prosser and Trigwell, 1999), administered on entry to and exit from the

Table 8.1 The RUFDATACT Framework and PG CAP

Reasons and purposes of the PG CAP evaluation	To provide data on what appeared to have a tangible and desired effect on learning and teaching in a certificated training programme for new lecturers To feed into ongoing review of course To gain credibility with colleagues and senior management, who, in a research-intensive institution, are unlikely to give credence to evaluation which is untheorised, and lacks substantive data and rigorous analysis	
Uses	Development of course Dialogue about course with participants and others Annual review of course Quality audit Reaccreditation data	
Foci	Are there changes in conceptions and practice of course participants, with reference to theoretical links between lecturer conceptions and student learning? (Trigwell and Prosser, 1996)	Does the course appear to work better for some people/disciplines? (subgroup analysis)
Data and evidence	Changes in conceptions and practice: Longitudinal measures: • Approaches to Teaching Inventory • participants' reflective writing • interviews and focus group with participants • end-of-course questionnaire and discussion • feedback from other colleagues (e.g. Heads of School)	Subgroup analysis: • motivation questionnaire • participants' reflective writing • interviews with participants
Audience	Board of Studies, course participants, Heads of School, senior management, mentors, external examiner, Quality Director, Higher Education Academy, Quality Assurance Agency, other educational developers (community of practice)	
Timing	Annual, ongoing questionnaires at start and end of each cohort Continuous, more informal, discussions with participants and others	
Agency	Evaluation done by internal educational developers	
Context	Many complex factors, e.g.: • many participants attend because of probationary requirement, not intrinsic motivation • different interest groups with different perspectives on value of LDPs • competing tensions: research and teaching; Research Assessment Exercise is a real pressure • disciplinary differences and varying commitments to teaching: important to recognise disciplinary variation • support from senior management, but senior management team likely to change • good support from most Heads of School • time pressures of course participants in early years of lecturing career	
Theory of change	That the programme will help staff develop as reflective practitioners who gain confidence from their knowledge of L&T, and gradually contribute to a more student-focused culture in their subject area. So change is anticipated at the individual level and, over time, at the discipline level and then institutional level, as a critical mass of staff who have been through the programme affect institutional cultures	

course, acknowledging the difficulty of distinguishing quantitative data trends with a small sample. Qualitative data came from participants' reflective writing and interviews. The qualitative data gave more interesting results, as individuals explained how their attitude and approach to student learning had developed. The ATI does not focus, for example, on changes to practice, and the qualitative data suggested that these were more significant than conceptual changes.

The importance of developing lecturers as reflective practitioners (e.g. Schön, 1983) is another common theory of change behind LDPs (e.g. Rust, 2000), and the second PG CAP theory of change was that the reflective practitioner model of professional learning can help teachers to critically work through what this might mean for them. Quantitatively, the End of Course Questionnaire (adapted from Rust, 2000) aims to chart in what ways PG CAP participants feel they have changed as a result of the course, self-scoring on a Likert scale against a number of statements. This is an opportunity to test several levels of the theories of change, such as how helpful reflection is perceived to have been. Qualitatively, the reflective writing which is done throughout the course is specifically aimed at helping participants think critically about the relationship between theory and practical applications. However, using such data for evaluation purposes raises ethical and validity concerns if the participants are writing, as in this case, for assessment purposes. Participants were asked post hoc if relevant excerpts can be used for evaluation. Even so, data must be treated with care, as they may be writing what they think course tutors wish to hear – a possible disadvantage of local evaluation. Triangulation with other sources is required to test whether these narrative data are valid.

Great value is attributed by new lecturers to the acquisition of practical skills which make them feel more confident and in control (Rust, 2000). In the PG CAP evaluation, the third theory of change related to the development of practical skills and confidence. The End of Course Questionnaire again tested participants' perception of their skills development, eliciting responses to statements such as 'I am more skilled as a teacher of my discipline', and 'I am able to plan better courses and lessons as a result of this course.' Qualitatively, discussions and open written responses at the end of the course asked participants to comment on specific ways in which their teaching had developed, and to what they attributed that development. As attribution is a significant problem in evaluation (did they really change their practice because of the LDP, or simply because they had two years' experience?), participant statements about attribution are helpful.

In the learning literature, motivation is a significant factor in learning (e.g. Vallerand et al., 1992; Boulton-Lewis et al., 1996; Biggs, 1999; McAlpine and Weston, 2000), and the fourth theory of change postulates that the programme will have different effects on individuals with different types and levels of motivation, and perhaps from different subject groups. The initial PG CAP evaluation hypothesised that motivation levels of probationary 'conscripts' could be a key learning factor, and so a Motivation Questionnaire was designed. Like the ATI, this questionnaire was completed on programme entry and exit, to explore how attitudes to the programme had developed and to chart disciplinary differences. Participants indicated their reasons for doing the course, against ten statements, analysed later into extrinsic, intrinsic or strategic reasons. An extrinsic reason, for example, was that a participant attended the course 'Because my head of department told me to' or 'To pass probation.' An intrinsic motivation would be 'Because I want to become a better lecturer.' A strategic motivator was 'To help me move on in my career.' The questionnaire also elicited the level of motivation for participating in the programme (high, medium, low), and any changes to motivation between the start and end of the programme. Results can be cross-tabulated with subject discipline and ATI results, if the cumulative sample size is sufficient to plot this relationship. Qualitatively, participants' reflective writing also provided comments and stories which illustrated different experiences of the LDP, and confirmed the need for further subgroup analysis to draw out disciplinary differences.

A significant amount of work was put into the PG CAP evaluation over a period of years, and a great deal of learning took place during this period. Of relevance to the question of whether local initiatives can inform national approaches to evaluation, it was salutary that attempts to use quantitative measures were hindered by small numbers of participants. Some kind of quantification might be possible if a national longitudinal approach was adopted, but that would entail commitment to collecting data over a period of years. For this local evaluation, the qualitative data were richer, but were not sufficient in themselves to demonstrate patterns of outcome – the different positions and experiences of individuals on the programme were not easily reducible to such patterns. A commitment to gathering such qualitative data nationally over a period of time could again be helpful. What the PG CAP certainly did demonstrate, however, is the value of taking a structured approach, RUFDATACT, which ensured some consistency in evaluative practice, and attention to the theories of change.

Conclusion

In comparing the large-scale, national evaluations with the smaller, local initiatives, it is clear that the large-scale approach to evaluation offers high-level, high-volume data coverage and, potentially, an objective external perspective, but may produce outcomes of limited relevance for specific institutions and LDPs, with their own history, identity and needs.

Smaller-scale evaluations, on the other hand, focus on particular institutions, allowing for closer attention to detail and appreciation of the local environment. Although the former view may serve wider, political purposes, this chapter suggests that 'zooming in' on the local context (Diezmann and Watters, 2006) has far greater potential for meaningful evaluation. The chapter advocates a purposeful approach which acknowledges local strengths and needs, and also addresses the nature of lecturer development programmes: they are not simply academic courses – they are highly political change initiatives, and the political context needs to be part of the evaluation. The theory of change underlying the programme needs to be articulated. If the theory of change is tacit, as it often is (Trowler and Bamber, 2005), then a useful opening discussion for the evaluation will establish what the LDP is specifically trying to change and how. Just as importantly, *why* the change works should be asked, not in terms of 'does it work?', but 'what is it about the programme that works for whom?' (Pawson and Tilley, 1997). Lecturer Development Programmes are likely to produce uneven developments, which might not be picked up by large-scale, broad brush evaluations. If engineering lecturers are finding the programme less helpful than biology lecturers, for example, then subgroup analysis of this finding is needed. Similarly, the cycle of development can vary, with participants being able to fully demonstrate their learning only some time after completing the programme. As these findings are picked up in local evaluations, the course team can then tackle any evaluation findings which imply that the change initiative is not effective, for whatever reason, and the theory of change can be adapted. Their next iteration of the change initiative will be to adjust expectations, and reformulate the change theory: this would be difficult with a broad brush approach which was not situated within the local context.

A number of lessons can be drawn from the evaluations described above, which may be illustrative when considering whether a national model or framework for evaluation is feasible or desirable. In favour of a national model is the fact that evaluation is an educative process, and it would be helpful to create a national dialogue around LDPs and their value. This could be especially timely at this stage, when most UK LDPs are reaching maturity, following their introduction post-Dearing (NCIHE, 1997). The process of striving for some shared understanding about desirable LDP outcomes and processes would take the higher education sector beyond the very loose framework of the Professional Standards Framework against which LDPs are accredited (HEA, 2006).

Against a national framework or model for evaluation, however, is the reality that evaluation is a socio-political process, and that any evaluation has to work with the socio-political context in which it is set. If an evaluation is divorced from its setting, then the setting cannot be part of the evaluation, as it should be. If, for example, resistance to staff development from heads of department is an issue, this should form part of the evaluation. If other institutional policies affect staff commitment to the LDP, that should figure in the evaluation. The more context-specific an evaluation, the more likely it is to reflect the realities on the ground (Henkel, 1998). Furthermore, the iterative nature of evaluation in a theory of change approach is more difficult to achieve when national resources have to be marshalled, rather than small-scale local ones.

Ideally, then, evaluations should be carried out locally, with full cognisance of local cultures and contexts – just like the LDPs themselves. The theories of change for the programme should influence the design and conduct of the evaluation. However, this could be informed by a national organising framework, such as RUFDATACT, which could guide programme teams in taking a structured approach to their evaluation. It is not inconceivable that some 'indicators of effect' or 'indicators of enhancement', along the lines of those produced in the Scottish higher education sector to aid preparation for Enhancement-Led Institutional Review (QAA, no date) could help local evaluators to frame their evaluations within some broad national parameters. Such indicators could include, for example, evidence (to be defined flexibly, according to local context), that:

- the aims of the LDP have been met, to some extent;
- LDP participants have given careful thought to their practices in learning and teaching;
- student learning has been supported;
- learning and teaching practices have improved in some way;
- programme participants have greater confidence;
- departments and subject groups have, on balance, been affected positively by staff doing LDPs.

Arguably, such broad indicators hardly constitute indicators at all. However, LDPs generally aim at enhancement, and enhancement is no simple 'product' to pin down – 'quality enhancement can only blossom in the context of a flexible, negotiated evaluative model' (Filippakou and Tapper, 2008).

Acknowledgement

This chapter is adapted from Bamber, V. (2008) Evaluating lecturer development programs – received wisdom or self-knowledge? *International Journal of Academic Development* 13 (2), 107–116.

Endnote

1. Pre-1992 and post-1992 refer to institutions which gained university status in the UK before and after this date respectively.

References

Bailey, D. and Littlechild, R. (2001) Devising the evaluation strategy for a mental health training program. *Evaluation* 7 (3), 351–368.

Bamber, V. (2002) To what extent has the Dearing policy recommendation on training new lecturers met acceptance? Where Dearing went that Robbins didn't dare. *Teacher Development* 6 (3), 433–457.

Bamber, V., Walsh, L., Juwah, C., and Ross, D. (2006) New lecturer development programs: a case study of Scottish higher education institutions. *Teacher Development* 10 (2), 207–231.

Becher, T. and Kogan, M. (1980) *Process and structure in higher education*. London: Heinemann.

Biggs, J.B. (1999) *Teaching for quality learning at university*. Buckingham: SRHE and Open University Press.

Blackler, F. (1995) Knowledge, knowledge work and organisations: an overview and interpretation. *Organisation Studies* 16 (6), 1021–1046.

Boulton-Lewis, G.M., Wilss, L., and Mutch, S. (1996) Teachers as adult learners: their knowledge of their own learning and implications for teaching. *Higher Education* 32 (1), 89–106.

Coffey, M. and Gibbs, G. (2001) The strategic goals of training of university teachers. Paper presented at 8th International Improving Student Learning Symposium. Manchester, UMIST, 4–6 September.

Coffey, M. and Gibbs, G. (2002) Measuring teachers' repertoire of teaching methods. *Assessment and Evaluation in Higher Education* 27 (4), 383–390.

Connell, J.P. and Kubisch, A. (1999) Applying a theory of change approach to the evaluation of comprehensive community initiatives: progress, prospects, and problems. In Fulbright-Anderson, K., Kubisch, A.C. and Connell, J.P. (eds) *New approaches to evaluating community initiatives volume 2: Theory, measurement and analysis*. Washington, DC: Aspen Institute.

Creswell, J.W. (2003) *Research design: qualitative, quantitative and mixed methods approaches*. 2nd edn. Thousand Oaks, CA: Sage.

Diezmann, C.M. and Watters, J.J. (2006) Structuring reflection as a tool in qualitative evaluation. Paper presented at HECU Conference, Lancaster. Available at: http://www.lancs.ac.uk/fss/events/hecu3/documents/diezmann_watters.doc (accessed 25 May 2010).

Entwistle, N., Hanley, M. and Hounsell, D. (1979) Identifying distinctive approaches to studying. *Higher Education* 8 (4), 365–380.

Filippakou, O. and Tapper, T. (2008) Quality assurance and quality enhancement in higher education: contested territories? *Higher Education Quarterly* 62 (1–2), 84–100.

Gibbs, G. and Coffey, M. (2000) Training to teach in higher education: a research agenda. *Teacher Development* 4 (2), 31–44.

Gibbs, G. and Coffey, M. (2004) The impact of training of university teachers on their teaching skills, their approach to teaching and the approach to learning of their students. *Active Learning in Higher Education* 5, 87–100.

Gosling, D. (2008) *Educational development in the United Kingdom. Report for the Heads of Educational Development Group*. London: Heads of Educational Development Group. Available at: http://www.hedg.ac.uk/documents/HEDG_Report_final.pdf (accessed 3 March 2008).

HEA (Higher Education Academy) (2006) *Professional standards framework*. Available at: http://www.heacademy.ac.uk/assets/York/documents/ourwork/professional/ProfessionalStandardsFramework.pdf (accessed 13 October 2007).

Henkel, M. (1998) Evaluation in higher education: conceptual and epistemological foundations. *European Journal of Education* 33 (3), 285–297.

Ho, A.S.P. (2000) A conceptual change approach to staff development: a model for program design. *International Journal for Academic Development* 5 (1), 30–41.

Jacobs, C. (2000) The evaluation of educational innovation. *Evaluation* 6 (3), 261–280.

Kember, D. and Kwan, K.P. (2000) Lecturers' approaches to their teaching and their relationship to conceptions of good teaching. *Instructional Science* 28, 469–490.

Knight, P. (2006) *The effects of postgraduate certificates: a report to the project sponsors and partners*. Milton Keynes: The Open University.

Lawson, R.J, Fazey, J.A. and Clancy, D.M (2006) The impact of a teaching in higher education scheme on new lecturers' personal epistemologies and approaches to teaching. Paper presented at the 14th Improving Student Learning Symposium, Improving Student Learning through Teaching, University of Bath, 4–6 September.

McAlpine, L. and Weston, C. (2000) Reflection: issues related to improving professors' teaching and students' learning. *Instructional Science* 28 (5–6), 363–385.

Marsh, H.W. (1982) SEEQ: a reliable, valid, and useful instrument for collecting students' evaluations of university teaching. *British Journal of Educational Psychology* 52 (1), 77–95.

NCIHE (National Committee of Inquiry into Higher Education) (1997) Higher education in the learning society. Committee chaired by Sir Ron Dearing. Available at: http://www.leeds.ac.uk/educol/ncihe (accessed 31 July 2007).

Newman, I., Ridenour, C.S., Newman, C., and DeMarco, G.M.P. (2003) A typology of research purposes and its relationship to mixed methods. In Tashakkori, A. and Teddlie, C. (eds) *Handbook of mixed methods in social and behavioral research*. Thousand Oaks: Sage. pp. 167–188.

Pawson, R. and Tilley, N. (1997) *Realistic evaluation*. London: Sage Publications.

Prosser, M. and Trigwell, K. (1999) *Understanding learning and teaching: the experience in higher education*. Buckingham: Open University Press/SRHE.

Prosser, M. and Trigwell, K. (2006) Confirmatory factor analysis of the approaches to teaching inventory. *British Journal of Psychology* 76 (2), 405–419.

Prosser, M., Rickinson, M., Bence, V., Hanbury, A., and Kulej, M. (2006) *Report: formative evaluation of accredited programs*. York: Higher Education Academy.

QAA (Quality Assurance Agency) (no date) *Enhancement-led institutional review*. Available at: http://www.qaa.ac.uk/reviews/ELIR/default.asp (accessed 16 July 2009).

Ramsden, P. (1991) A performance indicator of teaching quality in higher education: the course experience questionnaire. *Studies in Higher Education* 16 (2), 129–150.

Reynolds, J. and Saunders, M. (1987) Teacher responses to curriculum policy: beyond the 'delivery' metaphor. In Calderhead, J. (ed.) *Exploring teachers' thinking*. London: Cassell Education. pp. 195–213.

Rust, C. (1998) The impact of educational development workshops on teachers' practice. *International Journal for Academic Development* 3 (1), 72–80.

Rust, C. (2000) Do initial training courses have an impact on university teaching? The evidence from two evaluative studies of one course. *Innovations in Education and Training International* 37 (3), 254–261.

Saunders, M. (2000) Beginning an evaluation with RUFDATA: theorizing a practical approach to evaluation planning. *Journal of Evaluation* 6 (1), 7–21.

Schön, D. (1983) *The reflective practitioner: how professionals think in action*. London: Temple Smith.

Stefani, L. and Elton, L. (2002) Continuing professional development of academic teachers through self-initiated learning. *Assessment and Evaluation in Higher Education* 27 (2), 117–129.

Sullivan, H., Barnes, M., and Matka, E. (2002) Building collaborative capacity through 'theories of change': early lessons from the evaluation of health action zones in England. *Evaluation* 8 (2), 205–226.

Trigwell, K. and Prosser, M. (1996) Changing approaches to teaching: a relational perspective. *Studies in Higher Education* 21 (3), 275–284.

Trigwell, K., Prosser, M., and Waterhouse, F. (1999) Relations between teachers' approaches to teaching and students' approaches to learning. *Higher Education* 37 (1), 57–70.

Trowler, P. (ed.) (2002) *Higher education policy and institutional change: intentions and outcomes in turbulent environments*. Buckingham: SRHE and Open University Press.

Trowler, P. and Bamber, V. (2005) Compulsory higher education teacher education: joined-up policies; institutional architectures; enhancement cultures. *International Journal for Academic Development* 10 (2), 79–93.

Vallerand, R.J., Pelletier, L.G., Blais, M.R., Briere, N.M., Senécall, C., and Vallieres, E.F. (1992) The academic motivation scale: a measure of intrinsic, extrinsic and amotivation in education. *Educational and Psychological Measurement* 52 (4), 1003–1019.

9

Evaluation Matters in a National, Funded Academic Development Project

KOGI NAIDOO AND ALISON HOLMES

Introduction

With any research project, particularly a national, funded project, evaluation is a key focus for both the funding agency and the research team who invest resources, which include expertise, time and finances. For accountability and delivery on agreed goals which may include the success of the research initiative, for instance assessment of impact, evaluation 'matters'. The evaluation of academic development is a fraught subject and one that continues to challenge the profession (Kreber and Brook, 2001; Bamber, 2008). In this chapter, we provide an account of a national, funded project aimed at demonstrating the impact of academic development on teachers' and students' success; in other words, the evaluation of the effectiveness of academic development.

The underlying objective of the project, which was conducted in New Zealand universities between 2005 and 2008, was to establish the effect (if any) on student learning outcomes, of academic developers working in partnership with disciplinary based academic staff to implement a teaching and learning enhancement initiative (TLEI) within large first year classes (i.e. more than 100 students) where retention and engagement had been identified as problematic issues. This was a high stakes project, but one which was considered worthy of a NZ$400,000 research grant by the New Zealand Council for Educational Research (NZCER) in its annual funding round in 2005. The focus of this chapter is an exploration of the evaluation issues associated with this project. The intention is to illustrate that evaluation matters and is a necessary part of the accountability process that includes disseminating findings through publications and presentations, and fulfilling reporting requirements as outlined in the funding agreement. Evaluation measures from the perspectives of both the funding agency and the research team members are considered. The chapter also probes the extent to which the evaluative measures chosen are appropriate and transferable. This is achieved by means of presenting an overview of the research design process, the evaluation and impact measures, and project management strategies for successful project completion. The chapter concludes with a consideration of the evaluative measures that may be transferable to other large-scale research projects.

The Research Project

This NZCER funded project involved all eight New Zealand universities. It stemmed from many years of discussion and engagement among the staff of Academic Development Units (ADUs) through the Association of Staff Development Units in New Zealand (ASDUNZ) on the topic of evaluation of our practice. The project gained further impetus from the report of a study on the impact of academic development on student learning outcomes commissioned by the New Zealand Ministry of Education, and carried out by researchers at Massey University (Prebble et al., 2004). Two of the key points raised in this report were first, that there was little systematic research into the impact of academic development on student learning outcomes, and second, that the study had uncovered evidence of poor achievement in large first year level classes, particularly those with significant numbers of Māori and Pacific Island students. Members of the team who carried out the study for the New Zealand Ministry of Education proposed taking on the challenge to investigate, through a systematic study, the impact of academic development on student learning outcomes. A research proposal was developed collaboratively, funding was obtained and commitment was given by academic developers from all eight New Zealand universities to undertake the project within their own institutions.

This large-scale project encompassed a number of strands of activity and the stated aims were to:

- investigate academic development provision in New Zealand universities;
- evaluate the impact of academic development practice on student learning success and learning outcomes;
- identify/develop indicators and measures for enhanced student learning outcomes in targeted first year courses;
- have a better understanding of processes of teaching and learning in universities in these specific areas, focused on in the project;
- identify teaching practices that support the achievement of desirable student learning outcomes amongst diverse groups;
- develop TLEIs with teachers: strategies, methods and resources for teaching;
- identify the permutation of factors associated with TLEIs that account for the extent and nature of their influence on student learning;
- develop the capacity of teachers to investigate and change their practice in a scholarly way;

- review academic development practices and the development needs of academic developers;
- document practice and add to the evidence in academic development research literature.

In summary, the project aimed to address the following broad issue: 'How can academic development more effectively enable university teachers to enhance first year students' engagement in the learning process, learning outcomes and student success?'

The Project Process

The philosophical statements underpinning this project are: student learning is enhanced through engagement in the learning process (Kuh, 2008); academic development is successful where particular conditions exist that engage staff members (Bamber, 2008); teacher practices are modified as a result of engagement with academic developers or engagement with courses of study designed to impact on teaching practice (Gibbs and Coffey, 2004); and teacher conceptions and practices of teaching change as a result of developing an inner awareness of effect. These statements of teaching philosophy are not dissimilar to the outline of the 'theory of change' approach to academic development interventions discussed by Bamber in the previous chapter.

The basic structure of this research project was to have eight subprojects running concurrently across New Zealand universities, all with the same approach to evidencing the impact or effectiveness of a TLEI on student learning outcomes. These subprojects constituted individual strands of one overarching project. Each team member from individual universities, working in partnership with a disciplinary-based academic staff member responsible for teaching a large first year student cohort, would implement a defined TLEI and examine, through a range of evaluative measures applied over three iterations of that TLEI within the course, the effect, if any, on student learning outcomes.

If a positive impact was observed, we could confidently say that academic development interventions contribute positively to student learning outcomes.

This project is much more than a series of individually designed interventions from which researchers could identify successful inputs. In this case, systematic assessment of the effects of academic development on learning and teaching was dependent on the collaborative effort of the project team to design data collection methods that would provide tangible evidence of impact. In many situations, interactions between developers and disciplinary-based academic staff are characterized by short-term, one-off activities with people whose roles, intentions and priorities change regularly. Sustained strategic changes occurring on an incremental, ongoing basis with developers supporting and advising academic staff on implementing change are infrequent but generally regarded as effective. This longer-term project was designed to effect sustained strategic change in the teaching and the courses targeted.

Figure 9.1 shows a conceptualization of the relations between academic development, teaching practices and student learning outcomes.

Evaluative Measures

A range of evaluative measures were applied throughout this project. This involved both qualitative and quantitative approaches to data collection.

Qualitative Measures

The emphasis in this project was on partnership arrangements between teaching staff and academic developers. This meant that the teaching staff played a major role in the design and implementation of the TLEI, the observations being recorded during the project and the sharing and dissemination of results and resources.

A survey was carried out with the disciplinary-based staff at different points through the project to determine their level of experience of teaching large first year classes; the support they would like from the academic development unit; and what aspects of facilitating student learning they found most challenging.

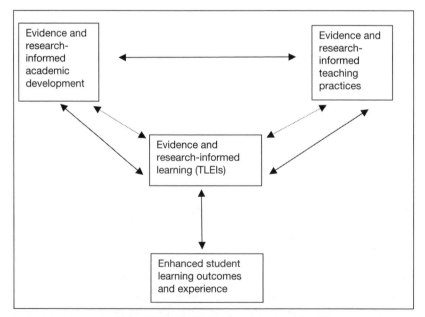

Figure 9.1 A Conceptualization of the Relations between Academic Staff Development, Teaching Practices and Student Learning Outcomes in the Project.

This survey provided us with baseline data on teacher perceptions of academic development.

The academic developers themselves completed a survey drawn up by the project co-ordinator responding to questions regarding the general provision of support for teachers of large first year student cohorts; what impact they believed that support has on student learning; what approaches academic developers offered to staff; and what additional institutional support staff could access.

Qualitative data from students regarding their learning, their perceptions of the teaching they experienced and their understanding of the intentions of the TLEI were obtained by means of recorded focus group discussions and questionnaire responses.

Taken together, these baseline data enabled us to 'measure' project outcomes in terms of changed approaches and practices by teachers, students and academic developers; further engagements between the teachers and the academic developers; the development of new networks or the strengthening of existing ones; and the development and transformation of teachers' thinking about their roles in learners' achievements – thus identifying impact.

At the design stage of the project we engaged a 'critical friend' from the UK who has extensive experience in project support, evaluation and monitoring of projects of a similar nature. This increased the rigour of the design, and his regular input during the project was an internal evaluation mechanism of both the project processes and outcomes. The research design and data collection strategies as originally conceived are depicted in Table 9.1. These methods and

Table 9.1 Research Design: Research Methods and Data Collection Strategies

Baseline data	Intervention	Impact data
Historical • student achievement • attrition rates Student data • focus groups on student experience of classes – week 8 of class[a] Teacher/teaching team • experience of teaching first year students • barriers and challenges Academic development • institutional context • specific to specific course	• Teaching skill development • Curriculum review • Assessment review • Structured, explicit programme developed and implemented in partnership with teacher/teaching team. Documented for potential replication	Collected for each cycle of implementation Class profile Student data • student achievement • attention/retention rates • focus group of students – week 8 • student evaluation instrument[b] Teacher/teaching team • interview – experience, sense of satisfaction[c] Academic developers • self-reflective • electronic journal for later reference

a   Focus groups same in baseline data collection and later evaluations.
b   Instrument – brief questions on course experience and teaching, same for *all* universities.
c   Teacher interview schedule same for each university.

strategies were chosen to enable team members to collect data to address the following questions:

- Has student learning improved?
- Have teacher practices changed?
- Have academic developer practices changed?

Quantitative Measures

Baseline quantitative data on student numbers and demographics, student success as determined from examination results and attrition rates, from a two-year time frame prior to the first iteration of the TLEI and after each of the three iterations was collated. These amassed data provided significant scope for seeking evidence of any change as a result of the teaching intervention. Each institutional subproject was overseen by institutional team leaders (members of the core team). Each team had responsibility for developing and designing its own TLEI, evaluating the research and collecting data in accordance with its own institutional ethos and situation. For the overarching project, the project leader focused the data collection on the workings of the academic developers and the teachers and collecting, collating and presenting the data required by the funding body for its milestone reports. These common data were used for the overall project findings and final project outcomes which included institutional case studies, practitioner guides, student success indicators and other project outputs. Table 9.1 charts the research design, research methods and data collection strategies.

Evaluation and Impact Measures

In this section we reflect on the various evaluation and impact measures used in the project. This was a complex project, a superproject with eight subprojects using an action research methodology. With the fluid nature of the research design and methods employed, the evaluation measures became a movable feast. At the research project level we were evaluating the impact of the work of teachers working in partnership with academic developers implementing TLEIs (three iterations of the course). We were investigating impacts, if any, on teachers, the academic developers and the students (success rates). At a second level, we were also evaluating the project processes – the extent to which the project was meeting its aims as set out in the research proposal. The funding body required quarterly updates on the project's progress and outcomes (project milestones, reporting, publications and dissemination of research findings and outputs). This required the project teams to monitor, reflect on and report back at all stages of the project.

During the course of the project, through the data analysis, it became apparent that there was a link between sustained engagement with teachers and the improvement of student learning outcomes. Most of the subprojects showed some level of enhancement in student learning outcomes as determined by examination results. However, it would still be problematic to claim that there was a directly attributable causal link between academic development and student learning outcomes. The qualitative research data provided much richer information about the development of relationships and ongoing developments with both teachers and students. Using the analogy of student engagement as a prerequisite for optimal learning, one could infer that this ongoing, collaborative team member engagement is a demonstration of learning for all involved – the students, the teachers and the academic developers. In addition, since there was a different TLEI in each institution, the project demonstrated that it is not the nature of the TLEI per se that is important but rather the sustained work in partnership with teachers in their professional practice that has a positive impact.

The project was the vehicle which motivated the team members to collaborate with a common purpose and goal, working on mutually agreed and shared TLEIs, raising the profile and credibility of academic developers' and teachers' engagement with scholarship, and working in partnership at both institutional and national levels in New Zealand.

That evaluation matters was clear to the project team from the outset. The overarching goal of the project was to evaluate the impact of academic development work on student learning outcomes, but we were also mindful that a large multi-year, multi-party project would not succeed without leadership and management. The next section outlines some of the project management strategies used which we also evaluated from the perspective of project process.

Project Management and Leadership

The need for a strong project manager and the allocation of tasks (Baume et al., 2002) is important not only to the success of the teamwork approach, but also for the contribution this makes to the professional development of the team and participants beyond the parameters of the project. The project manager, therefore, was key to the projects 'success'. Using the funder's imperatives the project manager ensured the reporting demands were met and worked constantly to maintain team cohesion. Collaborative activity, whilst often demanded in funding proposals, is actually very costly to achieve (Holmes, 2004). Some specific strategic leadership strategies that contributed to the project success are outlined below.

Task Management Strategies

- Milestone plans and reporting at two levels: national milestones mapped against project goals, and institutional milestones mapped against institutional project plans which served as time lines and action lists.

- Being flexible and adapting to institutional contexts (e.g. case study design) and meeting institutional ethics requirements for the project methodology.
- Timely, regular communication and correspondence (updates, follow up and reminders using group emails).
- Recording of meetings, and sharing reports and institutional data on a project wiki.
- Regular reporting on progress, challenges and successes.

The task management strategies worked to keep the project on track and to maintain momentum. The frequent, regular communications and reports prevented project imperatives from slipping and flagged potential problems. This also served to prompt those who were behind or struggling to seek support and advice from the team. An example of support and renegotiation occurred when one team member had to withdraw owing to work pressures. TLEIs were developed according to local needs whilst maintaining integrity with the overall project intentions.

Collegiality Strategies

- Equality of team members: teachers and academic developers as co-researchers.
- Regular meetings in partner institutions: meeting institutional team members who hosted the national core team for project presentations, sharing reflections and obtaining evaluation feedback.
- Reflection at team meetings to build team collegiality and community in a supportive environment.
- Evaluation and review: ongoing reflection.
- Critical friend to bring external perspective and fulfil roles of peer evaluator and mentor.

Collegiality strategies served as the glue to keep the project on track when participants were feeling overwhelmed by demands on their time or other priorities. They also served to alert the teachers to their role in the wider project. Each team member showed a high level of commitment to the common purpose and a strong sense of obligation to maintaining the team dynamic. While this section describes how we achieved the evaluation of the second level of project evaluation, the following section outlines other evaluative strategies that we purposively adopted to research the link between academic development and student learning outcomes.

Evaluation Measures: Impact of the TLEIs

Measures of project success included the impact on different stakeholders: the University, teachers, academic developers and students. Also focused on is the extent to which the research objectives were achieved.

Impact on the University

All team leaders within their own institution committed to presentations of the research and providing position papers for senior managers with responsibility for learning and teaching issues. Many of the projects were the topic of discussions at senior committee level. Two examples of positive impact are that in one university the lead teacher has been asked to chair a new university committee directly as a result of engagement with this project, whereas in another the TLEI has been adopted on a much wider basis across the university.

Impact on the Teachers

The survey results with the disciplinary-based teaching staff provided evidence that many of them came to understand how their practice impacts on students' approaches to learning and their levels of engagement within the classroom. Eliciting information from the teachers was quite difficult but the project team came to realize that our research project was not necessarily as high a priority for the teachers as it was for the academic developers. Nevertheless, there is a strong indication that many of the teachers valued the sustained engagement with the academic developers.

Impact on the Academic Developers

The importance of the role of academic development has been underpinned by our ability to demonstrate to the university and the wider community the value of sustained partnerships between academic developers and teachers within their discipline. In addition, the indications of a link between academic development and student learning outcomes are very important, and again underpin the role academic developers play within institutions.

A range of evaluative tools and measures have been used to collect this information – surveys, focus groups, reflective logs and verbatim notes. The opportunity to develop strong networks and partnerships and to observe ongoing changed practices in our teachers is yet another invaluable impact.

Impact on the Students

The success rate across all the project sites indicated after three iterations that student measures of success (pass rates) had improved from the baseline data. The impact on students noted in one TLEI was that new technologies were introduced which supported student learning and changes were made to the facilitation of learning because of the introduction of these technologies. In addition, students reported positively on seeing their teacher engaging in professional development for their benefit.

Achieving the Research Objectives

Research is of no benefit if the findings are not shared (Association of American Universities et al., 2009). To ensure we fulfilled this objective a team member was nominated coordinator of dissemination. The dissemination plan identified many opportunities for raising awareness of the project by writing position papers for individual universities, giving conference presentations and writing up the planning process, before any major findings were available. Subsequent strategies encouraged the use of further position papers to enhance the level of knowledge about the project in the individual institutions.

Specific Dissemination Strategies

- Strategic dissemination using position papers (institutional and national) to obtain high-level support.
- Showcasing progress through seminars and workshops, conference presentations and publications.
- Adapting the final report to useful outputs for different parties.

The dissemination strategies over the duration of the project ensured that both progress and impact could be demonstrated. Several publications and conference presentations arose from the project at various stages.

Higher education in the UK is littered with final project reports and resources gathering dust on shelves (HEFCE, 1998). This downgrades the value of the work that projects achieve. The funding body in this case, NZCER, agreed that the final project outputs would be a series of practitioners' guides for teachers, academic developers and funding bodies. The guide aimed at teachers comprises an overview, a guide about each project and a collection of teachers' views about academic development. The guide for academic developers features a common overview, a case study of each project and a reflection on the role of academic development. The final guide for the funding body is an overview of the whole project: a cross-case analysis with an extensive review of the research conclusions.

There were over fifty presentations and other outputs from this project which provide avenues for external critique and evaluation of the overall project.

Transferable Evaluation Strategies

The national project set up to systematically demonstrate the effect of the work of academic developers on student learning outcomes in a changing environment has demonstrated a positive impact through its comprehensive evaluation framework. This impact is evidenced by ongoing network relationships; developmental activity by teachers in other contexts through connections with this project; and developmental activities by the project teachers in other areas of their work, by ripple effects such as the request to chair an elearning committee as a direct result of the involvement with this project and ongoing engagement with technology in teaching where it was not evident before. The evaluation framework and methodology adopted, resonating with the model proposed by Debowski in Chapter 2, has enabled the team to assess the impact of the TLEIs on student learning outcomes; the positive benefits of academic developers working in partnership with staff to effect sustainable change; and the effectiveness of the project management strategies.

The overall project design, characterized as an overarching national project, enabled the collation of specified data from eight different individual institutional case studies. The protocols for collecting pre- and post-experience for teachers, academic developers, student focus group questions, etc. could be replicated or be the basis for further investigation in other contexts. The outcome of this design has been that the individual institutional members, whilst contributing data to the national project, have also been able to carry out research in a way that suited their individual contexts, contributed to institutional needs and demands, and facilitated local research publications; therefore, this aspect of the project design is readily transferable to other contexts, within an institution, discipline or across institutions.

Conclusion

Reflecting on the design of the TLEIs, the end point of the intervention may not have looked at all like the original intention, but that is the nature of the work of academic developers. It is also the source of many of the unexpected outcomes or ripple effects from this project. The consistent use of data collection instruments in and across the projects (in addition to locally decided data collection activities) meant that, even though the intervention may have changed significantly, focus still remained on the students' experiences of the course and their success. The focus remained with a linking of data collected after each iteration of the specified course with the baseline data that were collected.

The role of leadership is central to ensuring the success of a large, longitudinal multi-party project such as this. The leadership role involves project management, ensuring data are collected and approving protocols. It also creates opportunities for reflection and sharing. In addition, leadership involves getting to know the team members and making good use of their expertise, strengths, values and aspirations.

It was important for the leader and the members of the national and institutional project teams to maintain a balanced perspective. Revisiting the funding criteria and the project goals regularly assisted in maintaining perspective and focus. Being a part of the project also afforded the team a basis to use the opportunities for collaboration to extend networks on both personal and professional levels. This was a highly valued situation for the academic developers. From a benchmarking (or benchlearning) perspective this project outlines a process for the successful execution of a multi-party, multi-year project with complex goals and intentions. As with all aspects of education, it is the relationships which underpin the outcomes, and in this respect this project had its fair share of challenges, which were overcome because of the deliberate collegiality strategies in place. What the project described does show is that extensive and iterative evaluation of academic development inputs and processes is strenuous, complex and time consuming – but what is also clear is that all stakeholders in the project were in agreement that evaluation matters.

References

Association of American Universities, Association of Research Libraries, Coalition for Networked Information, National Association of State Universities and Land-Grant Colleges (2009) Call to Action. *Educause* 44 (2), 6–7. Full document available at: http://www.arl.org/disseminating_research_2009 (accessed 9 August 2009).

Bamber, V. (2008) Evaluating lecturer development programs: received wisdom or self-knowledge? *International Journal of Academic Development* 13 (2), 107–116.

Baume, C., Martin, P. and Yorke, M. (2002) *Managing educational development projects*. London: Kogan Page.

Gibbs, G. and Coffey, M. (2004) The impact of training university teachers on their teaching skills, their approach to teaching and the approach to learning of their students. *Active Learning in Higher Education* 5 (1), 87–100.

HEFCE (1998) Evaluation of the fund for the Development of Teaching and Learning. HEFCE 98/68 (para 5.38 on the availability of information from previous initiatives).

Holmes, A.J. (2004) Learning from co-ordination. In Martin, P. and Segal, R. (eds) *Learning from Innovations*. Milton Keynes: Open University. pp. 37–55.

Kreber, C. and Brook, P. (2001) Impact evaluation of educational development programs. *International Journal for Academic Development* 6 (2), 96–108.

Kuh, G. (2008) High impact practices: what are they, why they matter to student success and who has access to them. Keynote presentation at 32nd HERDSA International Conference: The Student Experience, Charles Darwin University. Darwin, 6–9 July.

Prebble, T., Hargraves, H., Leach, L., Naidoo, K., Suddaby, G. and Zepke, N. (2004) *Impact of student support services and academic development programs on student outcomes in undergraduate tertiary study: a synthesis of research.* Report to the Ministry of Education, Wellington, New Zealand.

10

Impact Evaluation and its Implications

KATHLEEN GRAY AND ALEX RADLOFF

Introduction

'In terms of effects on higher education practice, [. . .] we would earn at best an A for effort, but probably a C for impact', according to Christopher Knapper's (2003) 'report card on educational development' (p. 7). Weimer (2007) concurs that 'faculty development has not had much of an impact . . . despite nearly thirty years of effort' (pp. 5 and 6). This chapter is a reflective response to these comments about impact, based on a broad review of the concept of impact, analysis of a body of evidence from one academic development unit (ADU)'s annual reports over a three-year period and a number of years' experience in academic development (AD) leadership and management roles in four different Australian university settings.

Academic development's urge to make an impact may be connected with general pressures on universities to evidence outcomes that have socio-economic value and build social capital (Lee and McWilliam, 2008; Gosling, 2009). How great are the expectations about transforming learning and teaching that can fairly be placed on AD, within this context? Academic development has high visibility at present, thanks to recent national governments' higher education funding initiatives. In the UK, for example, the Higher Education Funding Council is concerned to assess 'the impact of a national policy to enhance teaching quality and status' (Gosling, 2004, p. 136). In Australia, the Carrick Institute for Learning and Teaching in Higher Education (2007), now the Australian Learning and Teaching Council, seeks 'high impact' through funded AD projects that support or maximise strategic change. The 'significant impact on higher education in Hong Kong' of the University Grants Commission's teaching quality agenda has been noted by Law and colleagues (2007).

This chapter is intended to offer a perspective that academic developers and the many other stakeholders in AD work may use to form a richer and more rounded view than the idea of impact often affords, of the outputs, outcomes and effects of such work. We start by considering the idea of impact in a range of evaluation contexts, and review more and less considered uses of this term in the literature of AD. Taking as an illustration our own practice in one ADU – as this was documented in a series of annual reports – we reflect what it was that seemed most important to convey about its impact and how this changed over time. We draw out the many possible dimensions of impact which a critical analysis of impact needs to consider. We conclude with a discussion of the pros and cons of using the language of impact in relation to AD work, either to describe its aims or as a criterion for its evaluation.

Considering the Meaning of Impact

Impact is a term often used in higher education management and development. But why do we use it, what do we mean by it, and how aptly does it describe the work of AD? Popular dictionaries define the noun and the verb 'impact' as the physical energy of striking, colliding with, compressing or otherwise forcefully contacting an object and, metaphorically, a significant or strong influence or effect. They may offer examples of its usage that involve the experience of physical discomfort, the employment of heavy or sharp instruments, the disruption of schedules and overturning of opinions. Nothing in these definitions is especially suggestive of empowerment, transformation, advancement or other hopeful descriptions for what higher education may achieve.

In socio-technical usage, the term often points to a need to evaluate potentially undesirable after-effects or detriments from a development project, for example, environmental impact assessment, which focuses on 'mitigation of any harmful environmental impacts likely to arise' (Jay et al., 2007, p. 288) or health impact assessment, used for 'detecting health problems, their causes and the policy context' (Putters, 2005, p. 700). In contemporary higher education, we often encounter impact used with this sense of foreboding, in discussions concerning what a university may face arising from the impacts of socio-economic forces, national or transnational policy agendas, or executive decisions, for example – not to mention in debates about the future socio-economic impact of higher education itself. The idea of impact in such discussions implies a possible threat or at least the challenge of unwanted change, and the need for strategic action or countervailing response to manage, exploit or neutralise the impending situation – for examples of such usage see Bacsich and Ash (1999) and Beer and Chapman (2004). Although we cannot rule it out, this is not typically the sort of impact that AD would wish to have.

Impact is also used in evaluating the outcomes of organisational and community development, which is a reasonable way to frame some AD work. Here too the term can convey negative or unintended consequences; thus, 'Three [authors] found organizational culture change initiatives produce a diverse and unplanned impact on employees' (Plakhotnik and Rocco, 2006, p. 95). Using the idea of impact may reflect a problematic approach to evaluation in this context; for example, 'The term "impact" has a unidirectional, authoritarian connotation that does not capture the character of initiatives that are fundamentally social and organizational in nature' (Mackay et al., 2002, p. 145). At best, the intention of this usage of impact is to analyse outcomes for a wide range of stakeholders, a feature often missing in discussions of the impact of AD: 'It further becomes clear that although impact assessment is about systematic analysis, it is also centrally about *judgements* of what change is considered "significant" for whom, and by whom; views which will often differ' (Roche, 2001, p. 363).

Individual impact in the workplace, another perspective that may be used in evaluating AD work, has been defined as the difference that a person's existence makes to increasing or reducing output (to paraphrase Dur and Glazer, 2005). However, it often has a cluster of further nuances when used colloquially, particularly in business management environments, to describe personal or professional achievements – such as visibility (having celebrity or superhero attributes); forcefulness (making sure that things get shaken up); immediacy (making sure to be unavoidably 'in your face' here and now); or defining (dominating or displacing other influences). Although these kinds of impact may be admired in some quarters, academic developers may be ambivalent about aspiring to them.

A quality management approach to categorising desirable impacts in higher education is offered by Shah et al. (2007, p. 138), using broad-brush criteria such as 'positive benefits', 'outcomes . . . worth the cost' and 'reform resulting in many initiatives'. A technology management approach to cataloguing positive impacts in university elearning is taken by IMS Global Learning Consortium (2007), using the criteria of access, affordability and quality as major elements, with adoption, accountability, organisational learning, interoperability and innovation as secondary considerations. Even these two management-influenced interpretations of 'impact-as-a-good-thing' are not particularly insightful ways to capture the aims or to evaluate the work of AD.

Reading the Idea of Impact in Academic Development

Impact is often used in the AD literature to capture the goals and achievements of a range of activities, as for example in the theme of Baume et al.'s (2002) book on AD project management. Given the range of possible meanings of impact that we have canvassed, what effects are academic developers really trying to ascribe to their work? This is an important question because words are our stock-in-trade. As Barrett et al. (2004) point out, 'Through our use of language academic staff developers engage and endeavour to persuade and change the perceptions and behaviour of faculty members in their teaching and learning, and in general in their profession as academics' (p. 135).

Close reading of recent AD literature shows that impact is often equated or conflated with other words which are not entirely synonymous and which have a range of implications for evaluating AD work. The implicit meanings include achievement, accomplishment, change, consequence, contribution, difference, effect, impression, influence, results, returns, outcome, output, reform and success. We have termed such usage rhetorical in the sense of seeking to persuade and to accentuate the positive. Many papers that do not explicitly use impact in their titles nevertheless use it interchangeably with other words in their discussion in this way.

This usage of impact is commonly applied to evaluating one of the key components of AD work at present, namely providing initial professional development in learning and teaching for academic staff. Examples include Rust (2000); Gibbs and Coffey (2004); Prebble et al. (2004); Smith and Bath (2004); Dearn (2005); Postareff et al. (2007); Stes et al. (2007); and Hanbury et al. (2008). In all cases the term 'impact' is used in a one-dimensional sense, as a synonym for effectiveness. Although these studies may look at indirect or long-term impacts, for example on students or on institutional culture, the design of impact assessment is circumscribed to improving effectiveness of AD programmes. It does not extend to examination of unintentional, undesirable or disruptive effects, or comparative effects and opportunity costs in relation to learning and teaching improvement initiatives not mediated by academic developers.

Other occurrences in the literature go beyond the rhetorical and undertake more deliberate deconstruction or sustained interpretation of the idea of impact in AD. We have termed this approach 'conceptual usage' and summarise its key points here. According to Kreber and Brook (2001), impact is something that can be assessed on six levels, from lowest to highest: participants' perceptions and satisfaction with a programme; participants' beliefs about teaching and learning; participants' teaching performance; students' perceptions of staff's teaching performance; students' learning; and the culture of the institution. Smith (2004) takes a similar view of impact as something that can occur at the level of the organisation, the department, the experience of the students taught by the participants, the careers of the participants, and the individual participants – although she concludes, inviting idiosyncrasy, 'ultimately you must choose how you wish to define impact for your own purposes in assessing it' (p. 101). Underlying the concept of layers or levels of impact is Kirkpatrick's (1998) and Guskey's (2000) conceptualisation of various levels of significance in the evaluation of staff development programmes, progressing from satisfaction through learning and application, to organisational support and to impact on the core business of the organisation.

What characterises these examples is a desire to express the high point attained in a piece of AD work; such a stratified sense of impact has the effect of focusing attention on the stages and levels of change. However, there are other ways of looking at the impact of AD. For example, Devlin (2006) raises questions of precise impact, negative impact and ultimate impact in discussing the role of teacher conceptions in improving teaching; although these are not defined further, they are suggestive of non-hierarchical features of impact. In another example, Wisker (2006) relates impact to three conceptual models of evaluation – accountability, improvement and scholarship – indicating a variety of philosophies that may underpin the conceptual usage of impact in AD. Given this range of qualitative nuances of impact, it seems important not to become so focused on working through the levels of change that we fail to address other aspects of our influence on the nature of change.

However, Lee (2005) has commented that academic development units 'are obliged to constantly demonstrate their usefulness, effectiveness and value' (p. 19). Thus academic developers' interest often lies not in conceptualising impact multi-dimensionally, but in using the idea to convey the sense in which we are 'effecting positive change in our institutions' (to paraphrase the discussion of impact in Fry et al., 2004). Of course, AD works in a context where it is not the sole agency seeking to make a difference to learning and teaching – as illustrated by Bakker (1995), Volkwein and Carbone (1994) and Zepke et al. (2003). So in seeking or claiming to have an impact of its own, AD is not operating in a vacuum, but in a context where other impacts, intended, acknowledged or otherwise, are also occurring.

From our reading we have found impact applied to many separate and fragmented activities where it risks inflating expectations but delivering no results. The idea of impact may make more sense when applied within a larger framework or system of understanding AD; one which goes beyond piecemeal evaluation of operational activities such as running workshops, awards schemes and quality assurance processes, and takes an integrated approach to addressing the big-picture issues that impede the advancement of learning and teaching in the institution or the community. It is a challenge to find circumstances in which AD records management and knowledge management (what Sword, 2008, calls the 'longitudinal archive') can sustain inquiry into how the term 'impact' serves us when we attempt to frame the outcomes of AD on this scale.

Reading Annual Reports for Evidence of Impact in an Academic Development Unit

We next critique the role played by ideas of impact in our own motivations and achievements, based on our experience of working in an ADU, using annual reports as an illustration. Our experience is based on five years' work in this ADU in an academic super-faculty of a large multi-campus Australian university of technology, comprising ten schools, 19,000 students from diploma to doctorate level and 1,100 academic and administrative staff. The ADU's approximately twenty-five staff did four main types of work: leadership and collaboration in teaching and learning; advice and coordination for student affairs, curriculum development, and quality assurance and improvement; directing strategically targeted projects; and consolidated planning and reporting.

For the purpose of exploring our ideas then and now about the system-wide impact of AD, we reviewed ADU annual reports that summarised the purpose and outcomes of the work of the ADU. These annual reports offer documentary evidence over three years of changing conceptions of impact at different periods and in different aspects of the ADU's work, through analysis of their style, structure and organising principles.

The 2003 annual report is six pages long, plus seventy-six pages of appendices. The main section of the report uses the university's strategic plan and work-planning template as its organising framework, and provides layers of detail: tabulated main headings in this section give functional and discrete summaries of strategy and policy; programme and course development, renewal and amendment; quality assurance of programme and course operations; the student experience; and staff capability building. Subsections supply further dot-pointed elaboration on aims, actions, highlights and directions. These in turn point to appendices.

The 2004 annual report is twelve pages long. As its organising framework it uses the university's teaching and learning strategy (an up-to-date version had not existed the year before). Its layout emphasises the work as a collaborative enterprise within the super-faculty and across the university, and its main headings consistently stress a unifying role and purpose; for example, supporting planning, policy and systems, supporting educational quality improvement and supporting organisational restructure. Under each heading is a cryptic description of achievements, more actions-focused and less a representation of processes than in the previous year's report.

The 2005 report is four pages long and gives an account of our work but was compiled by other ADU staff following our moves to other universities. It is organised as a series of snapshots, with main headings based on most popular programmes, innovations in learning and teaching, programme accreditations, new and renewed programmes, and academic policy and management achievements. In telling very short stories about activities and awards, this report attributes the outcomes to the super-faculty as a whole. The role of the ADU is entirely between the lines in the accomplishments reported; the influence of the ADU on the wider planning, policy and systems of the university and the intellectual and scholarly dimensions of the ADU's work are not mentioned.

When we initiated the annual reports in 2003, we deliberately tried to communicate what our work was and what its value was, in relation to our explicit mission to raise the profile of learning and teaching and build a culture of shared engagement in learning and teaching quality improvement. It seems to us now that the tenor of these annual reports changed distinctly from one year to the next, even though we had not envisaged such evolution – the 2003 report emphasises the extensive presence of ADU work, whereas the 2004 report emphasises the accomplished performance of the work. The 2005 report represents the work differently again, as something tightly and seamlessly woven into the fabric of a larger and more powerful organisational unit. As a coda to our review, in 2006 no annual report was published. Over three years, conceptualisation of AD impact, as it was expressed in the reporting of the connection between the ADU's aims, activities and outcomes, shifted from volumetric to systematic to anthropomorphic to ineffable.

We now see that every year's report was crafted to convey impact in such a way as to make a good impression, with the 2005 report moving closest of all to adopting a media and marketing style of impression management. We realise that we were aligning our outward-facing purpose in undertaking such annual reporting with Skaerbaek's (2005) description of annual reporting as not at all unimportant, but primarily strategic – not so much for 'objectivist theoretical use' in management decision making as for 'impression management purposes'. Furthermore, it seems to us that the act of deliberately trying to document impact inevitably has an effect on the impact. The process and form of documentation used to demonstrate impact, whether managerial report or scholarly output, may put pressure on the future of AD work by 'showing up' a less-than-perfect status quo or may lead senior staff to decide that enough has been achieved for now and it is time to move on to a competing institutional priority.

Based on our review of impact assessment, we see that these reports do not tell the full story of impact. In rereading the reports we recollect the unrecorded challenges – intractable staff, disengaged managers, administrative inertia and incompetence and the sheer number of person hours it took to get the outcomes we reported. Also, even though our annual reports used the language of key performance indicators to organise what we accomplished, there are some aspects of the work, for example, in website and course guide development, whose ripple effects will never be known. In addition, the reports give no inkling of the residual impacts of AD work on institutional strategy and policy; by deciding to focus on the areas that we did, we may have alienated university management by ignoring certain activities and privileging others. Furthermore, the reports do not assess the impact that the (difficult) reality of AD work had on the ADU's capacity to develop and retain staff with expertise and to plan for succession. However, whereas producing the reports did not wholly capture impact, the reports bear testimony to their time and succeed in recording our work, managing our knowledge about it and giving a professional account of it.

Our annual reports were never intended to be independent objective evaluation studies. We would have expected the ADU's programmes to undergo more formal institutional review and evaluation at some stage. We can only speculate about how we might have suggested framing the terms of reference for such an evaluation, with regard to:

- the stated mission and goals and wider engagement with/endorsement of them;
- the measurable contribution to meeting specific institutional targets/goals;
- the nature of the workplace changes that the work engenders;
- the efficiency of our processes; and
- the opportunity cost and benefit-to-cost analysis.

However, given the likelihood of who might sponsor such a review and their expectations of what AD should accomplish, the assessment of impact in such a context may be influenced more by organisational imperatives than by what we know about effective learning and professional development.

Assessing Impact versus Evaluating Effectiveness in Academic Development

Rereading our annual reports yielded some insights that surprised us. Looking back we see that the process of annual reporting was a voluntary, internal discipline of self-review and self-affirmation that had a positive impact on us as academic developers. When we were doing the AD work and writing the reports we were associating our ideas of impact with our desire to make a difference for the better in our university, in a way that changed markedly from year to year. Our reflections have led us to a more complex and multi-dimensional typology of aspects of impact, each of which may be viewed along a spectrum or as a dichotomy. There is a possibility that this approach to evaluation will show impacts which, in some instances, may be inter-related, as:

- acceptable or troublesome;
- client-centred or academic-developer-centred;
- core to mission or peripheral;
- incremental or exponential;
- immediate or deferred;
- individual or collective/group;
- internal or external;
- planned or accidental;
- self-sustaining or one-off;
- short-term or persistent;
- technical or cultural;
- visible or invisible.

The challenge of applying this typology in evaluating AD is that the findings may not be predictable or serve the interests of AD. There are variations in the level of risk and control associated with some of these aspects of impact, therefore an evaluation of AD that is based on the idea of impact assessment must be prepared to deal with the consequences. Evaluation of AD which identifies deleterious impacts does not necessarily position or empower AD to manage them for the benefit of the university or in the interests of AD.

The reality of review, and the benefits of being self-critical about AD, have been noted: 'It is of importance to critically examine the role and impact of educational development centres, and analyse to what extent they are capable of taking a broader and more central role as instruments for quality and organisational development' (Havnes and Stensaker, 2006, p. 8). Irrespective of whether we use impact assessment to evaluate AD work, we have a scholarly obligation to preserve and share with stakeholders, colleagues, and even with competing interests, our evidence about the effect of what we do on what we value. If we choose to use it, impact assessment requires at the very least more rigorous evidence. In a principled approach, this evidence necessarily will rely on external evaluation and validation, with benchmarking and self-regulation as starting points. Evaluation of impact will be based on more than one source of evidence, and efforts to improve impact will be open about and will engage with unforeseen and unwanted effects as well as just the good news. Given the competing forms of impact with which AD's stakeholders have to deal, it is important for an ADU to uphold an explicit set of core values, whatever these may be, and to be guided by evidence as to whether the actions it takes to serve these values are correlated positively with fundamental improvements. If we do not say what is important and why, somebody else may speak on our behalf whose orientation to improving the quality of learning and teaching may not be the same as ours.

Conclusion

Current usage of the term 'impact' in AD literature is loose, overly focused on good news and curiously at odds with less optimistic usage in relation to other elements of change in higher education. This is perhaps an illustration of the 'serious and complex problem with the field, from an intellectual as well as a structural point of view' (Lee, 2005, p. 20). Impact appears to be used often for rhetorical value, and this is a concern if it conveys the nature of the work ineptly to stakeholders, or worse, reflects unrealistic or unethical thinking about the work. But the very fact that rhetorical usage is prevalent suggests a growing sense of imperatives – to show return on investment (accountability), to continuously improve practice (development) and to provide evidence of what makes a difference (adding to new knowledge). The urge to describe the impact of the work may be a symptom of the pressures to rationalise or reinvent it in the current context of higher education.

From our reading and reflection, we conclude that the concept of impact is multi-dimensional, whereas its usage is a double-edged sword. In using the idea of impact, academic developers must be careful what they wish for. There is a danger that, when used rhetorically, impact can produce exaggerated or misleading claims for what the work is about or what it can actually achieve. There is a risk that, even when used deliberately, impact will set up expectations of high-powered performance and create high levels of exposure to public critique and judgement. What do we do with all the evidence about impact, once we have brought it into the open? What if it does not support what we were doing? What if it shows something completely different that is inside or outside the reach of academic developers to work with, and that may or may not be what we value? Are we prepared and positioned to address such situations? There are positive reasons to use the idea of impact in AD. Doing work that is manageable, that we can be in charge of, and about which something can be claimed and recognised at key stages, is energising and meaningful. As a reminder of our aspiration and striving for improvement, using impact can give voice to a genuine and human urge to make a difference, right across the spectrum of AD orientations from the romantic to the strategic. Using impact can have a moral and ethical dimension, if we believe in the power of AD to make a difference and if we are willing to identify ourselves formally as AD professionals. However, the dangers of building unsound expectations in terms of impact around such work outweigh possible advantages. On balance, we would prefer that academic developers eschew the use of the term in self-evaluation of AD work in which they are immersed; in our view, 'effectiveness' is a better term to use in these circumstances.

Acknowledgement

This chapter is adapted from Gray, K. and Radloff, A. (2008) The idea of impact and its implications for academic development work. *International Journal for Academic Development* 13 (2), 97–106. It is reprinted here by permission of the publisher (Taylor and Francis Ltd; http://www.tandf.co.uk/journals).

References

Bacsich, P. and Ash, C. (1999) The hidden costs of networked learning – the impact of a costing framework on educational practice. In *Proceedings of ASCILITE*. Brisbane: Queensland University of Technology, 5–8 December.

Bakker, G. (1995) Using 'pedagogical-impact statements' to make teaching and research symbiotic activities. *Chronicle of Higher Education* 41 (27), B3.

Barrett, T., Botha, J., Chan, S., Mason, C., and Tisdall, C. (2004) The power of language and conversation in fostering engagement in academic development. In Elvidge, L. (ed.) *Exploring academic development in higher education: issues of engagement*. Cambridge: Jill Rogers Associates. pp. 127–135.

Baume, D., Martin, P., and Yorke, M. (eds) (2002) *Managing educational development projects: effective management for maximum impact*. Abingdon: RoutledgeFalmer.

Beer, G. and Chapman, B. (2004) *HECS system changes: impact on students*. Canberra: Australian National University Centre for Economic Policy Research. Discussion Paper 484.

Carrick Institute (2007) *Leadership for excellence in learning and teaching program: guidelines and supporting information – 2007*. Available at: http://www.altc.edu.au/system/files/ leadership%20Program%20Assessment%20Report%20April%20200720v1.0.pdf/ (accessed 27 May 2010).

Dearn, J. (2005) The role and impact of faculty development on learning and teaching outcomes in higher education. *Educational Developments* 6 (1), 1–11.

Devlin, M. (2006) Challenging accepted wisdom about the place of conceptions of teaching in university teaching improvement. *International Journal of Teaching and Learning in Higher Education* 18 (2), 112–119.

Dur, R. and Glazer, A. (2005) *The desire for impact.* CESifo Working Paper No. 1535, Category 4: Labour markets. Rotterdam: CESifo.

Fry, H., Hewes, I., Kiley, M., Marincovich, M., Meyer, J.H.F., Pearson, M., and Way, D. (2004). Conceptual frameworks in action. In Elvidge, L. (ed.) *Exploring academic development in higher education: issues of engagement.* Cambridge: Jill Rogers Associates. pp. 59–70.

Gibbs, G. and Coffey, M. (2004) The impact of training of university teachers on their teaching skills, their approach to teaching and the approach to learning of their students. *Active Learning in Higher Education* 5 (1), 87–100.

Gosling, D. (2004) The impact of a national policy to enhance teaching quality and status, England, the United Kingdom. *Quality Assurance in Education* 13 (3), 136–149.

Gosling, D. (2009) Educational development in the UK: a complex and contradictory reality. *International Journal for Academic Development* 14 (1), 5–18.

Guskey, T.R. (2000) *Evaluating professional development.* Thousand Oaks, CA: Sage.

Hanbury, A., Prosser, M., and Rickinson, M. (2008) The differential impact of UK accredited teaching development programs on academics' approaches to teaching. *Studies in Higher Education* 33 (4), 469–483.

Havnes, A. and Stensaker, B. (2006) Educational development centres: from educational to organisational development? *Quality Assurance in Education* 14 (1), 7–20.

IMS Global Learning Consortium (2007). *Learning impact 2007: the summit on global learning and industry challenges.* Available at: http://www.imsglobal.org/learningimpact/ (accessed 1 April 2007).

Jay, S., Jones, C., Slinn, P., and Wood, C. (2007) Environmental impact assessment: retrospect and prospect. *Environmental Impact Assessment Review* 27 (4), 287–300.

Kirkpatrick, D. (1998) *Evaluating training programs: the four levels.* 2nd edn. New York: Berrett-Koehler.

Knapper, C. (2003) Three decades of educational development. *International Journal for Academic Development* 8 (1/2), 5–9.

Kreber, C. and Brook, P. (2001) Impact evaluation of educational development programs. *International Journal for Academic Development* 6 (2), 96–108.

Law, E., Joughin, G., Kennedy, K., Tse, H., and Yu, W.M. (2007). Teacher educators' pedagogical principles and practices: Hong Kong perspectives. *Teaching in Higher Education* 12 (2), 247–261.

Lee, A. (2005) *Knowing our business: the role of education in the university.* Callaghan, NSW: Australian Council of Deans of Education.

Lee, A. and McWilliam, E. (2008) What game are we in? Living with academic development. *International Journal for Academic Development* 13 (1), 67–77.

Mackay, R., Horton, D., Dupleich, L., and Andersen, A. (2002) Evaluating organizational capacity development. *Canadian Journal of Program Evaluation* 17 (2), 121–150.

Plakhotnik, M. and Rocco, T. (2006) Organizational culture: a literature review of the AHRD [Academy of Human Resource Development] 1994–2005 Proceedings. In Plakhotnik, M. and Nielsen, S. (eds) *Proceedings of the fifth annual college of education research conference: urban and international education section, 29 April.* Miami: Florida International University. pp. 94–99.

Postareff, L., Lindblom-Ylänne, S., and Nevgi, A. (2007) The effect of pedagogical training on teaching in higher education. *Teaching and Teacher Education* 23, 557–571.

Prebble, T., Hargraves, H., Leach, L., Naidoo, K., Suddaby, G., and Zepke, N. (2004) *Impact of student support services and academic development programs on student outcomes in undergraduate tertiary study: a synthesis of the research.* Report to the Ministry of Education, New Zealand.

Putters, K. (2005) HIA, the next step: defining models and roles. *Environmental Impact Assessment Review* 25 (7–8), 693–701.

Roche, C. (2001) Impact assessment: seeing the wood *and* the trees. In Eade, D. and Ligteringen, E. (eds) *Debating development: NGOs and the future.* Oxford: Oxfam GB. pp. 359–376.

Rust, C. (2000) Do initial training courses have an impact on university teaching? The evidence from two evaluative studies of one course. *Innovations in Education and Teaching International* 37 (3), 254–262.

Shah, M., Skaines, I., and Miller, J. (2007) Measuring the impact of external quality audit on universities: can external quality audit be credited for improvements and enhancement in student learning? How can we measure? In *Proceedings of the Australian Universities Quality Forum: evolution and renewal in quality assurance, Hobart, 11–13 July*. Melbourne: Australian Universities Quality Agency. pp. 136–142.

Skaerbaek, P. (2005) Annual reports as interaction devices: the hidden constructions of mediated communication. *Financial Accountability and Management* 21 (4), 385–411.

Smith, C., and Bath, D. (2004) Evaluation of a university-wide strategy providing staff development for tutors: effectiveness, relevance and local impact. *Mentoring and Tutoring* 12 (1), 107–122.

Smith, H.J. (2004) The impact of staff development programs and activities. In Baume, D. and Kahn, P. (eds) *Enhancing staff and educational development*. Abingdon: RoutledgeFalmer. pp. 96–117.

Stes, A., Clement, M., and Van Petegem, P. (2007) The effectiveness of a faculty training program: long-term and institutional impact. *International Journal for Academic Development* 12 (2), 99–109.

Sword, H. (2008) The longitudinal archive. *International Journal for Academic Development* 13 (2), 87–96.

Volkwein, J.F. and Carbone, D. (1994) The impact of departmental research and teaching climates on undergraduate growth and satisfaction. *Journal of Higher Education* 65 (2), 147–157.

Weimer, M. (2007) Intriguing connections but not with the past. *International Journal for Academic Development* 12 (1), 5–8.

Wisker, G. (2006) Educational development – how do we know it's working? How do we know how well we are doing? *Educational Developments* 7 (3), 11–17.

Zepke, N., Leach, L., and Prebble, T. (2003) Student support and its impact on learning outcomes. Paper presented at 26th Annual HERDSA Conference: Learning for an unknown future, Christchurch, 6–9 July.

11

Evaluation of Academic Development

Looking to the Future

LORRAINE STEFANI

The chapters and case studies in this book provide affirmation of the complex nature of academic development, the multiple interpretations of the nature and scope of the development project and the problematic nature of evaluation of the effectiveness of academic development.

Nevertheless, these same chapters and case studies bear witness to the idea that over the last three decades academic development has progressed from an informal set of 'teaching improvement' activities to a scholarly field of study and practice (McDonald and Stockley, 2008). In its relatively short history, academic development has moved from the fringes to the mainstream of higher education (Kahn and Baume, 2003), and although that is an achievement to be proud of, it also has implications for the expectations of what academic development and developers can reasonably achieve.

These expectations are not in any way well articulated within institutions. As many of the chapter and case study authors in this book attest to, the remit of academic development has vastly expanded into increasingly significant roles, including change agents and policy leaders. This has not of course occurred within a vacuum. Universities and higher education institutions have undergone massive transformation over the past two decades. It is therefore not surprising that the field of academic development has also undergone transformation.

This shift from the fringes to the forefront for academic development has not happened overnight. In 1987, Ingrid Moses, a highly respected academic developer, founding Director of the Centre for Learning and Teaching at the University of Technology, Sydney and later Vice Chancellor of New England University, New South Wales, published a report of a survey she had carried out of educational development units in Australia, the UK, the USA, West Germany and Sweden, which concluded that 'in all these countries, educational development seems to be carried by the enthusiasm of those who are engaged in it' (Moses, 1987, p. 476; reported in Candy, 1996).

There is ample anecdotal, if not published, evidence that staff development in general was often viewed as deficit oriented, seen to be a matter of remedying perceived shortcomings in people's current level of skill. Murmurings of this view can still occasionally be heard, particularly in some research-led institutions.

A decade on from Ingrid Moses's report, universities were being conceived of and described as 'learning organizations'. A learning organization is one that seeks to create its own future; that assumes learning is an ongoing and creative process for its members; and that develops, adapts and transforms itself in response to the needs and aspirations of people both inside and outside of itself. Definitions of the 'learning organization' stem primarily from the influential work of Peter Senge in his seminal publication, *The fifth discipline – the art and practice of the learning organization* (Senge, 1990). Senge's work in turn builds on the earlier writings of Donald Schön in which he states:

> we must become able not only to transform our institutions in response to changing situations and requirements, we must invent and develop institutions which are learning systems, that is to say, systems capable of bringing about their own continuing transformation.
>
> (Schön, 1973)

These sentiments would seem to be as relevant today as when they were first articulated, but universities as complex organizations do not necessarily live up to the aspirations that underpin the idea of a 'learning organization', perhaps because the concept is an ideal, a vision that various parts of organizations achieve or realize to varying degrees. Nevertheless, it is easy to see how an organizational learning perspective can provide a theoretical basis for academic development.

Taking such an idea as his premise, Phil Candy (1996) suggested that academic development should ideally be:

- Comprehensive and embracing the total spectrum of academic work;
- Anticipatory rather than reactive;
- Research-based and theoretically rigorous;
- Exemplary in terms of modelling best practice, especially in teaching/ learning methodologies;
- Embedded in the institutional culture and context;
- Reflective and encouraging reflective awareness of practice, and geared towards the notion of lifelong personal and professional development.

Candy termed this the CAREER model of academic development (Candy, 1996).

In today's terms, this framework set out by Candy (1996) is still highly relevant and the chapters and case studies in this book would indicate this. The chapters by Debowski and Gordon, for example, show just how extensive is the development agenda; the case studies coming from one research-intensive university show both the depth and the breadth of the work being carried out. Many of the case studies show the anticipatory as opposed to reactive nature of development programmes; virtually all of the chapter authors argue strongly for a research-led, evidence-based approach to academic development. There is a strong sense of modelling best practice in the chapters by Cathy Gunn, Roni Bamber, and Claudia Stanny and Jane Halonen.

There remains a question mark regarding whether or not academic development is embedded in the institutional culture and context. Kathleen Gray and Alex Radloff, in their cautionary note on the language we use with respect to evaluation of our practice, highlight an issue often talked about, but rarely written about: the substantive impediments to institutions becoming or aspiring to become learning organizations – the intransigence of some staff members, the defensive interpersonal behaviours, some of which may well harp back to the days when a deficit-orientation to development was the norm, but which have significant impact on the exchange and flow of information. Some of these intransigent staff become senior managers in institutions and carry their prejudices with them into these powerful roles.

Academic development within any institution is dependent on high-level support. It should be obvious from mission statements, statements of institutional vision and values that academic development is an integral aspect of the fabric of the institution. Faculty deans and heads of department could promote academic development for all of their staff members. In this book the case studies indicate an institution within which academic development is valued, in which the developers are responsive to changing circumstances and where the developers work in partnership with staff across the institution. That is not to say that the picture is perfect but the positioning of the Centre for Academic Development (CAD) accountable to the Deputy Vice Chancellor (Academic), and the size of the Centre, with over sixty-five staff members, is testimony to a significant level of support.

Nevertheless, the staff within the CAD, along with colleagues from similar centres locally, nationally and internationally, are on a constant quest to find appropriate evaluative measures for their work.

The key messages arising from this book are that academic development sits within the broad framework of organizational change, development and transformation; that our practice is multi-faceted and entails a multi-agency approach which most likely requires visual models to depict the interconnectedness between the academic development centre or unit and other influences within the institution; that our practice should be research and evidence based; and that evaluation should focus on the processes by which developers effect change in attitudes and academic practice.

What is clear is that there is no simple one-size-fits-all approach to evaluating our practice; rather, there is a need to consider a research and evidence base for evaluative practice itself. The overarching research objectives of evaluative approaches could encompass identification of the extent to which a coherent body of knowledge about learning and teaching and the student learning experience has been developed across the institution as a result of the work of academic developers; and determining how learning environments, learning and teaching practices, curriculum design, development and delivery and, most importantly, the student learning experience have changed as a consequence of academic development policies, strategies and implementation across the institution.

This in turn may require the leaders of academic development centres and units to place a stronger emphasis on research into and development of appropriate, contextualized, informative and meaningful evaluation strategies.

There can be no doubt about the constantly evolving nature of academic development work. As most of the contributors to this book assert, academic development plays a transformative role in higher education institutions and yet it is also clear that academic developers themselves recognize that to further elevate our status we need to subject our practice to robust and scholarly evaluation. The questions that Shelda Debowski poses in Chapter 2:

- How are we progressing in improving our impact and effectiveness?
- How does academic development make a difference to the organisation?

provide an excellent starting point for scholarly institutional research. A strong message coming through the chapters and cases is that reporting on inputs alone provides a shallow basis for evaluation of effectiveness or impact. To reflect on and interrogate the outputs of our practice, our interventions and our inputs, will help us to frame responses to Debowski's questions.

Krause's view (Chapter 5) that we can use the information emanating from student surveys to frame our practice and therefore provide tangible evidence of contributing to the enhancement of the student learning experience is appealing. Likewise, the idea of evaluating whether the processes we use within our practice are in alignment with the expected outcomes, as suggested by Kreber (Chapter 4), offers a promising approach to determining our effectiveness. Although not articulated as such, this approach can be discerned through some of the case studies. Matiu Ratima for example shows the beginnings of this approach in his case on evaluating academic development for Māori staff and students, a field which is itself in its infancy. Hints of this strategy can also be discerned in the cases presented by Barbara Kensington-Miller on peer support, and Gunn and Donald on evaluating elearning processes. These cases may be close to what Kreber has in mind when she suggests that case studies can provide valuable insights into the context within which academic practice interventions are occurring. A different angle on evaluation is provided by Gunn in Chapter 6 where she outlines the design-based research approach to elearning, but it is consistent with the idea of evaluating our processes.

The idea of national benchmarking frameworks for evaluation, as hinted at by Bamber in Chapter 8, may be more appealing to senior managers in institutions than to developers themselves. However, it could also be interpreted as a significant elevation of the importance of academic development to the transformation and growth of higher education institutions.

As Gordon hints in Chapter 3, academic developers themselves need to be responsive and capable of adapting to changing circumstances and learning environments. Although this may be considered unpalatable for many developers, if we value our role as organizational change agents, value having moved from fringe activity to mainstream practice, we may have little choice but to accept that we too are subject to the multifarious accountability measures imposed on the wider institution. Better that we develop our own evidence-based evaluation strategies than to have evaluative measures imposed upon us by external bodies. It is to be hoped that the chapters and case studies in this book will provide the basis for the development of new evaluative strategies and protocols which will enable academic developers to show very clearly the contribution we make to enhancing the student learning experience and to organizational development and transformation.

References

Candy, P. (1996) Promoting lifelong learning: academic developers and the university as a learning organization. *International Journal for Academic Development* 1 (1), 7–18.

Kahn, P. and Baume, D. (eds) (2003) *A guide to staff and educational development*. London: Kogan Page.

McDonald, J. and Stockley, D. (2008) Pathways to the profession of educational development: an international perspective. *International Journal for Academic Development* 13 (3), 213–218.

Moses, I. (1987) Educational development units: a cross cultural perspective. *Higher Education* 16, 449–479.

Schön, D.A. (1973) *Beyond the stable state: public and private learning in a changing society*. Harmondsworth: Penguin.

Senge, P. (1990) *The fifth discipline: the art and practice of the learning organization*. New York: Doubleday.

Contributors

Roni Bamber is Director of the Centre for Academic Practice at Queen Margaret University, Edinburgh. The Centre for Academic Practice is responsible for enhancing learning, teaching and research at the University. Previously she was Director of Educational Development at Heriot-Watt University. She has worked as an educational developer for 10 years, and has participated in numerous initiatives, including the Scottish Enhancement Themes. Prior to this, Roni was a lecturer in Spanish for 18 years, teaching in four different universities around the UK. Roni has had significant experience in other academic activities, such as course leadership, curriculum consultancy, external examining, and quality audit. Her current research is in the area of the implementation and evaluation of staff development programmes, and introducing change in universities.

Ian Brailsford is an academic advisor in the Centre for Academic Development at the University of Auckland. He was appointed in 2006 after a decade with the University of Auckland History Department, first as a full-time graduate student, then as a part-time tutor while completing a PhD and, finally, as a contract lecturer. Ian currently teaches on the University Postgraduate Certificate in Academic Practice, university-wide Doctoral Skills Programme and coordinates training for graduate teaching assistants and laboratory demonstrators.

Susan Carter has coordinated the Student Learning Centre Doctoral Programme at the University of Auckland since 2004. Her fields of research include medieval, Renaissance and fantasy literature, but her focus is now on the practice, process and pedagogy of the doctoral degree. Her research on the doctorate ranges between the experiences of candidates, the structure of the thesis, the support of doctoral students, and the way that institutional and national policy affects candidate experience.

Shelda Debowski is Winthrop Professor (Higher Education Development) and Director of Organisational and Staff Development at the University of Western Australia. Her portfolio includes responsibility for academic staff development, organizational analysis and development, leadership and researcher capacity building and professional development of all university staff. Shelda also directed the development of teaching and learning services for the University from 2003 to 2005 and has contributed to several university advisory boards. She was President of the Higher Education Research and Development Society of Australasia (HERDSA) from 2005 to 2009 and

President of the International Consortium for Educational Development (ICED) from 2008 to 2010. She is a Fellow of HERDSA, the Australian Institute of Management and the Association of Tertiary Education Managers, and the Chair of the editorial board for the Higher Education Research and Development journal published by HERDSA.

Claire Donald has been a learning designer and flexible learning advisor since the late 1980s. She has been involved in educational research, teaching and technology-supported design and development work in the private sector and in the tertiary education sector. Her disciplinary fields of research and teaching are mainly in science education and more recently in postgraduate education. Her research interests include concept development, the learning design process, support strategies for learning design and professional development for elearning. She has a PhD in science education from the University of the Witwatersrand, Johannesburg.

George Gordon was the founding Director of the Centre for Academic Practice at the University of Strathclyde in Glasgow. He retains a functioning association with the Centre and the University in the role of Research Professor, in addition to being an Emeritus Professor. He is presently Chair of the Society for Research into Higher Education. He has published widely on aspects of staffing, academic and professional development, leadership and management, and quality assurance and enhancement in higher education. He is a former head of an academic department and a former Dean of Arts and Social Sciences.

Barbara M. Grant is a senior lecturer in the Academic Practice Group, a division of the Centre for Academic Development at the University of Auckland. She advises academic staff on aspects of their teaching, supervision and research. She has taught courses on graduate research supervision and thesis writing for many institutions at home and abroad and has organised and facilitated many residential and non-residential writing retreats for academic women (and sometimes men and women) within and outside New Zealand. Barbara's research interests lie in the area of post-critical accounts of higher education, including enquiries into the supervision of graduate research students, academic identities, research methodologies for social sciences and academic writing.

Kathleen Gray is a senior research fellow in the Faculties of Medicine and Science at the University of Melbourne. Her PhD examined the transition from classroom to web-based learning and teaching in higher education. She has extensive experience as a university teacher, and has also held a wide range of academic development roles in educational technology, educational quality assurance, curriculum design and policy implementation. Recent research projects include implications of new and emerging web technologies for learning and teaching in higher education, and for academic standards, practices and management.

Cathy Gunn is the Head of the eLearning Design and Development Group within the Center for Academic Development at the University of Auckland. Her work in the field of academic development focuses on innovation and capacity development for elearning. She has worked in various roles, mainly in a large research-intensive university since the early 1990s. Her research focuses on contemporary issues in elearning, including organizational change, academic development, evaluating the impact of information technology in education and the psychology of learning. A varied portfolio of publications reflects this breadth of experience. She recently served for four years as President of the Australasian Society for Computers in Learning in Tertiary Education (Ascilite), and maintains a presence in the international elearning community through this and other professional networks.

Jane S. Halonen is the Dean of the College of Arts and Sciences at the University of West Florida. A clinical psychologist by training, Dr Halonen's scholarly interests have concentrated on faculty development, quality standards in higher education, critical thinking and assessment. Winner of the 2000 American Psychological Foundation's Distinguished Teaching Award, she continues to teach psychology as a life-giving part of her workload. She has also served as the Chief Reader for Psychology's Advanced Placement Reading and co-directs the international Improving University Teaching conference.

Alison Holmes is a former Director of the University Centre for Teaching and Learning at the University of Canterbury. She has led the development of the Centre to encompass student and staff support for their academic endeavours. She has been actively involved in the development and running of Ako Aotearoa, the National Centre for Tertiary Teaching Excellence in New Zealand. This role encompasses the provision of support to all teachers in the post-compulsory education sector. She is a member of the Higher Education Academy in the UK. Her research interests are in the areas of educational collaboration and work-based learning.

Frances Kelly is a lecturer in doctoral skills development at the University of Auckland. She graduated with her PhD, in English, in 2003 and has since worked at the Student Learning Centre within the Centre for Academic Development. Her teaching is primarily in the Doctoral Skills Programme offered through the School of Graduate Studies. Frances's research interests are primarily in the area of doctoral education and academic writing.

Barbara Kensington-Miller spent 20 years as a secondary school mathematics and science teacher before returning to university to complete her Masters and Doctorate. She now works as a lecturer for the Academic Practice Group within the Centre for Academic Development at the University of Auckland. One part of her role is a special responsibility for supporting early-career academics in their teaching and/or research. To support the different groups and needs, Barbara has set up peer mentoring within a community of practice, which she evaluated through research. These have been within and across disciplines, and two groups from different cultures. Her other current research interest is exploring the socio-cultural norms of students and lecturers in a large mathematics lecture and how the lecturer can change these norms through the use of questions.

Kerri-Lee Krause is Chair in Higher Education, Director of the Griffith Institute for Higher Education and Dean (Student Outcomes) at Griffith University. Her role connects the student experience and outcomes with support for academic staff and curriculum development. Her research expertise spans broadly across higher education policy areas, with a focus on the quality and changing nature of the student experience, the changing nature of academic work and the implications of these changes for policy and practice. On the basis of her research, she provides advice to the sector on enhancing institutional quality, along with strategies for managing the changing student and academic staff experience in higher education.

Carolin Kreber is Professor of Higher and Community Education at the University of Edinburgh, where she is also presently Director of the Centre for Teaching, Learning and Assessment and Coordinator of the Postgraduate Certificate Programme in University Teaching. Main interests include interpretations of complex notions such as identity, autonomy and authenticity in relation to learning and academic practice and the different kinds of questions that can be asked as part of (the Scholarship of) Teaching and Learning, particularly the linkages between theoretical, instrumental and ethical deliberation.

Linda McLain is currently the Deputy Director of the Staff and Organisational Development Unit (SODU) at the University of Auckland and has worked in the university sector for more than 15 years as an academic and in professional and organizational development. Prior to coming to the University of Auckland she worked for seven years at Edith Cowan University in west Australia. She has also spent time in the public sector (Departments of Education and Training and the Ministry of Justice), in organizational development in Australia and at universities in Germany and the United States. She works in an environment where she can assist people to achieve their potential – by providing the opportunity to gain skills, abilities and behaviours which will make their jobs easier. Her major goals are to ensure alignment between the work of the SODU and the strategic objectives of the University, to build the SODU team, and to create alliances and partnerships with other areas of the University.

Kogi Naidoo is Deputy Director of the Centre for Learning and Professional Development, University of Adelaide, Australia, and Higher Education Research and Development Society of Australasia Fellow. She has extensive experience in teaching English and education, working in academic development, research and quality assurance in South Africa and New Zealand.

Her postgraduate research focused on developing course quality assurance mechanisms. In recognition, she received prestigious awards: SA Junior Technikon Fellowship, Ernest Oppenheimer Gold Medal, and South African Association for Research and Development in Higher Education Young Achiever Awards. Kogi led a national New Zealand project investigating the impact of academic development on first-year student learning.

Alex Radloff holds a PhD in Higher Education and her research interests include student learning, graduate attributes, change management and the professional development of academic staff. She has published and presented extensively on these topics. Alex has led a number of learning and teaching projects and facilitated a wide range of academic development programmes. Following more than 30 years as an academic, staff developer and senior executive in a number of Australian universities, Alex is now a consultant in higher education and adjunct professor at the Melbourne International Campus of CQUniversity.

Matiu Ratima is the Kaiwhakaako Māori (Māori Academic Developer) within the Academic Practice Group, Centre for Academic Development, University of Auckland. He is a PhD candidate in language education at Waikato University. His research interests include Māori academic development, language revitalization and student engagement. He currently teaches courses in academic citizenship and Māori culture and society. His work with the Centre for Academic Development is primarily focused on a programme to meet the developmental needs of Māori staff within the University. He also contributes to the academic development of all staff through workshops and programmes of teaching development, student engagement and institutional bi- and multicultural engagement.

Claudia J. Stanny is the Director of the Center for University Teaching, Learning, and Assessment (CUTLA), co-Director of the Quality Enhancement Plan, and an Associate Professor in Psychology at the University of West Florida. Claudia earned her BA, MA and PhD in Psychology from Florida State University. Claudia's scholarly work includes workshops, conference sessions, and consultation on teaching strategies, faculty development, and the assessment of student learning for evaluation of academic programmes. Her published research focuses on applied aspects of memory and cognition, teaching of psychology, and faculty development and assessment issues in higher education.

Lorraine Stefani is Professor and Director of the Centre for Academic Development (CAD) at the University of Auckland, New Zealand. She is particularly interested in promoting the role of academic development in organizational change and development. With responsibility for leading a team of over sixty staff, she has implemented a successful model for sustainable distributed leadership and leadership capacity building within CAD. She has extensive experience of educational change management and a high level of research output on a range of topics including e-portfolios/elearning, assessment of student learning and student engagement. She is a member of the inaugural governance Board of Ako Aotearoa, the New Zealand Centre for Tertiary Teaching Excellence.

Helen Sword is Head of the Academic Practice Group in the Centre for Academic Development at the University of Auckland, where she coordinates the Postgraduate Certificate in Academic Practice. She holds a PhD in Comparative Literature from Princeton University and has published widely on modernist literature, higher education pedagogy, academic writing and digital poetics. Her books include *Engendering Inspiration* (Michigan 1995), *Ghostwriting Modernism* (Cornell 2002) and *The Writer's Diet* (Pearson Education New Zealand 2007). She is currently working on a book entitled *Stylish Academic Writing: A Manifesto*.

Index